READING PAUL'S LETTER TO THE ROMANS

Society of Biblical Literature

Resources for Biblical Study

Tom Thatcher, New Testament Editor

Number 73

READING PAUL'S LETTER TO THE ROMANS

READING PAUL'S LETTER TO THE ROMANS

Edited by

Jerry L. Sumney

Society of Biblical Literature
Atlanta

READING PAUL'S LETTER TO THE ROMANS

Library of Congress Cataloging-in-Publication Data

Reading Paul's letter to the Romans / edited by Jerry L. Sumney.
     p. cm. — (Resources for biblical study ; number 73)
    Includes bibliographical references and indexes.
    ISBN 978-1-58983-717-1 (paper binding : alk. paper) — ISBN 978-1-58983-718-8 (electronic format)
    1. Bible. N.T. Romans—Criticism, interpretation, etc. I. Sumney, Jerry L. II. Series: Resources for biblical study ; no. 73.
    BS2665.52.R375 2012
    227.1'06—dc23   2012041814

Printed on acid-free, recycled paper conforming to
ANSI/NISO Z39.48-1992 (R1997) and ISO 9706:1994
standards for paper permanence.

For John Baxter and James Smeal

Together we read Romans for ourselves for the first time

Contents

Abbreviations

Primary Sources

1 Clem.	1 Clement
1 Apol.	Justin, *Apologia i*
1 En.	1 Enoch (Ethiopic Apocalpyse)
2 Bar.	2 Baruch (Syriac Apocalypse)
A.J.	Josephus, *Antiquitates judaicae*
Ann.	Tacitus, *Annales*
Apoc. Mos.	Apocalypse of Moses
Apol.	Tertullian, *Apologeticus*
Ars.	Ovid, *Ars amatoria*
B.J.	Josephus, *Bellum judaicum*
C. Ap.	Josephus, *Contra Apionem*
Civ.	Augustine, *De civitate Dei*
Claud.	Suetonius, *Divus Claudius*
Conf.	Augustine, *Confessionum libri XIII*
Ep.	Pliny, *Epistulae*; or Seneca, *Epistulae morales*
Epigr.	Martial, *Epigrammata*
Hist.	Tacitus, *Historiae*
Hist. adv.	Orosius, *Historiarum Adversum Paganos*
Hist. eccl.	Eusebius, *Historia ecclesiastica*
Hist. rom.	Dio Cassius, *Historia romana*
Hypoth.	Philo, *Hypothetica*
Ign. *Phld.*	Ignatius, *To the Philadelphians*
Inst.	Lactantius, *Divinarum institutionum libri VII*
Jub.	Jubilees
L.A.E.	Life of Adam and Eve
Nat.	Tertullian, *Ad nations*
Sat.	Horace, *Satirae*; Juvenal, *Satirae*; or Persius, *Satirae*
[*Subl.*]	Longinus, *De sublimitate*

Superst.	Plutarch, *De superstitione*
Tib.	Suetonius, *Tiberius*

SECONDARY SOURCES

AB	Anchor Bible
AcadBib	Academia Biblica
ANTC	Abingdon New Testament Commentaries
BDAG	Bauer, W., F. W. Danker, W. F. Arndt, and F. W. Gingrich. *Greek-English Lexicon of the New Testament and Other Early Christian Literature.* 3rd ed. Chicago: University of Chicago Press, 1999.
BECNT	Baker Exegetical Commentary on the New Testament
BZNW	Beihefte zur Zeitschrift für die neutestamentliche Wissenschaft
CBET	Contributions to Biblical Exegesis and Theology
CBQ	*Catholic Biblical Quarterly*
ConBNT	Coniectanea biblica: New Testament Series
CSEL	Corpus scriptorum ecclesiasticorum latinorum
CurBS	*Currents in Research: Biblical Studies*
EC	*Early Christianity*
HBT	*Horizons in Biblical Theology*
Herm	Hermeneia
HTR	*Harvard Theological Review*
IBT	Interpreting Biblical Texts
ICC	International Critical Commentary
JBL	*Journal of Biblical Literature*
JSNT	*Journal for the Study of the New Testament*
JSNTSup	Journal for the Study of the New Testament Supplement Series
KEK	Kritisch-exegetischer Kommentar über das Neue Testament (Meyer-Kommentar)
LCC	Library of Christian Classics
LNTS	Library of New Testament Studies
NIB	*New Interpreter's Bible.* Edited by Leander E. Keck. 12 vols. Nashville: Abingdon, 1994–2004.
NICNT	New International Commentary on the New Testament

NovTSup	Supplements to Novum Testamentum
NPNF1	*Nicene and Post-Nicene Fathers*, Series 1
NPNF2	*Nicene and Post-Nicene Fathers*, Series 2
NTS	*New Testament Studies*
NTR	New Testament Readings
OBT	Overtures to Biblical Theology
PCC	Paul in Critical Contexts
PCNT	Paideia Commentaries on the New Testament
RefR	*Reformed Review*
RGRW	Religions in the Graeco-Roman World
SBLDS	Society of Biblical Literature Dissertation Series
SBLSymS	Society of Biblical Literature Symposium Series
SCJR	*Studies in Christian-Jewish Relations*
SFSHJ	South Florida Studies in the History of Judaism
SNTW	Studies of the New Testament and Its World
TDNT	*Theological Dictionary of the New Testament.* Edited by G. Kittel and G. Friedrich. Translated by G. W. Bromiley. 10 vols. Grand Rapids: Eerdmans, 1964–1976.
TSAJ	Texte und Studien zum antiken Judentum
WBC	Word Biblical Commentary
WBComp	Westminster Bible Companion
WUNT	Wissenschaftliche Untersuchungen zum Neuen Testament

READING THE LETTER TO THE ROMANS

Jerry L. Sumney

Romans has been one of the most influential books of the New Testament. It was a text from Romans that moved St. Augustine to become a Christian. Martin Luther's reading of Romans led him to start the Protestant Reformation. John Calvin's reading led him to propose his doctrine of the predestination of all people. John Wesley's foundational experience came to him while hearing a reading of the preface of Luther's commentary on Romans. In scholarship of the nineteenth and twentieth centuries, Romans exercised more influence on the ways Paul and his theology were understood than any other letter, possibly more than all the other letters combined. Interpreters consciously outlined Paul's theology by following the themes of Romans. Only in the last two decades of the twentieth century did New Testament scholars begin to seriously question the wisdom of relying on Romans so heavily. Still, many leading scholars look to it as their starting point for understanding Paul.

Traditionally Romans has been thought of as the place where Paul sets out his theology systematically. Other letters have their content determined by problems in the church to which Paul is writing or some other element of the letter's occasion. But in Romans, it was said, Paul is free to say what he thinks without responding to specific problems. Thus, if you wanted to know what Paul really thought or if you wanted to describe Paul's theology, you should start with and focus on Romans. The last decades of the twentieth century saw interpreters begin to question this assumption and to question the primacy of Romans in understanding Paul's theology.[1]

---

1. Especially influential in shifting attention to the theology of other Pauline letters was J. Christiaan Beker's *Paul the Apostle: The Triumph of God in Life and Thought* (Philadelphia: Fortress, 1980). He set out a method for thinking about the letters and the theology in them that did not require interpreters to start with the theology of any

Scholars have increasingly recognized that Romans is not a text of systematic theology with no immediate context shaping the way Paul talked about the issues. In fact, some theological issues that are important to Paul are not even mentioned in Romans (for example, the Lord's Supper). Still, Romans is not only the longest of Paul's extant letters, it is also the one that provides the fullest explication of what he teaches on a range of issues—including why people need the gospel and how God addresses that need in Christ. As we will see, however, this exposition of his teaching is shaped by specific things he needs to accomplish with the letter. As a result, many interpreters now draw on Romans more carefully than some who have simply used it as an outline of Paul's theology.

Paul seems to have three related purposes in mind as he writes Romans. The first relates to his immediate travel plans. Paul writes Romans from Corinth. He has just completed a round of visits to congregations he had established earlier to take up a collection to deliver to the church in Jerusalem. The Jerusalem church, and perhaps the region as a whole, had experienced some significant financial problems. Paul had asked his churches to contribute to a fund designed to bring aid to the Jerusalem church. Paul envisioned this offering as more than a good deed designed to help the poor. As he saw it, this was an opportunity for his predominantly Gentiles churches to acknowledge their spiritual debt to and connection with the churches that had a predominantly Jewish membership. Tensions between these churches had been high, so high that Paul is afraid they will split and refuse to acknowledge the legitimacy of one another. He even fears that the Jerusalem church will not accept the gift he is bringing from his churches.

Paul thinks that having the predominantly Gentile churches make this gesture and provide this relief will calm the tensions. When Paul arrives in Jerusalem, then, he wants to be able to represent all the churches that have a large Gentile population. As you will see in the essays by Mark Nanos and Andrew Das, there is significant disagreement among scholars about the ethnic composition of the church in Rome and about its relationship to the Jewish community there. Most interpreters acknowledge, however, that one reason Paul writes Romans is to be able to include the churches of the city of Rome among those he represents as he goes to Jerusalem.

Paul's problem with claiming to represent the Roman churches is that

---

one letter. The subsequent work of the "Pauline Theology Group" of the Society of Biblical Literature furthered this work substantively. Much of the work of that group can be found in the four volumes entitled *Pauline Theology*.

he had never visited Rome as a missionary and so was not the founder of its churches. It is possible, though by no means certain, that the people who founded the Roman church were related to Paul's missionary team. Whether that is the case or not, he needs more contact with the churches in Rome to include them among those he represents in Jerusalem. So as he writes Romans, he needs to introduce himself, his apostleship (and so his authority), and his teaching in a way that will move the Roman church to consider him their apostle.

Second, Paul wants the churches there to sponsor a new missionary endeavor. He tells them that after his trip to Jerusalem he wants to begin a new mission in Spain. He has spent his time as a missionary and apostle in areas east of Italy, mostly in Asia Minor (today's Turkey) and Greece. Now he intends to turn west. He seems to want at least the financial support of the church in Rome, and perhaps more. He may need a guide or translator; he does not specify how he wants to be "sent on by you" (15:24). Paul tells about this travel itinerary and his reasons for it in Rom 15:22–33.

While Paul writes to introduce himself as an apostle and to claim them for inclusion with the collection, he also gives advice about problems in the Roman church. This seems particularly bold since he is trying to win them over. Still, Rom 14–15 deal with questions about religious dietary and calendrical regulations. It seems that at least some of these questions stem from differences in the ways church members think believers should observe the Mosaic law, but other questions are not so clearly related to that issue. Interpreters are divided over how much of the dispute revolves around Torah observance and how much around other questions. More broadly, Paul also takes up the topic of relations between Jews who are not in the church and Gentiles in the church and between Christ-confessing Jews and Christ-confessing Gentiles.

Romans was delivered to the Roman church by a woman named Phoebe. This is the reason Paul commends her to the Romans in 16:1–2. She was a deacon of the church in Cenchreae, a port of the city of Corinth. Having Phoebe deliver the letter and mentioning that he has gone through that region is how we know Paul is in Corinth when he writes Romans. The date of its writing is around 57. This is the last letter Paul writes as a free person. He will be arrested in Jerusalem and probably never be out of prison again.[2]

---

2. Interpreters who think Paul wrote the Pastoral Epistles often assert that Paul

There is much that you can learn from studying Romans from many perspectives and using many methodologies. Our knowledge of the early church is enhanced by many things in Romans. We find information about non-Pauline churches outside of Palestine, about the varying social statuses of members of the church, and about the church's relationship with the Roman Empire. All of these and more are legitimate and important goals for studying Romans, and knowledge of all of them is needed to understand Romans. The purpose of the essays in this book is to help readers understand this letter. Since Romans is a religious document intended to argue for particular religious and theological views, the focus of this volume is on its theology. Other kinds of issues are raised because of the ways the positions taken on them influence how we understand the message and theology of the letter. Such study contributes to our understanding of the beliefs and practices of Pauline and Roman Christianity in the middle of the first century.

The first two essays of this book (those mentioned above by Nanos and Das) discuss the identity of the recipients of Romans and the relationship of their church to the synagogue. What you conclude about this question influences how you understand some theological matters and some other issues about the letter as a whole. The next essay draws attention to the ways some interpreters see political elements in the letter's language and theology. How the church understood itself in relation to the Roman Empire and how its language may reflect and oppose the empire's claims may also influence how we hear this letter. Sylvia Keesmaat's essay reflects the attention that has been given to this aspect of the context of Paul's letters and their recipients. She shows how significantly this way of viewing Romans can shift our understanding of its message.

The other essays each take up a theological theme that is important in Romans. The sequence roughly follows the sequence of the way these subjects become dominant in the flow of the letter's argument. There are two essays on the question of the place of Israel in God's plan, the topic that dominates Rom 9–11. What Paul says about this issue, like the question of

---

was released in Rome and then returned to the Aegean area rather than going on to Spain. They contend that he wrote those letters before he was arrested and sent to Rome a second time. In this view Paul was executed at the end of this second Roman imprisonment. The vast majority of critical scholars, however, reject that reconstruction and argue that Paul did not write the Pastorals and was never released from prison after his arrest in Jerusalem.

the identity of the recipients of the letter, has been understood in radically different ways. Both essays here reject the view that God's covenant with Israel has been concluded. They differ in the ways they see God remaining in covenant with Israel.

Each essay in the book begins with a brief account of the range of views taken on the topic it treats. The authors then present their own understanding of that issue, indicating why they think this represents the best interpretation. The authors do not represent a single perspective on the letter. The differences among them are intended to help readers think about the implications each issue has for our reading of the whole. Having these competing readings will, I hope, help you sharpen your own understanding as you see the strengths and weakness of the various positions taken.

Interpreters agree that Paul provides a thematic statement for the whole of Romans in 1:16–17. These verses read, "For I am not ashamed of the gospel, for it is the power of God for all who have faith, for Jews first and also Greeks. For in it the righteousness of God is revealed from faith for faith. Just as it is written, 'The just will live by faith'" (author's translation).

These verses are packed with import as Paul hints at many things he will discuss in the rest of the letter. We will point to some of those topics here as preparation for the essays that follow. First, we might note that the gospel is a manifestation of the power of God, not Christ. This suggests that the work of Christ, as Paul sees it, is to demonstrate and make present the power of God. God remains the source of the gospel, with Christ as the one through whom that source is active.

This thematic statement also assumes that everyone (Jews and Gentiles) need the gospel. While Paul does not say why that is the case in these verses, he spends all of 1:18–3:20 demonstrating that everyone does need it. He first explains why Gentiles need it, and then he turns to show that Jews also need it, even though they already had the law and are in a covenant relationship with God.

There are extensive discussions about the meaning of the word "faith" in Romans and in all of Paul's use of it. As we think about the meaning of this word, it may help to think about English words that have many meanings. Consider the word "set." It might be a noun or a verb. As a verb it means, among other things, to put something down or to prepare a trap; as a noun it might refer to a group of China dishes or a certain amount of tennis. It might even refer to a predetermined length of time, a set amount of time. This is just a small sample of the meanings for this small word that you find in a dictionary. Just as "set" has many and different meanings, so do many Greek words. The Greek word usually translated "faith" is *pistis*, and the verb form (or cognate) is *pisteuō*, often translated "to have faith" or "to believe." But *pistis* has a wide range of meanings that include faith, faithfulness, and trustworthiness.

Scholars continue to disagree about the meaning of *pistis* in various places in Romans, including in these opening verses. In this place, though not in all, I think the word means "faithfulness." Thus, the middle sentence of verses 16–17 says that God's righteousness is revealed "through faithfulness for faithfulness." That may seem no clearer than the previous translation, but the rest of Romans helps us fill out the meaning. The first reference to faithfulness refers to the faithfulness of Christ; that is, to the faithfulness to God and God's will that we see in Christ's willingness to do God's will through his ministry, cross, and resurrection. This life and death of faithfulness then creates faithfulness in those who hear the message about it. So the phrase means that God's righteousness is revealed through the faithfulness of Christ and his faithfulness produces faithfulness in others.[3] The essay by Katherine Grieb explores what Paul means when he talks about God's righteousness and how it comes to expression in the work of Christ. Joel Green then explores the various images Paul uses to describe how the work of Christ gives expression to God's righteousness.

Paul says in 1:17 (and expands on that expression in 3:21) that the Scriptures of Israel speak of this revelation of God's righteousness. Paul uses the Scriptures to interpret what has happened through Christ, more than he sees them as predictions of some sort. His mention of Scripture here signals a clear connection between God's presence and acts among the Israelites and what God does through Christ. This raises important issues that Paul must address throughout Romans. The essay of Francis Watson discusses the way Paul sees the law's place in the church. This was a central issue in the life of the first-century church, an issue that would determine the course of the church's history. Watson argues that Paul contends that faith in Christ rather than Torah observance should be the central identity marker for church members. Rodrigo Morales takes up the

---

3. Other interpreters argue that "from faithfulness to faithfulness" means that the faithfulness of God leads to the faithfulness of Christ. This interpretation, even more powerfully than the one offered in the text, maintains a focus on God as the actor in salvation, in the gospel.

issue of the way Paul uses Scripture in Romans. Scholars disagree about how much Paul takes into account the original context of the verses he quotes from the Hebrew Bible. Many think he pays little attention to that context, others argue that he is very careful about reflecting that original meaning in his use of a passage. Morales sets out this dispute more fully and then discusses Paul's use of Scripture as one who is convinced Paul does draw on the original context of that earlier writing.

Paul sees the gospel as a new revelation of God's righteousness. This means that the gospel is an eschatological event; that is, it is an end-time happening. Paul saw the coming of Christ as an event that initiated the end of all things. Through Christ, God's purposes for the world were finally being accomplished. Yet it was clear that the will of God was not yet being done. So while the end-time had begun, he looked forward to the conclusion of the end-times. In the course of Romans, he compares Christ to Adam. Just as Adam was the first human of the previous time, so Christ is the first person of the end-time. James Dunn's essay explores Paul's understanding of what it means to set Christ in an eschatological context in such a way that you can speak of him as a "second Adam." Ann Jervis continues the exploration of the eschatological nature of the gospel by discussing what Paul says in Romans about the presence of the Spirit in the lives of believers. Paul thinks that having God's presence in one's life is an end-time gift of God. Jervis describes what Paul says this presence of the Spirit means in the present for believers' lives.

Our thematic verses in chapter 1 have another curious turn of phrase. Verse 16 says salvation is for all, Jews first. For non-Jewish readers, then and now, this seems startling. Rather than having all people be completely equal in every way, this phrase gives priority to Jews. The essays of Elizabeth Johnson and Caroline Johnson Hodge draw out ways to understand what Paul says about the relationship between Jews and Gentiles within the church, as well as the relationship between the church and the earlier covenant between God and Israel. They focus on what Paul says in the difficult section that makes up chapters 9–11 of Romans.

Chapters 12–15 deal with how the believers in Rome should behave. We must not see this section as unrelated to previous parts of the letter. Paul's thematic statement in 1:16–17 also points to these chapters. Remember that *pistis*, the word usually translated "faith," sometimes also means faithfulness. If it means "faithfulness" there, then it certainly looks for-. ward to this concluding explanation of what faithfulness looks like for the churches in Rome. Even if we understand *pistis* to mean "faith" or "trust" in 1:16–17, it still includes a reference to how people conduct their lives. When Paul speaks of faith, he does not mean that a person simply holds to a particular set of beliefs. Faith for Paul is an orientation of life. It includes what people believe, but also encompasses their attitudes and behaviors toward others. For Paul, if a person does not live as they should, that is good evidence that he or she does not have faith—at least not what he calls faith. What you believe and how you live are inextricably linked for Paul. The essay by Victor Furnish will explore the connections between the way Paul talks about the gospel in the preceding chapters and the expectations for behavior that he sets out in chapters 12–15.

Some interpreters argue that chapter 16 of Romans was added at a later time. Not only does chapter 15 end with a doxology that makes an appropriate end for the letter, but some ancient manuscripts put the doxology that concludes chapter 16 at the end of chapter 15. In addition, Paul sends personal greetings to more people in chapter 16 than he greets in any other letter. This seems strange because he has never been to Rome. Despite these problems, the majority of interpreters think chapter 16 was a part of the original letter. They note that it is present in nearly every ancient manuscript of Romans, and it is not until after the fifth century that it is actually absent from a manuscript—a manuscript that is a Latin translation of the original Greek. Further, many interpreters also think that chapter 16 fits at least one purpose of the letter quite well. If Paul intends to claim these churches as his in Jerusalem or to gain their support for his mission to Spain, it will help in this initial contact to refer to people in Rome whom he knows, especially when they are leaders in their church. Knowing these people gives him some additional credibility. In the language of rhetoric, it helps him establish his ethos.

Careful study of chapter 16 can also reveal a good deal about the people who are in Paul's churches, since it seems that many people he has known from other places are now in Rome. Among the things we learn from chapter 16 is that women play a significant role in the leadership of Paul's churches and in Paul's missionary efforts. While Paul has a reputation for restricting the place of women, this chapter shows what prominent positions they held as leaders and as coworkers in his mission.

Romans is in many ways a tightly constructed argument. Its parts flow from one another and the later parts depend on what Paul thinks he has established in earlier parts. At the same time, the argument of the letter (that is, its train of thought) is often hard to follow. There are some contorted arguments in some places (see especially chapters 9–11) and in others there seem to be leaps of logic that are difficult to follow. But working through the provocative and dense argumentation is worth the effort. At the end we see how Paul envisions the Christian message as something that affects and will eventually re-orient the entire cosmos. Simultaneously, he sees it as a message that currently reorients the believer's life, turning people to ways of living that make life more meaningful. Whether or not the reader is convinced by Paul's message, this letter sets out a grand vision. Interpretations of this vision, both good ones and inadequate ones, have been very influential in the development of Western culture. Identifying the roots of some of our understandings of ourselves as humans makes the study of Romans, then, an important undertaking.

For Further Reading

Bartlett, David L. *Romans*. WBComp. Louisville: Westminster John Knox, 1995. Bartlett provides an accessible text that will help beginning interpreters gain understanding of the issues involved with interpreting Romans and so prepare them for further study. This text can also serve as a good beginning commentary for nonspecialists.

Johnson, Luke T. *Reading Romans: A Literary and Theological Commentary*. New York: Crossroad, 1997. Johnson's accessible commentary gives special attention to the literary features of Romans. He also gives good attention to the theological issues raised throughout the letter.

Keck, Leander E. *Romans*. ANTC. Nashville: Abingdon, 2005. This excellent commentary brings the best of recent scholarship to a fairly wide range of readers. His attention to the theme of the righteousness of God and his careful, yet accessible, attention to difficult issues make this an outstanding resource for study of this letter.

Keck, Leander E., and Victor P. Furnish. *The Pauline Letters*. IBT. Nashville: Abingdon, 1984. This very introductory text covers all the Pauline letters. It provides a broad overview of issues and themes. Thus, it can serve as a good entrée into study of Romans.

To the Churches within the Synagogues of Rome

Mark D. Nanos

Paul did not use the label "Christian" in his letters, and it is widely recognized that in Paul's time "Christianity" did not exist in a formal, institutional sense. Instead, Christ-followers were still identifying themselves in Israelite/Jewish terms based on covenant affiliation with the one God who created a people from Abraham's descendants. Those who shared Paul's commitment to Christ were addressed and discussed, in terms of ethnicity, as Jews or non-Jews/Greeks, Israelites or members from the other "nations" (*ethnē*, usually translated "Gentiles"),[1] circumcised or foreskinned, and so on.

In spite of the common recognition of such historical factors, for the most part Romans continues to be discussed as if it is represents a time when Christianity, however labeled, is understood to have been something other than Judaism, and Christians to have been something other than Jews. On this reading, Jews who became Christians no longer hold their identity as Jews to be of covenantal value (the Mosaic covenant having been fulfilled and thus made obsolete). In other words, they are no longer Jews religiously, even if they remained ethnically Jews because of birth. If some Christ-following Jews "also" attended Jewish communal meetings (i.e., "synagogues"), these are separate from attending Christ-followers' meetings (i.e., "churches"): Christians and Jews represented separate group identities; they met separately and they upheld different foundational norms.

---

1. We derive ethnic and ethnicity from *ethnē*, which translates as "peoples" or "nations," i.e., "members from the nations" other than Israel; it can refer to members of the nation of Israel too.

The traditional position is generally presented in binary (this or that) theological terms, thus Christ or Torah (often labeled "law"),[2] concluding that Christ replaced Torah, making the latter obsolete for guiding life among Christ-followers—or that is how it should be (i.e., traditionally "Paulinism" is defined as a "law-free gospel").[3] Within a few centuries, no Christians, even (former) Jews who "converted," were permitted to attend Jewish meetings or practice Jewish rites or ways of life[4] and this was apparently the view of some (although by no means all) Christ-following non-Jews already in the early second century (e.g., Ignatius of Antioch).[5]

Following from these premises, the primary problems Paul addressed in Rome are understood to have arisen from the failure of some Christ-followers to respect this change of eons and to live "free of Torah" and Jewish identity (as most interpreters understand the "weak" in Rom 14), or alternatively, from the misguided teaching of those who promoted Torah and Jewish identity alongside of commitment to Christ. Secondarily, however, Paul called for his audience to avoid offending any "weak" Christ-following Jews (and perhaps "Judaized" non-Jews), and also not to think that God had rejected those Jews who did not (yet) share their commitment to Christ.

Those traditional ways of approaching Paul as well as Romans are easily challenged. I propose that Paul and his communities—including the community he did not found but wrote to in Rome—were subgroups of the Jewish communities that believed Jesus represented the dawning of the awaited age.[6] The Jews in these subgroups, Paul included, observed

---

2. "Torah" is a Hebrew word that denotes "teaching" rather than simply "law," including laws/commandments but also many other teachings, stories, warnings, consolation, etc. For Paul, "Torah" is not the opposite of "love" or "freedom" but embodies "teaching" about important values, including "commandments" that clarify how those whom God has "freed" from Egypt, from sin, and so on, are to treat ("love") others.

3. Mark D. Nanos, "The Myth of the 'Law-Free' Paul Standing Between Christians and Jews," *SCJR* 4 (2009): 1–21. Cited 29 August 2012. Online: http://escholarship.bc.edu/scjr/vol4/iss1/4/.

4. Second Council of Nicea, Canon 8; see James Parkes, *The Conflict of the Church and the Synagogue: A Study in the Origins of Antisemitism* (New York: Atheneum, 1979), 394–400.

5. See Ignatius, Ign. *Phld.* 6.1 for the first extant reference to "Christianity [*Christianismos*]" as a religious system, apparently coined to set it out in antithesis to "Judaism [*Ioudaismos*]" (see also Ign. *Magn.* 9.1).

6. See Mark D. Nanos, *The Mystery of Romans: The Jewish Context of Paul's Letter* (Minneapolis: Fortress, 1996).

the covenantal obligations of Torah, for they were Jews involved in a fully Jewish movement.[7] They argued that the awaited age gift of the Holy Spirit now enabled them to practice their commitment to the God of Israel according to the highest ideals of Torah. The non-Jews who joined them did not become Jews and were thus not under the Mosaic legislation (Torah) on the same terms as Jews; however, they were committed to lives of righteousness defined in Jewish communal terms and thus by Torah, for they met in Jewish groups, and thus according to the Jewish norms for these groups, and were enabled by the same Spirit of God.

Those in the Jewish community who did not appreciate non-Jews claiming full identity and rights within the Jewish community apart from proselyte conversion, a tradition providing inclusiveness, might react with confusion and disapproval. If such identity claims continued, such "guests" and Jews advocating such policies would likely be deemed dangerous and subject to discipline. Reactions along that line might stem from a desire to protect divinely commanded covenantal norms, including circumcision. Sociopolitical concerns would also arise, including fear that the community's rights would be compromised, resulting in punishment and perhaps elimination of these rights. In addition, consideration must be given to the simple cultural observation that in antiquity one's identity in a community was more central to one's sense of self than the cultural norms shaping post-Enlightenment notions of self. Complicated? Yes, but Paul's letters indicate just such complexities existed for these non-Jews in terms of how to negotiate Jewish communal identity while remaining non-Jews, rather than that they were experiencing the kind of already fully "Gentilized," separated communities and values usually championed in Paul's name.[8]

---

7. See Tacitus, *Ann.* 15.44. Ambrosiaster in the fourth century, in his commentary *Ad Romanos* (ed. H. J. Vogels; CSEL 81:1), described the earliest Christ-followers in Rome being taught to keep Torah by Christ-following Jews.

8. By way of analogy, consider the dynamics likely to arise if some small group within the Amish community began to teach non-Amish neighbors that they could avoid military service if they but attended Amish meetings without actually becoming Amish. Non-Amish neighbors who believed this would eventually find that this proposition was controversial. Amish leaders, upon learning of it, would likely seek to stop this breach of policy, for it posed a threat to their rights if they did not maintain compliance with the government's definition of who was Amish and thus entitled to avoid service, and it undermined communal identity standards. At the same time, the non-Amish boy seeking this right would be challenged by his family, friends, and

What happens if we read Romans anew based on the proposition that the audience to which Paul addressed the letter met together as subgroups of the larger Jewish community (or communities) of Rome? Do features of Paul's letter make better sense when approached from this contextual vantage point? Besides avoiding the disapproval and dismissal of the value of Judaism, what might be at risk for Christian identity and guidance? In this essay, we can only begin to explore why this approach is compelling. It is my opinion, granted, as a Jew and outsider, that in addition to the concern for historical probability being served, there are theological and spiritual gains for Christians when they are no longer tied to the negative binary (either/or) categories traditionally posed in terms such as Christians or Jews, Christianity or Judaism, Christ or Torah, freedom or obligation, grace or responsibility, faith or works (deeds/actions), moral or ritual, spiritual or physical, and so on. In keeping with Paul's own arguments, these categories are more realistically approached in this-*and*-that rather than this-*or*-that terms. Paul's beliefs and actions (his concepts of faithfulness to Torah and Christ) were not conceptualized in a Christianity *or* Judaism framework. Rather, for Paul and those under his influence, surprising though it may seem, being a Christ-follower was the ideal way to live out Judaism in the awaited age-to-come, which they believed had begun.

The Historical Context

Despite our wealth of information about Rome in the mid-first century c.e., surprisingly little is known about the Jewish communities there, and outside of Romans and Acts of the Apostles, which can be variously interpreted, nothing is known about relationships between the Jewish communities and Christ-followers there. Nevertheless, there are several topics to discuss.

---

civic leaders, for unpatriotic, misguided, and dangerous behavior. The Amish subgroup leader upholding this deviant policy, like Paul, would teach him to hold fast in the face of social pressure. How this would unfold in different local contexts would of course be different, yet certain developments would likely be common. Similarly, these are the kinds of complexity that I propose were faced by the non-Jews within the Christ-following Jewish subgroups. In his letters we see Paul's responses to those who have been persuaded by him and others to uphold a social identity that deviates from the prevailing Jewish and non-Jewish communal norms.

There is no evidence of any buildings from the time used for meetings of Jews or Christ-followers. There is no reason to suppose that Paul's use of the term "gatherings/churches" (*ekklēsia*) distinguishes his group from any other Jewish subgroup or its gatherings, which could equally be referred to as *ekklēsia*. The terms community, meeting, gathering, and assembly were general terms, just as they are today. Only later did "church/*ekklēsia*" come to refer specifically to Christian gatherings and buildings, while "synagogue/*synagōgē*" referred to Jewish gatherings and buildings.[9]

Paul appears to use *ekklēsia* not, as often claimed, to distinguish his groups from *synagōgē*, but rather to signify their identity as subgroups "meeting" specifically within the larger Jewish communities. The point was not to indicate a rival movement, but to indicate that these gatherings demonstrated that Christ had begun the restoration of Israel and the reconciliation of the nations already in the midst of the present age, as promised in Scripture. Interestingly, Paul does not use the term *ekklēsia* in Romans to refer to the overall community but only to one specific "gathering" in the house of Prisca and Aquila (16:3–5); almost certainly there were other gatherings in other locations.

Paul addressed households where meetings took place, and households were also the likely venue for many meetings among Jews. Of the few synagogue buildings that are dated to Paul's time or before, there are none in Italy.[10] There may have been some buildings in Rome, even large ones, that were referred to as *proseuchē* or *synagōgē*, but there is no evidence of it. Even if there were several large public structures, there were likely hundreds more small meetings to facilitate reading and discussing Scripture, worship and prayer, celebrating Sabbaths and other holidays, and other mutual interests and causes as well as social life in general.

In addition, the Jewish community of Rome, as elsewhere, likely consisted of many independent communities or subgroups, often unaware of if not intentionally distinct from each other for any number of reasons.

---

9. In general, non-Jews used *synagōgē* to refer to any kind of gathering together, including of animals, and *ekklēsia* was used to refer to many different kinds of gatherings, most formally to indicate the assembling of the citizens of a city to cast votes as equals.

10. See Anders Runesson, "The Synagogue at Ancient Ostia: The Building and its History From the First to the Fifth Century," *The Synagogue of Ancient Ostia and the Jews of Rome: Interdisciplinary Studies* (ed. Birger Olsson, Dieter Mitternacht, and Olof Brandt; Jonsered, Sweden: Åströms, 2001), 29–99, esp. 81–82.

These might include the distance between each other in this large city, differing interpretation and practice of Torah or level of acculturation, different cultural and ethnic backgrounds, dissimilar economic standing, and so on. Inscriptions in the catacombs of Rome suggest that there were at least eleven distinct synagogue communities by the third or fourth century C.E.; however, none of these synagogues have been dated as early as Paul's period.[11]

Similarly, Rom 16 indicates that there were already a number of small groups of Christ-followers, although only one household "gathering [ekklēsia]" is specifically noted (16:3–5). The total number of people addressed might have been as few as fifty based on Paul's greetings to less than thirty specific individuals. Even if there were several hundred, they would easily fit within the larger Jewish communities of Rome as subgroups. They may have still been largely unnoticed and probably not well understood. Their subgroup identity is suggested all the more if most or all of the members of the groups confessing Christ were composed of the nonelite, and thus likely dependent upon existing Jewish communal leadership and other communal resources. In other words, when we think about the "churches" of Rome we can think in terms similar to those of the "synagogues" of Rome, as "house-churches/assemblies" or "house-synagogues." That remains the case whether or not there were also other more formal buildings. But this still does not tell us much about the relationships between the Christ-following subgroups and the larger Jewish communities of Rome.

The Romans had granted Jewish communities certain privileges since the time of Julius Caesar (Josephus, A.J. 14.190–212; 16.52–53). Jews were permitted "to live in accordance with their customs and to contribute money to common meals and sacred rites," "to assemble and feast in accordance with their native customs and ordinances" (A.J. 14.214–216 [Marcus, LCL]; reiterated by Augustus, A.J. 16.162–165, 172). These rights for Jewish communities continued under Claudius and Titus. When these rights were occasionally denied, Jewish communities successfully appealed to the reigning emperor for judgment according to this precedent (Josephus, A.J. 14.213–267; 16.160–178, 278–312; 19.304–306).[12]

---

11. Leonard Victor Rutgers, "Jewish Ideas about Death and Afterlife: The Inscriptional Evidence," in *The Hidden Heritage of Diaspora Judaism* (2nd ed.; CBET 20; Leuven: Peeters, 1998), 45–71.

12. See full discussion in Miriam Pucci Ben Zeev, *Jewish Rights in the Roman*

This distinctive treatment leads us to ask whether the kind of anti-Jewishness found in Roman authors after the Judean Revolt was already prevalent among Romans when Paul wrote this letter in the mid-50s. There seems to have been a decisive negative shift after 70 C.E., following the Revolt. Vespasian and Titus appealed to their victory over the Judeans to legitimate the beginnings of their new (Flavian) dynasty—with unavoidable implications for Jews in general.[13] Even if the Jews of Rome were not directly involved in the Judean Revolt, such distinctions often become blurred in times of political crisis involving an ethno-religious group's identity (cf. Josephus, *B.J.* 5.2; 7.420).[14]

When Paul wrote Romans, however, Jews were in general still respected and held in high regard as good citizens who exemplified high ideals, even if upholding some seemingly strange ideas and practices.[15] This general respect toward Jews and Judaism, albeit mixed with some ambivalence, has seldom been factored into interpretations of Romans.

It is easy to see the attractiveness of joining Jewish subgroups for non-Jews who turned from the worship of other gods to the worship of the God of Israel in Christ. However, apart from "full" identification with the Jewish community by becoming Jews themselves through proselyte conversion, their ostensible "atheism" for not worshipping the Roman gods and their traitorous refusal to participate in familial and civic cult would be inscrutable if not dangerous (cf. Tacitus, *Hist.* 5.4–5; Juvenal, *Sat.* 14.96–106). That issue arose in the second century C.E. when the Romans began to identify Christians as something other than Jews and to develop punishments for neglect of proper behavior for Roman subjects who were not Jews (cf. the correspondence between Pliny the Younger and the emperor Trajan in ca. 110–12 C.E., *Ep.* 10.96.1–10; 10.97.98–117). But no similar evidence indicates that Roman authorities knew about "Christians" as a separate socio-religious group independent of Jewish communal life during the time Paul wrote to Rome.

World: The Greek and Roman Documents Quoted by Josephus Flavius (TSAJ 74; Tübingen: Mohr Siebeck, 1998).

13. Martin Goodman, *Rome and Jerusalem: The Clash of Ancient Civilizations* (New York: Alfred A. Knopf, 2007), 366–76, 428–77.

14. Consider, e.g., some today who fail to distinguish clearly between Islamic nations or so-called "insurgents/terrorists" and Muslim people, regardless of how vehemently these Muslims might be opposed to such people and policies.

15. Consider again the analogy with common opinions of the Amish.

The earliest mention of *christiani* arises in accounts of them being blamed by Nero for the fire of 64 C.E., language that probably indicates a subgroup identity within the Jewish community that was vaguely understood by non-Jewish Roman authorities rather than an independent religious association ("a 'superstition' of Jewish origin").[16] If Christ-following non-Jews were already neglecting familial and civic cult apart from affiliation with the Jewish communities of Rome, it seems highly unlikely that they were not known about immediately as a threat to the welfare of Rome, as well as to the interests of the Jewish communities and their relations with Roman authorities. The Jewish community's own rights to refrain from civic cult would be brought into question for not bringing any non-Jews into compliance with communal norms. I propose that the language in Romans suggests the beginnings of just such tensions regarding the non-Jews in these subgroups, but also that it implies that no hard break between the larger Jewish community and these subgroups had already been made. Paul sought to address intra-Jewish communal developments.[17]

In the past forty years or so, the traditional interpretations of Romans have argued that the Christ-followers Paul addressed in the mid- to late-50s C.E. were (presumably) already meeting separately from the Jewish communities of Rome as a result of an expulsion of the Jews from Rome during the reign of Claudius (usually dated to 49 C.E.). According to the construct, conflicts between Christ-followers and the larger Jewish community precipitated this expulsion.

This construct is based upon a reading of two early second century C.E. accounts. Suetonius briefly mentions a conflict regarding someone named *Chrestus* (Suetonius, *Claud.* 25.4), which led to an expulsion of the Jews for turbulence within their communities and, in Acts 18:2, Luke notes that Aquila and Priscilla were expelled from Rome along with "all" the Jews. The conclusion is then drawn that since the Jews were forced to leave Rome, the only Christ-followers who remained were non-Jews. Even if some Jews remained, the Christ-following communities were no longer a part of the Jewish community, by choice or default, because they were

---

16. Stephen Benko, *Pagan Rome and the Early Christians* (London: Batsford, 1985), 16, 20.

17. I read Rom 13:1–5 to be calling for subordination to the synagogue authorities (rather than Roman authorities) and payment of the temple tax by these non-Jews in just such an effort to demonstrate their commitment to the Jewish communities, albeit apart from becoming proselytes (*Mystery of Romans*, 289–336).

responsible for a cataclysmic disruption of life for, if not the expulsion of, some estimated twenty to fifty thousand Jewish people.

According to this view, the Christ-followers who remained developed their own identity as "Christians" and their ethos became more "Gentile" in contrast to "Jewish" values. Thus, when Jews began to return under Nero (beginning in 54 C.E.), those who were Christ-followers, including those who were formerly leaders within the Christ-following subgroups of the Jewish community, were not welcomed back without reservations. Rather, they were being greeted with the proposition that they needed to adopt a more "strengthened" (i.e., non-Judaism based) approach to Christian values, such as Paul is generally imagined to have upheld, for example, in Rom 14. This new lifestyle revolved around rejection of the Torah-defined ways of life that distinguished Jews from non-Jews, such as circumcision, Sabbath and other calendrical observances, kosher dietary customs, and so on.

There are many reasons to be suspicious of this construction: the sources are unclear and conflict with each other, and it is doubtful that Paul would have approached that level of ethnicity-based discrimination in the name of Christ with the arguments we meet in Romans.[18] Let us examine a few details.

First, it is highly unlikely that all or even much of the Jewish community was expelled from Rome by Claudius. Suetonius's report can be understood to indicate an expulsion of only those Jews involved in a disturbance, in direct conflict with the statement in Acts 18:2 that all the Jews were expelled. The silence of Jewish and Roman writers about this expulsion is all the more suggestive when we note that citizens, which at least a number of Jews in Rome were, could not be expelled without due process. Moreover, Dio Cassius writes specifically that Claudius did not expel the Jews of Rome but only restricted their meetings (*Hist. Rom.* 60.6.6–7). Further, while the author of Acts notes that the Jewish leaders in Rome have little firsthand knowledge of the Christ-followers and mentions the wholesale expulsion, he does not link this expulsion to a disturbance over Christ (18:1–4). The author of Acts may well know that it had nothing to do with disturbances related to claims about Christ. Whatever his source, it seems to have exaggerated the extent of any such edict. Luke's notice simply explains why Aquila and Priscilla, who are not explicitly identified

---

18. For a more detailed discussion, see my *Mystery of Romans*, 372–87.

as already Christ-followers, were in Corinth when Paul met these fellow Jews and leather workers, whom he stayed with "because he was of the same trade."

Second, it is unlikely that the expulsion mentioned was precipitated by disputes about Jesus Christ. Suetonius elsewhere discusses the *christiani* under Nero rather than the *chrestiani* (*Nero* 16.2), following Tacitus, who already knew of the *christiani*. This spelling suggests that Suetonius knew the difference and that he was not under the impression that the expulsion under Claudius had anything to do with Christ or Christ-followers, but with someone in Rome named *Chrestus*, a relatively common name in Rome.[19]

Third, it is curious to suppose that Romans would have expelled Jews without also expelling the non-Jews meeting in their midst. Would they be left in Rome to carry on meetings involving the name Christ and avoiding civic cult including to Caesar if such groups had provoked disturbances that had led to the expulsion of the Jewish community in the first place?

Fourth, most importantly, Paul's approach to the non-Jews in Romans is not what one might expect if they were in positions of power and using that power to exclude or discriminate against Jewish Christ-followers. If they appealed to the teaching of Paul or other leaders to legitimate such behavior, we could expect Paul to challenge these teachings and teachers much more directly, just as he had in other writings (cf. 1 Cor 1:10–6:20). We might also expect some direct instruction about respecting at least the five Jews mentioned in chapter 16, instead of just extending simple greetings and acknowledging their positions of authority in the community (two holding meetings in their house, which suggests a problem with the construction, and two others are "apostles").

Although a relatively new twist on this historical data, many recent interpreters matter-of-factly relay this construction in their introductions to Romans. Yet, the data do not provide a reliable foundation to build upon. Someone coming upon this construct who did not think it supported an interpretation of Romans already held would not likely be impressed that it constituted a reliable historical measure by which to limit the options for exploring the context for or meaning of Paul's message.

---

19. Suetonius also appears to be unaware that this supposed *Christus* was not actually in Rome at the time of Claudius, if that was to whom he meant to refer.

The Rhetorical Implications from the Letter

In the formal opening of the letter, Paul introduces himself in language that would make little sense to a Greco-Roman person apart from learning the story of Christ within the context of the Jewish communal narrative, one that can be developed from Jewish Scriptures but not elsewhere. He not only cites Jewish Scriptures, which he will continue to do more than in any other extant letter, some fifty-plus times, but he alludes to these Scriptures many more times. He apparently assumes that the recipients would be competent to follow his line of thought. Yet copies of these Jewish texts were expensive and apparently not well known outside of Jewish communities. How then would they know the Scriptures upon which his arguments were based apart from being socialized into Jewish communal life?

If these non-Jews attended Jewish communal meetings, they would hear the Scriptures read, translated, and interpreted in regular, weekly sermons.[20] Or are we to suppose that Paul expected those raised on Greek and Roman stories (but not those of the Bible) were meeting in households independent of Jewish communal affiliation, and that each already possessed these expensive scrolls (or had attendees who already knew them well enough from earlier exposure that they could now recite and explain them)? In addition, would they have competent readers and the educational programs sufficient to prepare them to understand Paul's Scripture-based arguments? Alternatively, are we to suppose that Paul simply overshot the competence of his recipients, playing on their respect for the authority of this source as a persuasive advantage?

Paul approaches his audience as if they are familiar with many concepts that would be foreign to non-Jews. In the first sentence, he makes the significance of the lineage of David central, that is, the idea that a king (i.e., messianic leader) as promised in Scripture was now on the throne of Israel, even though his descendants had been living under occupying empires for over six hundred years, and now lived under Roman rule. Paul presents the one who fills that role as having been killed by crucifixion, which was reserved for slaves and feared terrorists and carried out by the regime of Caesar, the one ruling the world from his home city, Rome. Roman readers would recognize that Paul's argument challenges the claims of the Roman

---

20. Cf. Philo, *Hypoth.* 7.12–13; Josephus, *A.J.* 16.43; *C. Ap.* 2.175; *B.J.* 2.291; Luke 4:16–22; Acts 13:14–15; 15:21.

empire; but how deeply would they resonate with this Jewish tradition apart from familiarity with Jewish communal interpretations and ways of negotiating the paradoxes such aspirations created?

There is not space to discuss many similar topics in the letter that seem to suggest a Jewish communal context, since for many interpreters they simply suggest some familiarity with Jewish Scriptures, as indeed did come to be the case in Christianity. Such topics are found throughout the letter. Several features in chapter 11, which discusses the topic of those Israelites/Jews who do not share Paul and his target audience's convictions about Jesus, support a strong case for intimate interaction, as well as the improbability of the kind of break that is central to the edict-of-Claudius constructions of the situation in Rome. Let us take a closer look at this particular chapter.

The Implied Jewish Communal Context of the Non-Jews Addressed in Chapter 11

The identity of the Christ-followers Paul addressed is a critical factor in determining how to approach the implications of his comments. Regardless of the actual makeup of the audience in Rome, it is important to hypothesize the makeup of the audience Paul imagined he would influence. More specifically, we need to identify whom he targeted with his various comments, perhaps even different groups at different points in different arguments. These specific people or subgroups are referred to variously as the author's "target" or "implied" or "encoded" or even "rhetorical" audience—that is, the ones whom the author seeks to persuade directly when the letter is read. When an author seeks to influence, the construal of the audience may already be shaped by how the author wishes for them to conceptualize themselves and their circumstances. This "rhetorical" dynamic can mislead the later reader who does not know the actual makeup of the original historical audience, author, and situation, including exactly how the author sought to influence that audience, and how the author chose to address them, or intentionally refrained from doing so. The author may also target different specific constituents among the audience imagined to receive the text, and do so disproportionately, either by ignoring certain other groups among the recipients, or addressing them and their concerns less or indirectly, even implicitly.

Throughout the letter there are indications that the members of Paul's target audience—the ones to whom he directs his attention specifically—

are non-Jews, because he describes some people as his Jewish compatriots in chapter 16. These audience members are identified as those from among "the nations" (*ta ethnē*) to whom Paul is specifically called to proclaim the message of Christ (e.g., 1:5–6, 13; 11:13–32; 15:15–16). Furthermore, in the midst of Paul's arguments, these non-Jews are often differentiated from "them," Jews about whom Paul writes, and in many cases "they" are Jews who are not Christ-followers (e.g., 3:1–3; 9:1–5; 10:1–2; 11:1, 11–32; 15:25–32). Although there is controversy about whether Paul was always targeting non-Jews throughout the letter, in 11:13 he says explicitly that he is targeting non-Jews, members from the nations other than Israel ("now I am speaking to you Gentiles"; NRSV), and this remains the case throughout this chapter.

Chapter 11 represents the culmination of the arguments Paul began in chapter 1, followed by the "therefore" of 12:1, which initiates a transition to the instructions that occupy the rest of the letter. Paul seeks to explain to non-Jewish Christ-followers the present anomalous situation in which many Jews (members of the nation Israel) are not persuaded about the meaning of Jesus at the same time that a number of members of the other nations, such as his addressees, are persuaded. This is the case even though the Scriptures, as Paul understands them, uphold the covenant promise that "all Israel will be restored," "removing godlessness from Jacob" (i.e., Israel), and "taking away their sins" (11:26–27).

Throughout the argument Paul instructs these non-Jews to resist any temptation to grow arrogant or suppose that they have replaced those Israelites who are "stumbling," that is, those Jews not joining Paul as heralds who proclaim the message of Christ to the nations. These non-Jews should not be concerned only about their own success. Rather, they are to recognize humbly the generosity (grace/favor/benefaction) of God toward themselves and, in reciprocity, to think and to live generously toward those who are temporarily suffering this fate, which is somehow, mysteriously, tied up with how God is bringing about the promised restoration of these members of Israel. Nevertheless, those Jews remain in the covenant relationship, albeit in some kind of disciplinary state. He seeks to clarify that, however inscrutable the plan may be, it involves some Israelites now requiring God's mercy for their present failure to be persuaded to proclaim Christ to the nations alongside Paul. This is similar to the mercy extended to these former idolaters from the other nations for their failure to be persuaded about the one Creator God. Now, although for different reasons, all are joined in equal need of God's mercy (vv. 25–32).

In making his case, Paul develops an allegory in which the non-Jewish audience is one shoot cut off of a wild olive tree and grafted among the many branches natural to a cultivated olive tree, which represent members of Israel (vv. 17–24).[21] By way of the olive tree allegory, Paul argues that God will not tolerate arrogant attitudes or behavior toward those branches suffering some kind of temporary state of harm, which are being cloaked in a divine "callus [*pōrōsis*]" to keep them, and the overall tree, protected until they are prepared to produce fruit.[22]

Paul's language presupposes that these non-Jews are involved in personal contact with Jews who do not share their views about Jesus, but whom Paul believes will, in due time. At the same time, these non-Jews must avoid behaving in arrogant ways that might turn these Jews away from considering this proposition. Moreover, if that should occur, God will punish these non-Jews severely; in metaphorical terms, they will be cut off from the tree, to which they were not natural in the first place. The image in the allegory of one wild shoot among many natural branches suggests a social situation in which the non-Jews are the minority group among a much larger and more diverse body of Jews; the non-Jews are not the majority or separated socially from the Jews whom they might negatively affect—although we must be careful not to make too much out of allegorical elements. In any case, the social connections implied in spelling out the role of these non-Jews in the divine plan for the restoration of these Israelites, and the price to be paid for failing to perform their part, are palpable. Actually, Paul makes them plain just before beginning this allegory.

Paul introduces the idea in verses 11–12 that some Israelites were suffering a temporary setback in their divine role as messengers of God enlisted to bring God's words to the nations. That has been to the immediate benefit of these non-Jews, but ultimately, Paul argues, their best interests will actually be served when these Israelites are restored to carrying out their special task. In his two uses of the metaphor of messengers running

---

21. See Mark D. Nanos, "'Broken Branches': A Pauline Metaphor Gone Awry? (Romans 11:11–36)," in *Between Gospel and Election: Explorations in the Interpretation of Romans 9–11* (ed. Florian Wilk and J. Ross Wagner; WUNT 257; Tübingen: Mohr Siebeck, 2010), 339–76.

22. See Mark D. Nanos, "'Callused,' Not 'Hardened': Paul's Revelation of Temporary Protection Until All Israel Can Be Healed," in *Reading Paul in Context: Explorations in Identity Formation* (ed. Kathy Ehrensperger and J. Brian Tucker; London: T&T Clark, 2010), 52–73.

but some temporarily tripping (which Paul draws on both before and after the tree allegory, and elsewhere throughout the letter), they are characterized as "stumbling," but forcefully declared "not fallen!" Thus, non-Jews should not think their own success is best gained by these Jews remaining unconvinced about taking the gospel message to the nations. In verse 12 and again in verse 15, Paul makes the comparative point that the return of those Jews will be exponentially more advantageous for non-Jews than it has been to date. Paul declares that these non-Jews' own aspirations will actually only be realized following the restoration of these Jews to their role as heralds of the gospel.

In verses 13–14 Paul tells these non-Jews that even his efforts toward them were motivated by his commitment to the ultimate restoration of those fellow Israelites. In other words, these non-Jews' interests are not even the ultimate goal of Paul's ministry! Rather, his work among them is a means to accomplish another end: "Now I am speaking to you Gentiles. Inasmuch then as I am an apostle to the Gentiles, I glorify my ministry in order to make my own people jealous, and thus save some of them" (NRSV).[23]

Note that it is not jealousy of these non-Jews that Paul promotes, as if he would have expected Jews to understand these non-Jews to be replacing them. That would have hardly made sense to any Jews who rejected this message as mistaken, since they would not then have seen themselves as missing out or supposed that these non-Jews have gained something worth gaining; they have decided already that this is not the case. Moreover, Paul seeks to make his fellow Jews "jealous," and, specifically, jealous "*of his ministry*," that is, of Paul's successful work among non-Jews. Jealousy bespeaks the desire to "emulate" (Gk.: *zēlos*; to want to gain for oneself), not to deny to the other per se; it is very different from wanting to provoke "envy" (Gk.: *phthonos*), a begrudging reaction to the good gained by another.

Paul wants his fellow Jews to join him in declaring the good news among the non-Jewish nations when they see the successful results of his ministry. He imagines that the Jews will recognize that his success

---

23. The case can be strengthened by alternative translation, but it is not necessary in order to make the point: "But I am speaking to you members of the nations: inasmuch then as I am an apostle to the nations, I think (about how to carry out) my ministry, if somehow I may make my flesh (i.e., fellow Israelites) jealous of me, and restore some of them."

represents their own promised destiny, the hope of Israel, so that they
will then conclude that they are not "yet" participating with him in this
special, covenant privilege, because they have not shared his conviction
that the age to come has begun with Christ. It is Israel's special calling
to declare God's words to the world (see 3:1–2!), at least when the day
arrives to initiate this special task. Paul believes that day has dawned with
the resurrection of Christ and calling of himself and others to be "sent"
(i.e., apostles) to the nations with this news, followed then by the full light
of that day.

Thus, in Paul's way of thinking, when he gains a positive response to
his ministry among non-Jewish nations, his fellow Jews who witness the
turning of these non-Jews from idolatry to the one God will see that a new,
promised stage has arrived. They will then recognize that the awaited day
has indeed begun among these subgroups composed of Jews and non-
Jews celebrating Christ. Israel must be in the stage of being restored (i.e.,
"saved," in common theological terms), and made ready to announce this
news, but some of them have excluded themselves. Rather than envy, that
is, begrudging Paul or his audience's claims of gaining good, they will
judge this behavior legitimate (i.e., "justified," "right-eous," in common
theological terms) and want to be a part of this awaited fulfillment of
Israel's covenant expectations (i.e., "to evangelize"). In Paul's terms, they
will join him in trusting that God has raised Jesus from the dead and
announce that God has initiated the dawning of the age to come with
this act.

Paul's relating of his motivation and plan for success among the non-
Jewish nations reveals much, but what does it suggest about the state of
the social situation in Rome? If a cataclysmic separation of the Christ-
followers into separate meetings, indeed, into rival and specifically non-
Jewish-oriented meetings, has already developed (as the traditional and
edict-of-Claudius constructions contend), then Paul's hopes for the positive reaction of Jews to his ministry among the nations would seem to be
misguided. How could he suppose that they will assess his mission in self-
authenticating terms? Would not any Jews who would learn of his mission
consider it independent of Jewish communal aspirations and dangerous?
Is this not even more the case if he claims to represent a Greco-Roman
"Christian" rather than a Jewish movement, which could be dismissed as
irrelevant? Could such activity result in the positive reconsideration that
Paul seems to anticipate and desire?

If the communal life of Christ-followers took place in groups that were no longer operating within the larger Jewish community, all the more if by definition purposefully separated from it, Paul could not reasonably suppose that they would assess these later developments positively. Jews who had already dismissed the claims of these groups would probably not only remain generally unaware of such non-Jewish communal activity, but would also regard any such news that reached them with indifference if not hostility. But Paul does not think that will be the outcome, and he glories instead in imagining how his ministry among the non-Jews will provide the positive catalyst for his fellow Jews to reconsider his message, moreover, to want to emulate his ministry.

I approach Paul's texts with the assumption that he was able to reason well, regardless of whether I agree with his conclusions, and in spite of the fact that it seems things did not turn out as he hoped they would. Nevertheless, it takes real, intimate contact within the community of those who practice Judaism for Paul to expect that his readers will understand his meaning and identify their own interests and experiences with these aspirations, as well as to suppose that his fellow Jews will react in the manner he describes. I do not understand how Paul could imagine this scenario, or expect his audience to do so, apart from continued identity within the Jewish communities as subgroups, as those who understand themselves to be models of the practice of Judaism, albeit as non-Jews. That conclusion is in keeping with how Paul interprets the significance of incorporating non-Jews within these Jewish subgroups as equal members of God's people, although they do not become Jews/members of Israel but rather represent those from the other nations who join alongside of Jews/Israelites. For Paul, this communal gathering thereby exemplifies the arrival of the end of the ages, when, according to Scripture, the wolf will graze with, rather than devour, the lamb (Isa 65:25).

For Further Reading

Campbell, William S. *Paul and the Creation of Christian Identity*. LNTS 322. London: T&T Clark, 2006. Campbell's approach to Paul and to the message of Romans, which is the focus of most of his monograph, is in many ways compatible with mine. Because he does not share the view that the audience was still in the synagogues or that Paul was Torah-observant, his arguments may be especially relevant for those who are interested in aspects of my interpretation of Paul or Romans, but not convinced of those elements.

Fisk, Bruce N. "Synagogue Influence and Scriptural Knowledge among the Christians of Rome." Pages 157–85 in *As It Is Written: Studying Paul's Use of Scripture*. Edited by Stanley E. Porter and Christopher D. Stanley. SBLSymS 50. Atlanta: Society of Biblical Literature, 2008. Fisk challenges interpreters of Romans to consider the logical strengths of constructing the situation in Rome and the message of the letter in the way proposed herein. His additional insights, largely drawn from intertextual observations, offer further support for exploring this hypothesis.

Nanos, Mark D. "The Jewish Context of the Gentile Audience Addressed in Paul's Letter to the Romans." *CBQ* 61 (1999): 283–304. In this essay I detail the historical and rhetorical bases for understanding the audience of Romans to be composed of Gentiles who are a subgroup within the Jewish synagogue.

———. *The Mystery of Romans: The Jewish Context of Paul's Letter*. Minneapolis: Fortress, 1996. In this book I offer an examination of some of the many new interpretive options that arise from reading Romans as targeting Christ-following non-Jews in synagogue subgroups whom Paul seeks to bring to a better understanding of who they are and how they fit into God's larger plan for themselves as well as "all" Israel.

Rutgers, Leonard Victor. *The Jews in Late Ancient Rome: Evidence of Cultural Interaction in the Roman Diaspora*. RGRW 126. Leiden: Brill, 1995. Rutgers evaluates the material and literary evidence important to any construction of the context of the recipients of Romans.

Slingerland, H. Dixon. *Claudian Policymaking and the Early Imperial Repression of Judaism at Rome*. SFSHJ 160. Atlanta: Scholars Press, 1997. Slingerland provides a comprehensive study of the expulsion by Claudius that challenges the conclusions upon which the prevailing constructions are based. His conclusions support the position advocated in this essay.

The Gentile-Encoded Audience of Romans: The Church outside the Synagogue

A. Andrew Das

For decades scholars have debated the purpose and occasion behind Paul's Letter to the Romans. Books have appeared with titles such as *The Mystery of Romans* and *The Romans Debate*. The letter has remained, as one scholar put it, an "enigma." One should not conclude, however, that the discussion has been fruitless or that no progress has been made. Several avenues of investigation have, arguably, been satisfied or proved dead ends, especially those that have not accounted for the manner in which the letter seems to address the specific circumstances in the Christ-believing Roman assemblies (see §1 below). The best clue to the letter's situation and purpose is with the encoded audience, that is, the audience as reconstructed from the letter itself and as conceptually distinguished from the *actual* original hearers. Despite the scholarly popularity of viewing the Roman congregations as a mixture of both Christ-believing Jews and Gentiles (non-Jews), the letter, when considered on its own terms, targets an exclusively Gentile audience. Whether or not Jews were physically present in the Roman congregations, Paul identifies his hearers as Gentile. At key points, especially the opening and the ending of the letter, Paul includes the audience within his Gentile ministry (see §2). Advocates of a mixed audience have therefore responded with a series of passages that, for many, indicate the presence of Jewish believers in Christ within the encoded audience of the letter. These passages have not proven particularly compelling (see §3). At the same time, the encoded audience members clearly demonstrate some familiarity with Judaism. The Roman "weak" are sympathetic with the Jewish faith even as the "strong" see little reason for observing Jewish customs. This awareness of the Jewish faith makes sense only if the young Christ-movement in Rome began in contact with the synagogues (§4). A consideration of the external evidence, including an edict of expulsion that took place under the emperor Claudius, offers a picture that dovetails remarkably with what may be gathered from the letter itself (§5). Paul does not intend for the Gentiles in the capital of a powerful empire to lose touch with the vital Jewish roots of their faith. This essay therefore represents a solution to the ongoing Romans debate that accounts for the full range of evidence.

1. A Concrete Situation in Rome

In the 1977 *Romans Debate*, as well as in the 1991 expanded second edition, Karl Donfried helpfully assembled a variety of perspectives regarding the occasion and purpose of Romans. Several of those points of view are no longer considered seriously viable. For instance, although the ancient textual tradition is not unanimous, Romans specialists now tend to agree on a sixteen-chapter version of the letter.[1] Few these days would consider Romans a mere summary of Paul's theology with no connection to the particulars of the Roman assemblies. The letter is far from comprehensive in its choice of topics, and the specific groups described in Rom 14–15 suggest a concrete situation. Disagreement persists on the significance of Paul's brief comments near the end of the letter about his desire to evangelize in Spain (15:24, 28) and his plans to return shortly to Jerusalem (15:26–28, 31). The apostle does not link these briefly mentioned plans with the content of the letter. He does not connect his request for a welcome in Rome (15:30–33) to his plans to go to Jerusalem or to Spain. The wide-ranging destination points—Rome, Jerusalem, Spain—in all probability serve less as the *purpose* of the letter than as a further consideration for why the Romans, whom Paul has not yet visited, should heed this stranger's advice. For that matter, Paul does not just emphasize where he is *going* but also where he *has been*. If the churches of Greece and Asia Minor have received his ministry, how much more should the assemblies in Rome? Were Jerusalem or Spain of greater significance for Paul, he would surely at some point have connected the letter's content with his upcoming itinerary.

---

1. See A. Andrew Das, *Solving the Romans Debate* (Minneapolis: Fortress, 2007), 10–23, also 23–24 n. 83.

Many interpreters continue to point to the interactions between the "strong" and the "weak" in Rom 14:1–15:6 as a clue to a concrete situation in Rome that Paul wishes to address. Since Paul's undisputed letters deal with particular situations in individual churches and regions, should Romans be an exception? Although Paul addresses the "weak" and "strong" in Corinth, his discussion in Romans differs considerably from First Corinthians. In his admonitions to the Corinthians, Paul warned against eating meat sacrificed to idols and against eating in idol temples, both nonfactors in his Romans discussion. He also does not refer to the Romans' "knowledge" or "conscience" (cf. 1 Cor 8:1–12; 10:25, 27–29). Instead, he refers to differences in the Romans' "faith" (Rom 14:1, 22, 23). The weak in Rome, unlike those in Corinth, eat vegetables (Rom 14:2) and observe the days (Rom 14:5). Paul is not summarizing or generalizing instructions originally given in a different context. The differences in his instructions appear motivated by the specific circumstances in Rome.[2]

At several points in the letter, Paul demonstrates awareness, at least to some extent, of the situation in the Roman assemblies. He praises the Romans' faith (1:8), their maturity (15:14), and their obedience as "known to all" (16:19). He refers to the "teaching" they had received (6:17; 16:17) and is confident that his instructions will serve merely as a "reminder" (15:14–15). The Romans appear to be aware already of his desire to visit (1:9–11, 13; 15:18–23). Even his comments regarding the collection for the Jerusalem saints assume prior knowledge of his efforts (15:26). Perhaps the Romans were also aware of criticisms of Paul, and Paul, in turn, knows this (3:8). As one who has yet to visit or meet many of the Roman believers, Paul's obliqueness is understandable as a matter of tact as he offers apostolic advice for the Romans. The apostle's general awareness of the situation in Rome suggests that his explicit identification of the audience should be taken seriously.

---

2. William S. Campbell even went so far as to refer to a "consensus" that Rom 14–15 are "specifically addressed to Rome" ("The Addressees of Paul's Letter to the Romans: Assemblies of God in House Churches and Synagogues?" in *Between Gospel and Election: Explorations in the Interpretation of Romans 9–11* [ed. Florian Wilk and J. Ross Wagner; WUNT 257; Tübingen: Mohr Siebeck, 2010], 172).

2. A GENTILE-ENCODED AUDIENCE

Paul greets "all" the Roman Christ-believers in 1:7. Toward the end of the letter, he returns to his relationship with the addressees and identifies them. He has also left clues to the encoded readers' identity in the body of the letter. With consistency, he repeatedly identifies the Roman audience as Gentile. In Rom 1:5–6 he writes, "We have received grace and apostleship to bring about the obedience of faith *among all the Gentiles* for the sake of his name, *among whom you also* are called of Jesus Christ" (emphasis added).[3] Paul is not reminding the Romans of the obvious fact that they live in a Gentile world. He is emphasizing that they, as Gentiles, are within the realm of his apostolic authority as one commissioned for the obedience of faith of *all* the Gentiles (v. 5); thus he writes "to *all* the beloved of God who are in Rome" (v. 7). In the same breath as verse 5's "all the Gentiles" (*en pasin tois ethnesin*), Paul adds "including yourselves" (*en hois este kai hymeis*, v. 6). His commission to bring about the obedience of faith of all the Gentiles serves as the rationale for his writing those in Rome. Likewise a few verses later in 1:13, "I do not want you to be ignorant, brothers and sisters, that I often planned to come to you (but was prevented until now), in order that I may reap some fruit among you just as I have also among the rest of the Gentiles" (*kai en hymin kathōs kai en tois loipois ethnesin*). Paul refers to "the rest" of the Gentiles in relation to his Roman audience. Although the Christ-believing congregations in Rome were already in existence long before he wrote or visited (Rom 15:23), the twofold identification of the Roman audience as Gentile at the beginning of the letter explains why they should heed the advice of the apostle to the Gentiles (11:13).

Even as Paul grounds his relations with the Romans in his apostolic commission to the Gentiles in chapter 1, so also in chapter 15. Indeed, these chapters should be interpreted in connection with each other in view of the extensive connections and *inclusio* formed by Rom 1:5–15 and 15:14–32.[4] In Rom 15:15–16 Paul directly addresses his audience and justifies his writing "boldly" to "you" Romans because of his calling as a "minister of Christ Jesus to the Gentiles." He writes to the Romans "*so that the offering of the Gentiles may be acceptable.*" He hopes, through contact

---

3. Unless otherwise noted, translations are from the NRSV, with modifications by the author.

4. James D. G. Dunn, *Romans 9–16* (WBC 38B; Dallas: Word, 1988), 857.

with the Romans, to fulfill his God-given responsibility to the Gentiles: "for I will not dare to say anything except what Christ has accomplished through me for the obedience of the *Gentiles*" (15:18). The logic in these verses repeatedly assumes that the Romans are themselves Gentiles and thus the rightful recipients of his ministry.

One other passage from the body of the letter should be briefly noted. In Rom 11:13 Paul writes, "Now I am speaking to you Gentiles. Inasmuch as I am an apostle to the Gentiles, I glorify my ministry if perhaps I might make my flesh [people] jealous and save some of them." Throughout chapters 9–11 Paul speaks to the Gentile audience *about* his own people. As in the opening and in the later announcement of his plans in Rom 15 (what is called the apostolic "parousia"), Paul consistently and conspicuously identifies his ministry to the Gentiles as the basis for his address of the Romans, and these passages form a pattern:

	Ministry	Recipients	Including
1:5–6	apostleship	Gentiles	the Romans
1:13	reap harvest	Gentiles	the Romans
11:13	apostle to	Gentiles	the Romans
15:15–16	minister to	Gentiles	the Romans

In each instance, (1) Paul refers to his apostolic ministry, (2) he identifies the Gentiles as the recipients of that ministry, and then (3) he explicitly includes the Romans. He is therefore identifying the Romans as within the sphere of his apostolic labors. Some have noted that the Greek word Paul uses for "Gentiles" (non-Jews) may also mean "nations" (*ethnē*). If these verses were merely saying that Paul and his audience were located in the midst of the "nations" of the world, a rather mundane point, then the repeated emphasis (1:5–6, 13–15; 11:13; 15:15–16) would be inexplicable. Paul has not yet visited Rome. Although the Romans have yet to meet him, they should heed his advice precisely because he is Christ's minister to the Gentiles and they are Gentiles.[5]

---

5. On 1:5–6, 13, 11:13, 15:15–16, and 15:18 as clear evidence for the Gentile-encoded audience, see Das, *Romans Debate*, 54–68.

3. Jews in the Audience?

Despite the explicit identification of the audience as Gentile, most commentators rely on certain passages from the letter for decisive evidence that the Roman congregations included at least a minority of Jewish Christ-believers. For instance, Paul turns to address a "Jew" and a "circumcised" individual in 2:17–3:1. However, these paragraphs employ a diatribal style from antiquity with a *fictive* interlocutor.[6] In other words, when the ancient author employed this device he or she was not addressing an *actual* member of the audience but was turning aside to dialogue with an imaginary discussion partner or "interlocutor" as a means of grabbing the audience's attention and furthering the point. The author would address the interlocutor with a vocative expression, then reject the proposed notion with words such as "May it never be" (*mē genoito*), and finally offer a statement in support of the negation (introduced with a particle such as *alla, ti oun, gar, ti de*). Turning to the fictive Jew would prove rhetorically powerful for the Roman Gentiles, some of whom had had prior experience with the Jewish community and who had adopted certain Jewish customs. The Gentiles would overhear the "Jew" addressed by Paul and would be forced to revise their understanding of their relationship to the Jewish faith.

Quite apart from the particular style of speech involved, interpreters who identify a Jewish minority in the Roman audience generally have not recognized that the description of the "circumcised" "Jew" in Rom 2:17–29 does not match the *Christ-believing* Jews assumed to be in the audience. The Jew of Rom 2 appears to be a non-Christ-believer whom Paul must scold for not living in a manner consistent with his or her Jewish confession: "'The name of God is blasphemed among the Gentiles because of you'" (2:24). "Those who are physically uncircumcised but keep the law will condemn you that have the written code and circumcision but break the law" (2:27). This Jew is put to shame by those circumcised in heart and empowered by the Spirit who, as will be clear at the judgment, live in a manner befitting the worship of the true God. As the letter continues (Rom 8:1–4), Paul returns to that Spirit-endowed individual, who has succeeded where those under the letter of the law have not. Romans 2:17–29

---

6. Stanley Stowers, *The Diatribe and Paul's Letter to the Romans* (SBLDS 57; Chico, Calif.: Scholars Press, 1981), 177; Runar M. Thorsteinsson, *Paul's Interlocutor in Romans 2: Function and Identity in the Context of Ancient Epistolography* (ConBNT 40; Stockholm: Almqvist & Wiksell, 2003), 124–30.

therefore anticipates what will unfold more fully later in the letter. The "Jew" of Rom 2 without the Spirit or the circumcision of the heart is simply not the same sort of Jew as the supposed Christ-believer in the Roman congregations. Recognizing that Paul uses the style of diatribe resolves the potential difficulty posed by such harsh words.[7]

In Rom 7:1 Paul writes to the Romans as those who "know the law," but he has just identified his audience in 6:19 as former slaves of, literally, "impurity" (*akatharsia*) and greater and greater "lawlessness" (*anomia*). This description would be appropriate only for Gentiles. The Jews, in adhering to Moses's law, avoided unclean foods and would have found such a description offensive. Advocates of a Jewish minority in Paul's audience, to a large degree, have not recognized a rather crucial point regarding 7:1–6: the law with respect to the husband and instructions on divorce, marriage, and remarriage have figured prominently in Paul's prior teaching of *Gentiles* (1 Cor 7:10–11, 39–40).[8] He traces this particular emphasis on marriage and remarriage from the law to Jesus' teaching, which the apostle now conveys. In other words, the particular aspect of the law with which Paul expects his audience to be familiar is precisely what has figured in early Christian teaching of the Gentiles and derives from Jesus' teaching. In singling out the "law *of the husband*" as his example, Paul offers yet another tell-tale sign that his audience is Gentile.

Furthermore, as for "knowing the law," Paul does not specify what level of knowledge he expects of his readers in Rom 7:1–6. The point Paul makes does not require any specific knowledge of the law. Ancient readers did not normally have written manuscripts available for study in the same way as the modern reader. Even if Paul's Gentile readers somehow had access to synagogue manuscripts of the Scriptures, only ten to twenty percent of the people were literate in a world where most people struggled to survive. While modern readers frequently recognize sophisticated and intriguing connections to Hebrew Bible passages behind Paul's letters, it is questionable whether Paul expected his Gentile readers to recognize these allusions. Knowledge of the original contexts of the biblical citations in Romans is not necessary to understand or appreciate the apostle's points.[9]

---

7. See Das, *Romans Debate*, 87–89.

8. Peter J. Tomson, "What Did Paul Mean by 'Those Who Know the Law'? (Rom 7.1)," *NTS* 49 (2003): 576–77.

9. See Christopher D. Stanley, *Arguing with Scripture: The Rhetoric of Quotations in the Letters of Paul* (London: T&T Clark, 2004), 136–70, note esp. 132–33.

Still, from a rhetorical standpoint, Paul's frequent mention of the Jewish Scriptures forces the Roman audience to understand itself in relation to the heritage of Israel.

In Rom 14:1–15:6 Paul advises the "weak" and the "strong." The weak "observe the day" while the strong do not (14:5–6). Are the "weak" observing Jewish Sabbath and festival celebrations? In 14:14 the weak see certain foods as "common" or "unclean" with a Greek word never used in the literature of the day to express purity concerns apart from Judaism (*koinos*; three times!).[10] Conversely, even as Moses's law prescribed ritual cleanliness (e.g., Acts 10:15; 11:9), in Rom 14:20 Paul declares all things "clean" (*kathara*). The "weak" are avoiding meat and wine in favor of a diet consisting of vegetables and water (Rom 14:21; cf. 14:17) "for the Lord" (14:6). Paul expresses concern that they might lose their faith if forced to drop these practices (14:20).[11] Jews historically resorted to such diets when they did not have access to their own markets. Most readers of Romans have thus concluded that the "weak" are Jewish.

On the other hand, the practices of the "weak" were precisely those adopted by *non-Jews* sympathetic toward Judaism. Josephus, the Jewish historian, boasted how widespread among Greeks and barbarians were Jewish Sabbath and food customs (*C. Ap.* 2.39 §282 [Thackeray, LCL]).[12] Several authors of this period noted how Romans would light lamps and close shops and businesses on the Jewish Sabbath.[13] One of Horace's friends did not wish to converse with him out of respect for the Sabbath and identified himself, jokingly, as "a somewhat weaker brother, one of the many" (*Sat.* 1.9.68–72 [Fairclough, LCL]; 65–8 B.C.E.). The humor depended on a perception of the widespread practice of the Jewish Sabbath among the masses.[14] The designation "weaker" matches Paul's language for the "weak" in Rom 14. Seneca lamented how "the conquered [Jews] have given laws to the conquerors," who have little understanding

---

10. Dunn, *Romans 9–16*, 818–20.

11. Paul is accommodating of the practices of the weak, but he would hardly have been so accommodating had pagan or neo-Pythagorean calendrical observances been at issue. The Christ-believing context is a problem for proposals that the weak are adherents of Gnostic or Hellenistic mystery religions.

12. See also *C. Ap.* 2.10 §§ 121–124 and Tertullian, *Nat.* 1.13.

13. Ovid, *Ars.* 1.413–416; Seneca, *Ep.* 95.47; Plutarch, *Superst.* 3.166a; Martial, *Epigr.* 4.4, lines 7–12; Suetonius, *Tib.* 32.2; Persius, *Sat.* 5.180–184.

14. Ovid assumes a general familiarity with the Jews' Sabbath in *Ars.* 1.75–76.

of the origin and meaning of such rites.[15] In the middle of the first century
C.E., Petronius distinguished between those who worship the "pig god"
(i.e., Jewish dietary laws) and those who are circumcised and observe the
Sabbath.[16] Similarly, Juvenal in the early second century C.E. (*Sat.* 14.96–
106) contrasted a father who merely observed the Sabbath and avoided
pork with a son who fully converted to Judaism and was circumcised (*Sat.*
14.96–101 [Braund, LCL]). Observing the days and abstaining from meat
were precisely what Gentile sympathizers of Judaism were widely recognized as doing.[17] Paul does not shy away from discussing Jews elsewhere in
his Letter to the Romans. His oblique description of the "weak" would be
appropriate for *non*-Jews observing such customs. Indeed, his description
of law-observant and non-law-observant lifestyles as equally valid (14:6,
17) would not be winsome or persuasive if the "weak" were Jews whose
very identity would be bound up with such practices.[18] Paul could treat
such customs as, ultimately, matters of indifference precisely because his
audience did *not* consist of Jews.

Interpreters have frequently found the proposal of a Gentile-encoded
audience to be difficult in view of the Jews who number among the Roman
congregations according to Rom 16. At least five of the individuals in this
chapter were most likely Jewish: Prisca, Aquila, Andronicus, Junia, and
Herodion. On the other hand, those who specialize in ancient handbooks
on letter-writing have drawn attention to the fact that ancient admonitions
to greet someone that employ second-person pronouns request the letter's
recipients to greet a *third* party.[19] Paul employs that form of admonition in

---

15. As quoted by Augustine, *Civ.* 6.11 (*NPNF* 1/2:120–21).

16. Fragment 37 (Poem 24 in Heseltine, LCL). See the discussion in Louis H.
Feldman, *Jew and Gentile in the Ancient World: Attitudes and Interactions from Alex-
ander to Justinian* (Princeton: Princeton University Press, 1993), 344, 346.

17. Many Gentile Christians would have shared with the Jews a wariness of meat
or wine offered to the gods and would have felt constrained to refrain from partaking
(Rom 14:3; cf. 1 Cor 8). On abstention from idolatrous meat and wine, see Philip F.
Esler, *Galatians* (NTR; London: Routledge, 1998), 92–116; for Jewish abstention, see
Dan 1:8–16; Jdt 12:1–14; Esth 14:7, 17 (LXX); Josephus, *A.J.* 4.137; *Vita* 13–14.

18. See especially John M. G. Barclay "'Do We Undermine the Law?' A Study of
Romans 14.1–15.6," in *Paul and the Mosaic Law* (ed. James D. G. Dunn; Tübingen:
Mohr Siebeck, 1996), 304–8.

19. Terence Y. Mullins, "Greetings as a New Testament Form," *JBL* 87 (1968):
418–26, esp. 420–21; Hans-Josef Klauck, *Ancient Letters and the New Testament: A
Guide to Content and Exegesis* (Waco, Tex.: Baylor University Press), 24–25.

Rom 16. He is therefore admonishing his hearers (the Roman congregations) to greet the people whom he names. The named people would be
outside the Roman congregations or perhaps newcomers into their midst.
Interpreters have also overlooked the fact that the Greek word sometimes translated "compatriot" (i.e., fellow Jew; *sungenēs*; e.g., 16:7, 11),
when employed in contexts of familial language (mother—16:13; brother,
sister—16:14, 15), means "*relative*" and not "compatriot" (cf. 9:3, with clear
modification). Prisca and Aquila (16:3) were a missionary couple closely
associated with Paul in his *Gentile mission*, as were also Paul's *fellow prisoners*, the missionary couple of Andronicus and Junia (16:7). Four of the
five most likely candidates for a Jewish identity in Rom 16 are associated
with Paul's Gentile missionary labors and thus offer further evidence for a
Gentile audience in Rome. Were Paul's coworkers assembling in Rome to
pave the way for his impending visit to the city and perhaps also to provide
assistance for his further labors in the west?[20] The apostle could well have
been commending their reception by the Roman audience. The continued
assertion of a mixed audience of Jews and Gentiles in the Roman congregations is, in part, a matter of scholarly inertia in the study of Romans that
demands more critical scrutiny and engagement.

4. The Relationship to the Synagogues

Although Paul's argument does not require any knowledge of the original
context of his biblical citations, the rhetoric of quotation will only function
if the encoded readers esteem the sacred texts of Israel. Although Juvenal
(*Sat.* 14.96–106, esp. 101) thought that some Gentiles studied the Jewish
Scriptures, that engagement appears to have been superficial, at best. Gentile authors from this period appear entirely unaware of the content of
the Hebrew Scriptures beyond Genesis 1 (Longinus, [*Subl.*] 9.9 and Ocel-
lus Lucanus). An appreciation of the Jewish Scriptures would presumably
indicate that at least some of the encoded Roman readership must have
had prior exposure to or interaction with the synagogues. To contend that
the encoded audience is Gentile does not exclude interaction with synagogue Jews. The precise nature of that interaction, however, is difficult to
discern from the Letter to the Romans.

---

20. See also Das, *Romans Debate*, 29–34.

The Gentile Christians in Rome are not likely meeting as a *subgroup* of the synagogues. When Paul calls the Roman addressees his "brothers [and sisters]" (*adelphoi*) at the beginning of the letter (1:13) and praises their faith (1:8), he also relays to them grace and peace from the Lord Jesus Christ (1:7). He reminds his "brothers and sisters" (*adelphoi*) that they have died to the law through the body of Christ (7:4, 6). As "brothers and sisters" they have received Christ's Spirit (8:9, 12) and are now "heirs with Christ" (8:17). He distinguishes the "brothers and sisters" *from* "Israel" in 10:1. The brothers and sisters are members of the one body of Christ (12:1–8). Paul uses the language of "brothers and sisters" for fellow believers in Christ. The one instance where he departs from that pattern in 9:3 he is careful to signal the departure with the qualifications "*my* brothers and sisters" and "according to the flesh." The Roman "brothers and sisters" are therefore fellow Christ-believers.

Although the Roman "weak" practice certain customs of the law, Paul does not identify them as Jewish or describe any practices that would go beyond Gentile interest in the Jewish God. Paul is not describing a non-Christ-believing, Jewish "weak." Paul admonishes the weak not to judge the strong in 14:3. He exhorts the weak again in 14:19 and 15:5. He would not have been in a position of authority to give directions to non-Christ-believing synagogue Jews in Rome. Rather, by addressing the weak he is thereby including them in the encoded audience of the letter, an audience that he has repeatedly identified as Gentile (e.g., 1:5–6, 13–15; 11:13–24). Paul is an apostle of Jesus Christ and may only admonish the weak as fellow believers in Christ. Furthermore, in 14:6 the weak observe the day "in honor of the Lord." In Rom 14:9 Paul clarifies and affirms *Christ* as "Lord" of both the dead and the living. In 14:14 Paul is persuaded in the Lord *Jesus*. In 15:6 Paul again speaks of "our Lord Jesus Christ." The weak are therefore observing the day for the sake of the Lord Jesus Christ. The weak appear to be Christ-believers whose relationship with the non-law-observant strong requires some direction. Furthermore, the Christ-believers appear to be meeting in their own venues.[21] To speculate about the Christ-believers meeting in the context of synagogue gatherings is to posit a situation to which Paul never refers and which is therefore unlikely.

---

21. Although Paul does not initially describe the Romans as meeting in their own "churches" or assemblies (*ekklēsia*), he mentions in 16:5 the "*ekklēsia*" that meets in the home of Prisca and Aquila.

Paul's failure to mention a non-Christ-believing contingent in his audience, or in relation to his audience, should be taken at face value.[22]

5. THE CLAUDIUS EDICT

In his *Lives of the Caesars*, the second-century Roman historian Suetonius recorded an event that took place in the late 40s of the first century C.E. (*Claud.* 25.4). The Emperor Claudius (41–54 C.E.) expelled the Jews from Rome at the instigation of "Chrestus." Suetonius appears to have confused the name "Christus," or Christ, with "Chrestus," a common name in Rome at the time. Christian writers suspected their secular counterparts of deliberately altering the spelling to imply that Christ bore the name of a lowly slave (thus Justin, *1 Apol.* 4.5; Tertullian, *Apol.* 3; *Nat.* 1.3.9; Lactantius, *Inst.* 4.7). On the other hand, Suetonius does not otherwise appear particularly well-informed about the early Christian movement, and Greek manuscripts of the New Testament continued to confuse the spellings even beyond the time of Suetonius.[23]

Since "Chrestus" was a very common name in the Latin inscriptions for slaves and freedmen in Rome, some have proposed that a slave or freedman was causing trouble in the Jewish community. Such an individual, however, would have been indebted to a patron and would not likely have been in a social position to cause such a loud uproar in a community that would require imperial intervention. Such an incendiary figure has left no trace in the historical record. Similarly, no evidence has been forthcoming for a messianic pretender or Jewish nationalist movement in Rome. Secular authors regularly commented on Roman Jewish customs but never on the Roman Jews as a *political* movement. The Jews of Rome lacked a single organizational structure or leader. "Chrestus" may have been a common name in non-Jewish circles, but of the hundreds of Jewish male names in Rome's inscriptions or in inscriptions elsewhere in the empire, Jewish parents did not name their boys "Chrestus." Yet another possibil-

---

22. For a fuller critique of the notion that the Roman believers represented a subgroup within the synagogues, see Das, *Romans Debate*, 115–48.

23. The meager reference to "Christiani" in *Nero* 16.2 proves little beyond a general awareness of the movement. The brevity of the "Chrestus" comment also permits a reference to the "Christ-*movement*" in Rome, that is, the advocates of "Chrestus," rather than to the presence of Christ himself; rightly Rainer Riesner, *Paul's Early Period: Chronology, Mission Strategy, Theology* (Grand Rapids: Eerdmans, 1998), 166.

ity is that "Chrestus" was an influential figure in the imperial household who caused trouble for the Jews. Again, no trace has been found of such an individual, and Suetonius's habit was to introduce less well-known figures to his audience. He would have introduced this otherwise unknown figure as "a *certain* Chrestus" (*Chresto quodam*). The "Chrestus" to whom Suetonius referred, on the other hand, did not require an introduction. Whether deliberate or not, a confusion by Suetonius of "Chrestus" and Christ remains the most viable interpretation.

Acts 18:2 offers corroborating evidence for Claudius's expulsion of the Jews. In Corinth Paul "found a Jew named Aquila … who had recently (*prosphatōs*) come from Italy with his wife Priscilla, because Claudius had ordered all the Jews to leave Rome." Priscilla and Aquila were forced to leave Italy as *Christ-believers*. Paul's first convert in Greece was Stephanas (1 Cor 16:15), and he baptized Gaius and Crispus (1 Cor 1:14–16). Paul never mentions Aquila and Priscilla among his "first converts." These recent arrivals in Corinth from the heated situation in Rome likely would not have associated with Paul in his labors unless they themselves were already followers of Christ. Acts 18:2 also corroborates the fifth-century author Orosius's 49 C.E. date for the expulsion (*Hist. adv.* 7.6.15–16). An extant inscription referring to Gallio as proconsul of Achaia provides an anchor for the dating of events in the book of Acts, particularly events in the immediate context of Acts 18.[24] In light of the Gallio inscription, Priscilla and Aquila's arrival in Corinth would agree with a 49 C.E. date for the expulsion. In the years 47–52 C.E. Claudius was actively working to curb foreign cults and to strengthen the old Roman religious rites. An expulsion of the "Chrestus" movement would be consistent with this time period. The rate of growth of the early Jesus movement would favor a late 40s date for the movement's ability to cause conflict in Rome.[25]

A long tradition in the interpretation of Romans has assumed that Claudius expelled *all* the Jews from Rome because of the Chrestus incident. Despite the continued assertions, a mass expulsion of all the Jews from Rome is historically implausible and physically impossible. Suetonius was the only Roman historian to record the event. Josephus, the first-century Jewish historian, attempted to depict the Jewish people in a better light for the Romans. Josephus would have had to explain an expulsion of

---

24. Jerome Murphy-O'Connor, "Paul and Gallio," *JBL* 112 (1993): 315–17.

25. See the more detailed argument in Das, *Romans Debate*, 155–61.

all the Jews from Rome had such an event taken place. A mass expulsion would have been an obvious counterexample that could not have been ignored. The Roman historian Dio Cassius (ca. 160–229 c.e.) said that Claudius had wanted to expel the Jews from Rome in 41 c.e. but could not because they were too numerous (*Hist. rom.* 60.6.6). The Jews in Rome numbered from twenty to fifty thousand, one-tenth of the Roman city's population on the upper end of the estimates.[26] To expel that many people would have been a major operation. Indeed, unlike the Claudius edict, Tiberius's expulsion of four thousand draftable-age Jewish men in 19 c.e. left its imprint in every historian of the period. Suetonius's original text may be translated in a manner that does not imply a mass expulsion: "He expelled from Rome the Jews [who were] constantly making disturbances at the instigation of Chrestus." Suetonius would not be referring to *all* the Jews in Rome but rather to those particular Jews *involved in* the Chrestus disturbance. The haphazard implementation of Roman expulsions is sure evidence that this translation is on the right track. The Romans regularly expelled, among others, astrologers, fortune tellers, and practitioners of eastern religious movements. Expulsions usually represented political posturing. In 161 b.c.e., philosophers and rhetors were banned from the city, a highly impractical decree in view of the city's educational needs. In 154 b.c.e. Epicurean philosophers were expelled but remained active and influential in the following years. Most likely, in view of the paucity of references by the historians of the period, Claudius's expulsion targeted those actually *involved* in the Chrestus incident, that is, the "Chrestus people."[27]

In a synagogue dispute over "Chrestus," the Jewish Christ-believers with their maverick claims would have been at the center of the conflict.[28] God-fearers who, by definition, were not Jews or Jewish converts would not have been fully integrated into the synagogue community. (Even converts to Judaism were of a second-tier status, albeit within the Jewish community.) Roman authors recognized circumcision as *the* boundary marker distinguishing the Jewish people. God-fearers maintained their primary identity in the *non*-Jewish world. Jewish advocates of "Chrestus," on the

---

26. On the population estimate, see Das, *Romans Debate*, 163–64.

27. See Das, *Romans Debate*, 144–46.

28. One cannot sharply separate, then, the actions of Rome from the Jewish community's leadership, as did Campbell, "Addressees," 178. Roman politics were a response to developments within the synagogues and would have depended on information from the synagogues for the targeting of those at the heart of the tensions.

other hand, would have been a serious problem for the Jewish community *from within*. In administering the expulsion, the emperor would have had to rely on the information that came from Jews. The Jewish advocates of Chrestus would have been the primary targets of the expulsion, and in the wake of their departure the non-Jewish followers of Christ would remain. After the conflict over Christ, these Gentiles would no longer have been welcome in the synagogues, at least for as long as they openly advocated Christ. They would then have needed to meet for the worship of Christ in their own venues. After the expulsion, newcomers to the now Gentile Christ movement may not have had the same prior exposure to the Roman synagogues and may have shared in the widespread attitude that the conquered peoples and their religious views were inferior. Roman literary sources, in particular, display a noticeable prejudice against Judaism. Such attitudes in the larger society would surely lead to questions and disagreement about the Gentiles' relationship to the Jewish religious heritage. Paul must therefore address that relationship in his Letter to the Romans.

Whereas Claudius understood the dispute over "Chrestus" to be a Jewish matter in 49 C.E., by 64 C.E. Nero singled out Christians as scapegoats for the burning of Rome. Within fifteen years of Claudius's edict, the new emperor could discern the difference between a Jew and a Christ-believer at a time when others in the empire would have found the movements indistinguishable. Nero's prescient recognition of the difference is understandable in view of his wife Poppaea's interest in the Jewish community. A Jewish actor by the name of Alityrus was also popular in Nero's court. After Claudius's intervention, many in the Jewish community would want the difference between themselves and the fledgling Christ-movement to be known to the emperor lest there be unwelcome attention or intervention again. Whether through direct influence by someone like Poppaea or through indirect influence, early Christian authors traced Nero's hostility toward their movement to "jealousy and envy," most likely on the part of Jews who shared social space with the first Christians (Clement of Rome, *1 Clem.* 5.2, 4, 5; Melito of Sardis in Eusebius, *Hist. eccl.* 4.26.9–10 [*NPNF* 2/1:205–6]).

A conservative reconstruction of the external evidence of the Claudius edict as an independent witness agrees with and parallels the internal picture from the Letter to the Romans:

1. A Gentile audience: Paul addresses Gentiles in the letter even as Gentiles in Rome would be the worshipers of Christ in the wake of a Jewish Christian expulsion.

2. An interest in the Jewish Scriptures: Emperor Claudius considered the "Chrestus" advocates a movement within the synagogue. Gentile God-fearers would have initially learned of Christ in the synagogues and would therefore have had an appreciation for and interest in the Jewish Scriptures, just what Paul assumes of his Gentile addressees. Since Jewish Christ-believers were the primary targets of the expulsion, the non-expelled, non-Christ-believing Jews would have remained a potential influence on the early Christian movement, both positively and negatively. Although, externally, the Jews appear to be distancing themselves from Christ-believers by the time of Nero, internally, the "weak" remain attracted to Jewish customs.

3. Questions over the Gentiles' relation to the Jewish religious heritage: As Gentile worshipers began to meet separately from the synagogues after the expulsion of the Jewish followers of Christ, many newcomers to the movement would not have had prior experience in the synagogues. Questions would, in time, emerge over the relationship between the Roman Gentiles and the conquered Jews' religious heritage in which the Christ-believing movement was rooted. This reconstruction corresponds to the internal evidence as Paul addresses differing views on Jewish customs in Rom 14–15. The letter repeatedly grapples with the role of Moses's law in the Roman communities.

CONCLUSION: HOW DECISIVE A BREAK?

The agreement of the internal evidence of the letter with a conservative estimation of the external evidence provided by the Claudius expulsion represents a unique strength of this essay's solution to the debate over the letter's audience and occasion. A decisive break took place as Christ-believers began to meet for worship apart from synagogue gatherings and as a distinctive Gentile Christ-believing identity began to emerge. Neither the internal evidence of the Letter to the Romans nor the external evidence of the events in the wake of the Claudius edict suggests that Jews and Christ-believers were still worshiping together. Nevertheless, this break was not a "parting of the ways" between Jews and Christ-believers. Many Christ-believers found Judaism attractive and, no doubt, continued to mingle among the Jewish inhabitants of Rome.[29] Jews and Christians

---

29. Bruce N. Fisk helpfully charted a range of views potentially held by the

labored in common trades. They were coming to Rome as immigrants, merchants, and slaves. They tended to live clustered among other immigrants and easterners. They shared a social context and the religious heritage and Scriptures of Israel. They buried their dead in the same locations. Nothing in the Letter to the Romans or in the external historical record would suggest that Christ-believers had broken all ties with the Jews of Rome. Clearly, the "weak" wished to maintain the practices that were appropriate for Gentile sympathizers of Judaism.

Paul's letter admonishes the Roman Gentiles against any arrogance at the expense of the Jewish roots of the Christian faith. He may level the advantage of the "Jew" in Rom 2–3. He may claim the privileges and prerogatives of Israel for the Roman Gentiles in Christ. By the end of Rom 8, the Gentiles number among God's beloved and elect, as had Israel of old. Nevertheless, in an ironic twist, Paul turns to his own people according to the flesh in Rom 9–11 and concludes that "all Israel will be saved" (Rom 11:26). Christ-believing Gentiles in the capital of the empire may be meeting separately from the Jews for the worship of Jesus, but the worship of Jesus cannot be severed from the historic privileges and heritage of Israel.

For Further Reading

Achtemeier, Paul J. "Unsearchable Judgments and Inscrutable Ways: Reflections on the Discussion of Romans." Pages 3–21 in *Looking Back, Pressing On*. Edited by E. Elizabeth Johnson and David M. Hay. Vol. 4 of *Pauline Theology*. SBLSymS 4. Atlanta: Scholars Press, 1997. Achtemeier offers one of the first cases for an encoded Gentile audience and critiques the evidence for a mass expulsion of the Jewish population from Rome.

Das, A. Andrew. "'Praise the Lord, All You Gentiles': The Encoded Audience of Romans 15:7–13." *JSNT* 34 (2011): 90–110. This recent essay offers a comprehensive look at one of the passages deemed an Achilles' heel of the all-Gentile-encoded audience.

Roman Gentile Christ-believers vis-à-vis Judaism: hostile opposition and exclusion, ignorance, benign indifference, and sympathy-affirmation-embrace ("Synagogue Influence and Scriptural Knowledge among the Christians of Rome," in *As It Is Written: Studying Paul's Use of Scripture* [ed. Stanley E. Porter and Christopher D. Stanley; SBLSymS 50; Atlanta: Society of Biblical Literature, 2008], 182–83).

————. *Solving the Romans Debate*. Minneapolis: Fortress, 2007. This is the most recent full-length defense of an all-Gentile-encoded audience. The book also includes a thorough examination of the external sources for the Claudius edict as well as a lengthy critique of the notion that the Roman Christ-believing Gentiles remained a subgroup within the synagogues.

Donfried, Karl P., ed. *The Romans Debate*. Rev. and enl. ed. Peabody, Mass.: Hendrickson, 1991. These classic essays represent a helpful introduction to the diversity of views regarding the situation and purpose behind Paul's Letter to the Romans.

Donfried, Karl P., and Peter Richardson, eds. *Judaism and Christianity in First-Century Rome*. Grand Rapids: Eerdmans, 1998. These wide-ranging essays provide indispensable background on first-century Roman Christianity and Judaism, the role of the Roman government in religious affairs, and the relationship between Jews and Christians in Paul's Letter to the Romans and in the period prior to the letter.

Miller, James C. "The Romans Debate: 1991–2001." *CurBS* 9 (2001): 306–49. Miller catalogs the range of views on Romans from the 1991 second edition of Donfried's *Romans Debate* until 2001.

Stowers, Stanley K. *A Rereading of Romans: Justice, Jews, and Gentiles*. New Haven: Yale University Press, 1994. A pioneering affirmation of an all-Gentile-encoded audience that seeks to reread the letter from the point of view of that audience in its social and literary setting.

Thorsteinsson, Runar M. *Paul's Interlocutor in Romans 2: Function and Identity in the Context of Ancient Epistolography*. ConBNT 40. Stockholm: Almqvist & Wiksell, 2003. Thorsteinsson primarily answers the problem posed for an all-Gentile audience by Paul's address of a "Jew" in Rom 2:17, but good portions of the book are devoted to a more comprehensive case for the Gentile-encoded audience.

Wedderburn, A. J. M. *The Reasons for Romans*. SNTW. Edinburgh: T&T Clark, 1988. This is an earlier study championing multiple "reasons for Romans." Wedderburn also stresses recognition of a concrete situation at Rome that Paul was addressing.

Reading Romans in the Capital of the Empire

Sylvia C. Keesmaat

For many years Romans was seen to be a systematic outline of Paul's theology. To be fair, this assumption was made partly because Paul had never been to Rome, and it was assumed that he was writing a letter that laid out his theology as a way of introducing himself to this community. In recent years, however, scholars have begun to explore how this city itself shaped the Christian community that made its home there and how the themes and arguments of the letter address the context of that community. What was it like to live at the center of an empire like Rome? What kind of messages did this empire send to those who lived under her control? What were the dominant images that shaped public life? What were the stories that fueled popular imagination and demanded appropriate behavior from those who believed them? And, most importantly, does this letter address those symbols, challenge the stories, and thereby create an alternative imagination for followers of Jesus in Rome? These are the questions that are before us.

Um, excuse me? Can I ask a question?

Of course you can.

Well, I've been reading Romans for most of my life, and no one has ever talked about empire before. What is the problem with reading the letter as an introduction to Paul's theology?

On the face of it, there is nothing wrong with reading the letter this way. Except for one thing. With few exceptions, Paul always wrote to Christian communities rooted in a particular place.[1] Rather than writing to Chris-

---

1. See 1 Cor 1:2; Gal 1:2; Phil 1:1; 1 Thess 1:1. The exception to this is, of course, Ephesians, widely thought to be a circular letter, although its Pauline authorship is questioned. But even Ephesians is a circular letter to communities in a certain geographical area. All biblical references are to the NRSV, unless otherwise noted.

tians in general in these letters, Paul directs his writing to a specific people and the circumstances that they face in their particular context.

But if Paul had never met the Romans, would he have known enough about their context to address it?

Imagine that you are writing a letter to someone you had never met who lived in Washington, D.C., or New York City. You would still be able to address their context. You might ask if they had been to the Obama inaugural, or if they had ever visited ground zero. You might even offer an opinion on an event that happened in one of these cities. In the ancient world, Rome had enormous stature. News traveled throughout the empire about the city, its architecture, and its rulers. More than that, however, what happened in Rome dictated the behavior of the rest of the empire. The story of Roman military might was circulated in art and on coins, portrayed in architecture, talked over, and retold in song. Roman law and societal structures shaped daily interactions throughout the empire.

That is all pretty general knowledge, though.

You are right, but Paul and the churches in Rome had even stronger connections. Romans 16 shows that Paul personally knew quite a few of the leaders of the churches in Rome. He worked with some of them (Prisca and Aquila, v. 3), he was imprisoned with others (Andronicus and Junia, v. 7), and others had provided support for him. These people would surely have conveyed to Paul a clear picture of what life in the capital was like.

Part of that picture would have been this: in the year 49 C.E. the emperor Claudius ordered all Jews expelled from Rome. Whether they were in fact all expelled is debated, but it seems clear that over these years the churches in Rome would have taken a turn away from Judaism in order to avoid persecution. When the Jews returned to Rome in 54 C.E., by permission of the new emperor, Nero, Jewish Christians would have returned to churches that had lost their Jewish leadership and attempted to distance themselves as much as possible from Judaism.

Wouldn't they have welcomed their Jewish sisters and brothers back with joy?

They might not have been pleased to discover that some previous targets of Roman persecution had decided to return to their community. This might draw negative attention. There are various suggestions in the book of Romans that this community itself had undergone persecution under Roman rule (see Rom 5:3–5; 8:18–39, esp. vv. 35 and 38; 12:14). And now some Jewish Christians, who seem to be handy scapegoats for the empire, have returned to their community. This can only raise the question of God's justice—a theme that runs throughout Romans.

I'm not sure I have ever noticed the word "justice" occurring more than once in the Letter to the Romans.

That is because it is usually translated as "righteousness." In Greek the word *dikaiosynē* is used to translate two Hebrew words, "righteousness" (*tsedaqah*) and "justice" (*mishpat*). The Greek word *dikaiosynē*, therefore, has both of those meanings. Since the word "righteousness" doesn't have much meaning in our culture (except when we call someone self-righteous), I will use "justice" as the translation in order to retain the social, political, and cultural overtones that are in the Greek. That way you will be aware of those overtones in the letter.

So why would this suffering raise questions of God's justice?

How well do you know the Psalms? In Romans Paul cites Pss 10, 18, 44, 71, 94, 110, and 143, all of which are psalms of lament. When these psalms cry out to God for justice, what are they looking for?

Usually for enemies to be crushed and defeated and for God's faithful people to be vindicated.

Exactly. In these psalms God acts in justice and faithfulness when (often Gentile) oppressors are defeated and God's people are rescued. This is what God's covenant faithfulness looks like. And this story is not that different from the story of Rome, where those blessed by the gods (the Romans) defeat the barbaric pagan hordes.

If these are the stories that surround you, then a group of Jews who have been expelled by the empire, even if they have come back, look like the ones who have been abandoned by God. In fact, Paul spends Rom 9–11 arguing against precisely this point. According to Paul, God has *not* abandoned his people (11:1, 11–32).

So this community could be thinking that because the Jews are suffering they are no longer chosen by God?

Precisely. In a situation of Gentile boasting (11:17–24; 14:10) Paul is telling another story, one where suffering does not signify defeat.

What you have outlined here are themes of suffering and justice that can be found throughout Israel's Scriptures. They are much wider than the context of these Christians in Rome. I once heard a presentation where the speaker argued that since Paul was dealing with a story much larger than the story of Rome he would not have addressed Rome directly. Paul was writing about much larger issues: death, sin, and the defeat of evil at the

*hands of Jesus. To say that he was addressing the Roman Empire would be
to limit the cosmic scope of his vision and his writings.*[2]

That would be a compelling argument, except for one thing. Throughout the biblical story the people of Israel need to learn how to be faithful to the covenant God in their particular time and place. Moses does not warn the Israelites in Deuteronomy in merely abstract terms about choosing the path of death, rather he names the idolatry of Canaan and the threat of acting like they are still in Egypt (Deut 4:3; 12:2–4; 29–31; 16:21–22; 17:16; 18:9–14; 24:17,21; 29:16–18; cf. Lev 19:36). Similarly, the prophets call Israel to faithfulness not merely by pointing out grand cosmic themes but by rooting those themes in the specific unfaithful practices of Israel and Judah, with regard to this land and these people and these political alliances.[3]

Faithfulness to the covenant God is always embodied in particular historical situations and contexts. Conversely, the challenges to such faithfulness, the power of evil, death, or injustice (*adikia,* as Paul puts it), are always embodied in particular narratives, particular idolatrous practices, particular symbols. There is no way to address the large themes without talking about what they look like in *this* place with *this* people.

*Say that I accept your premise that Paul would have been aware of the
context of the churches in Rome. It is still not clear that he addressed the
Roman Empire in this letter. He doesn't mention the empire once, he doesn't
refer to any emperors, and he doesn't explicitly say anything about the imperial story.*

That is correct. And yet, the symbols, vocabulary and structure of the empire underlie the world that he describes in Romans.

*Why doesn't Paul just come out and say that he is challenging Caesar
and the empire?*

Paul doesn't need to make such an overt statement. It is similar to that old campaign where Christians said "Jesus is the Real Thing" as a cultural reference to the Coke campaign that proclaimed "Coke: the Real Thing." If

---

2. This argument was made by John Barclay in a paper entitled, "Why the Roman Empire Was Insignificant to Paul" (presented at the Pauline Epistles Section at the Annual Meeting of the Society of Biblical Literature, San Diego, Calif., 19 November 2007).

3. E.g., Isa 5:8–10; Jer 5:26–29; Hos 5:13; 7:11–13; 8:1–10; Amos 2:6–8; 3:9–11; 4:1–3; 5:10–13; 6:4–8; 8:4–6; Mic 2:1–2; 3:9–11.

they had spelled it out, "Jesus, Not Coke, is the Real Thing," their assertion would have lost some of its power.

I have no idea what you are talking about. Perhaps that isn't the best example.

Actually, it proves my point entirely. When I was a kid, everyone knew that this Christian slogan challenged an advertising claim. It didn't need to be spelled out. But now it does. In the same way, Paul's language in Romans didn't need to be spelled out at the time, because everyone understood what he was doing. It is only now that we have to do the clumsy work of explaining the reference.

So you are saying that because we are no longer living in the context of ancient Rome we don't catch all the allusions?

Exactly. Let me give you a more current example. If in an election year I were to go on a lecture tour entitled "Jesus for President!" that phrase alone would convey a challenge to the story of American presidency.[4] Or if I had a bumper sticker that said "God Bless the Whole World. No Exceptions," it is likely that you would see this as a challenge to the more prevalent bumper sticker that says, "God Bless America." Or, if I had a slogan that said, "Amish for Homeland Security," you would understand that I was saying something about the current militaristic nature of the Department of Homeland Security and that I was suggesting a less-violent alternative.[5] These examples make sense to us because we know the larger cultural context of the allusions. Paul didn't need to be more explicit because at the time his allusions made sense in terms of the wider cultural narrative. For us, however, two thousand years later, a little explanatory work is necessary.

I think an example from Romans would be helpful.

Consider the first six words of the epistle: "Paul, a slave of Jesus Christ."[6] Just imagine how this would have sounded in the context of an

---

4. This is the title of a book by Shane Claiborne and Chris Haw (*Jesus for President: Politics for Ordinary Radicals* [Grand Rapids: Zondervan, 2008]) that contrasts the gospel message of Jesus with the "gospel" of both Rome and contemporary American culture.

5. This last example is from the film *The Ordinary Radicals: A Conspiracy of Faith at the Margins of Empire* (Philadelphia: Jamie Moffett Media Design and Production and Another World Is Possible, 2008), DVD.

6. The word Paul uses here, *doulos*, is most accurately translated "slave," although many translations use "servant" instead.

empire governed by status and a culture governed by an honor/shame dynamic. Rather than introduce himself in language designed to increase his social standing, Paul deliberately uses a phrase that identifies himself with those at the bottom of the social ladder.

If that were at all confusing for his listeners (for really, who would want to listen to a letter from a slave), Paul qualifies the statement. He is a slave of the Messiah, Jesus, and set apart for the gospel of God.

The word "gospel" (*euangelion*) itself often referred to the "good news" of an imperial military victory. Paul not only uses this word, he also carefully qualifies it. We can better catch the sense if we translate "gospel of God" as "the proclamation of the triumph of God" (v. 1).[7] Similarly, this is the proclamation of the triumph of his son (vv. 3, 9). After hearing this a few times, when Paul gets to "I am not ashamed of the gospel for it is the power of God for salvation to everyone who has faith, to the Jew first and also to the Greek" (1:16), he has definitively set the gospel he is proclaiming over against the imperial gospel that dominated the cultural experience of his audience.

Paul's proclamation of triumph is about the son of Israel's God, a messiah descended from Israel's most famous king and who was designated son of God in power, by his resurrection from the dead (1:1–4). Caesar was also described as the son of royalty and the gods, hence the gospel of God describes a royal ruler who has all the designations that applied to Caesar.

Moreover, this son of God, who has power and royal lineage, has "risen up" to enact justice and triumph over the nations. That, too, is language that would be used of Caesar, but Paul roots resurrection language in the Psalms, where Israel appeals to God to "rise up" and save her from her enemies.[8] The implications are clear: whose gospel has triumphed? The gospel of God, not Caesar. Lest we think, however, that Paul is merely asserting the triumph of another oppressive ruler, as the letter progresses the paradoxical nature of that triumph becomes evident, for this is the son who became a servant (Rom 15:8), and who was given up to death for us all (8:34).

Paul ends his greeting with a phrase that he commonly uses in his letters: "grace to you and peace from God our Father and the Lord Jesus

---

7. This translation is from Neil Elliott, *The Arrogance of Nations: Reading Romans in the Shadow of Empire* (PCC; Minneapolis: Fortress, 2008), 152.

8. In addition to many others, the following psalms, quoted by Paul in Romans, appeal for God to "rise up": Ps 94:16; 44:23; 44:26.

Christ" (1:7). This phrase continues the challenge to the imperial story. In the context of an empire that proclaimed peace, the Pax Romana, as its greatest achievement, Paul proclaims another peace, a peace not only from God our Father, but also from a new Lord, the Lord Jesus Christ. In an empire in which Caesar was the only one to be called Lord in this sense, Paul not only names Jesus the Messiah, as Lord, but asserts that he offers a different peace.

Well, if Paul begins with phrases that undermine the imperial story, he moves pretty quickly to theology. The whole theme of the letter in Rom 1:16 and 17 is clearly about salvation, righteousness, and faith. It seems that he abandons imperial allusions in favor of the themes of biblical hope.

In fact, he doesn't abandon imperial allusions at all. This God of Israel is proclaimed as the one whose justice (*dikaiosynē*) is revealed through faith, for faith (*ek pisteōs eis pistin*; 1:17). Justice and faith. These two words, evoking deep resonances with Israel's Scriptures, challenge the imperial ideology at its core.

It was, after all, the goddess Iustitia (justice; the Latin equivalent of the Greek *dikaiosynē*) who was so closely identified with the reign of Augustus. And one of the lauded virtues of the Augustan reign was none other than *fides* (faith or faithfulness, which is the Latin equivalent of the Greek *pistis*). Where does the world meet righteousness and faith? In the imperial narrative of Caesar or in the story of Israel as reinterpreted in the light of the story of Jesus? As Israel's faith was always formed and lived in the shadow of empire, so also is the faith that Paul commends to the Christian community in Rome at the heart of the empire.

These programmatic verses, then, pick up the themes of the empire and powerfully reinterpret them in the context of another story, the story of the God of Israel, who has come to bring salvation through another Lord, Jesus. Paul draws deeply on that story, particularly those parts of Israel's Scriptures where the faithfulness of God is questioned in the face of oppression.

It seems to me that you are suggesting that these classic theological terms were also heavily loaded political terms.

That's right. And they have been political terms throughout much of Israel's story. The language of salvation indicated that Israel's God would come and defeat her enemies.[9]

---

9. The references are extensive: Pss 13; 18*; 25; 35*; 36*; 37; 68; 79; 118*; Isa

Paul heightens his critique, however, in the next few verses where he criticizes those who practice *adikia* (injustice, usually translated wickedness). His description of those who have darkened minds (v. 21), who have exchanged their glory for images of animals (v. 23), who practice degrading sexual immorality (vv. 24–27), and who are full of every kind of evil (v. 25–31) is a fairly accurate portrayal of the lives of the recent emperors, particularly Caligula. Others of that time described Caligula as cruel and malicious; he had family members murdered and engaged in outrageous and humiliating sexual predations, with both men and women. He had an incredible arrogance and divine pretensions.[10] The very empire that was supposed to be a manifestation of the goddess Iustitia (justice) was ruled by those who demonstrated the most rampant injustice.

I thought that these verses were standard Jewish diatribe against Gentiles?

They sound like that unless you happen to know the more recent historical happenings in the capital. In Rome these verses have an all-too-clear referent in the imperial house. The irony would not have been lost on Paul's audience.

But these verses do describe a wider situation. The fall into idolatry, which is so clearly illustrated by the lives of the Caesars, is something that has been found throughout all of history. Indeed, Paul's alludes in Rom 1:22–23 to Ps 106:20, where Israel exchanged her glory for that of an idol. The story Paul is telling has particular relevance for the Roman context, but it also has a wider, cosmic scope.

That is precisely the point of the next few chapters. Paul outlines how the story of Israel has cosmic implications for all of humankind, implications as wide as the story of Rome.

I am assuming you are referring to the story of Abraham in Rom 4 and Adam in Rom 5?

Exactly. Paul counters the grand sweep of the Roman mythology of salvation to the world with the story of Israel, which has similarly far-

---

25:6–12; 33:2–6; 46:12–13; 51:4–8; 52:7–12; 62:1–12 (* = psalms quoted by Paul in Romans).

10. According to Neil Elliott (*Arrogance of Nations*, 80), "it would be difficult to imagine a career that better illustrated the precise sequence that Paul describes:

arrogant refusal to honor the divine creator;

the turn to idolatry and worship of the creature;

a descent into defiling sexual lust;

and finally an expansive catalogue of cruelty and outrage."

reaching implications. So the promise to Abraham that he would inherit the world (4:13), a promise of blessing for all nations (Gen 12:3), is a challenge to the Roman myth of peace to the ends of the earth. And, unlike the Roman story, which situates evil in the barbarian hordes that resist Roman civilization and rule, Paul tells the story of sin and grace, death and life as one that runs through the heart of everyone, including himself (Rom 5–7). Rather than justice coming through the rule of Caesar, the son of the gods, it is the rule of Jesus that brings the free gift of justice to all (6:17).

But if the emperors were as bad as the description in Rom 1, why would anyone have thought that they would bring justice and peace?

The story is believable because those at the top of the social ladder *did* experience the abundance and justice that the imperial story promised. It works the same way in our society—even though only a few at the top really benefit from certain economic practices, those further down the social ladder buy into the story and strive to reach the top.

When Paul wrote this letter, Nero was just beginning his rule. As with all new rulers, the poets were quick to sing his praises. There was a hopeful feeling in the air. The rot, so to speak, had not quite set in.

In fact, Rom 8 subverts this ethos of hopefulness. When Nero came to power he was praised for restoring the Augustan age of renewal. The poets proclaimed that under his rule the earth would be fertile and abundant, and animals would be prolific and docile.

The reality, of course, is that the economic practices of the Roman empire were devastating for the land. In places where war had not brought environmental devastation, the extraction of resources did. Mining, clear-cutting for fuel and building, the systematic clearing of forests and pastureland for grain, along with the exploitation of small landowners, left a devastating legacy. As the empire exhausted the land in the areas close to Rome, it needed to expand more and more to meet its voracious needs.

Wait a minute. Are you saying that Paul's audience would have been aware of environmental degradation? Are you saying that this was actually an issue in the first century?

Yes, I am. People were writing about it at length.[11]

So when Paul was talking about creation groaning, he wasn't just talking about a general result of the curse?

---

11. J. Donald Hughes, *Ecology in Ancient Civilizations* (Albuquerque: University of New Mexico Press, 1975), 99–127.

No, Paul was talking about very specific things: destruction of forests, erosion, the silting up of the harbors—all of it a result of Roman economic practice. When Paul, in an epistle written to the heart of the empire, depicts creation as "groaning" (8:22), he directly subverts the official story of Rome. This portrayal of creation brings to expression the pain that the story of empire has carefully covered up. No such cover-up suits Paul. Creation is groaning and in naming this Paul exposes the lie at the heart of the empire's depiction of reality.

But there is more. Paul also indicates that creation is waiting for the freedom that will come with the revealing of the children of God (8:21). This challenges the imperial story in two ways. First, according to Rome, the emperor is the one who images the gods and engages in a glorious rule over the world. In Paul's story the agent of creational restoration is not Augustus or any emperor; rather, it is the restored people of God who bring abundance and peace as part of their creaturely calling. The image-of-God language, usually reserved for the king, is applied to those children of God, who are conformed to the image of Jesus (8:29). In this way the special status of the emperor as image of God is challenged by this motley assortment of people who claim to be followers of a different Lord.

Second, the abundance and fertility of the empire are rooted in the power and strength of Roman military might. Violence is the basis of all the empire offers. As Romans 8 progresses, Paul indicates that the children of God who will exercise right rule over creation are those who bear the firstfruits of the Spirit and hence groan in travail with creation itself (v. 23). That is to say, not violent rule over creation, but suffering with creation fits the children for the redemption of their bodies and entrance into glory.

This is starting to make sense in terms of the context you outlined at the start. In the end it seems that suffering is central to this story Paul is telling.

Yes, but not in the usual way. Remember that for this small beleaguered church, the power of Rome as conqueror was all pervasive and the story of the imperial conqueror had all the appearances of being true. The whole of Romans 8:17–39 concerns the meaning of this suffering that the believing community and, indeed, the whole of creation is experiencing. Does such suffering mean that a successful charge has been brought against those whom God has called (v. 33)? Does it mean that they have been condemned (v. 34), that God's love has been withdrawn (v. 35), and that the oppressor is victorious? Does it mean that Caesar, in fact, saves?

In short, you seem to be suggesting that their suffering is prompting them to ask if maybe the imperial narrative is true. And if it is true, then that would change everything for them, wouldn't it?

Well, yes. And one of the things it would change is how the Christian community responds to such suffering. The Scriptures of Israel interpret the suffering of the people in a number of ways. Suffering could mean that the enemies of God have triumphed. In that case God needs to come and defeat those enemies (see n.9). Or suffering could represent the birth pangs of the new age and those who suffer do so precisely *because* they are the faithful followers of God (this is more common in the prophetic literature, e.g., Isa 50:4–9; 52:13–53:12). While in some of these cases the defeat of God's enemies is still envisioned, in other texts the Gentiles will be welcomed into Israel as followers of the God of Jacob (Isa 56:3–8; 66:18–21).

Given these different narrative strands, how should the Christian community respond to the violence of empire? Should it take up the cry of the psalms of lament and demand that God come to grind the nations into dust, defeat the evildoer, and enable his people to oppress their foes?[12] Is that the story of those who follow Jesus?

Paul's answer, along with his quotations from Pss 118:6, 110:1, and 44:22, weaves together other strands from Israel's Scriptures into an entirely new cloth. With the psalmist he asserts, "If God is for us, then who is against us?" (Rom 8:31; cf. Ps 118:6). Unlike the psalmist, who has already been rescued from his oppression, however, Paul is asserting God's presence in the *midst* of such oppression. His confession in 8:34 that Jesus is seated at the right hand of God alludes to Ps 110:1, but unlike the ruler of that psalm, whose enemies become his footstool, the Messiah called Jesus intercedes even for those who have killed him (cf. Luke 23:34; Rom 5:8–10). And Paul's echo of Ps 44:22 answers the pleas of the psalmist for God to arise and save his suffering people, not by the vanquishing of their oppressors, but with the paradoxical assertion that those who suffer are not the defeated, but are more than conquerors (Rom 8:37).

Paul is still using the language of conqueror here. I'm not sure I understand your point.

Notice that Paul rejects the narratives about salvation that have plot lines concerning who is victor and who is conquered. He is saying that those suffering at the hands of Rome are more than conquerors, not because

---

12. See, for example, Pss 10:15–16; 94:23; 140:9–11; cf. Pss 18:29; 34:16; 69:22–28.

they are enacting violence on anyone, but because they are *suffering*. The Messiah who died and was raised is, paradoxically, the one in the position of authority at the right hand of God, and those who suffer are the ones who are—not conquered—more than, indeed above, the conquerors (Gr. *hypernikōmen*). Imperial categories of victory have been replaced with suffering love. The narratives of salvation that link the savior with conquest have been replaced with the story of a savior who died and was raised. The way to respond to the violence of the empire is to bear it, thereby revealing that one is part of the family of Jesus (8:17, 29) who cannot be separated from God's love and so will be raised like Jesus. It is such love, such relentless solidarity, that enables the Roman Christians to bear the suffering that they experience at the hands of their persecutors (12:12–21).

This would have been a hard message to hear over the Roman story of conquest.

It is precisely because this story was so hard to hear that Paul is so full of sorrow for his fellow Jews. As far as he is concerned, they have been totally unable to hear this story.

I'm not sure I follow. Isn't his sorrow in Rom 9–11 about the fact that his fellow Jews are not followers of Jesus?

That is putting the problem in its broadest terms. Another way to describe it would be in terms of Israel's historic interactions with the pagan empires that threatened her. In Rom 9–11, it becomes clear that some Jews have engaged in certain works in order to bring salvation. Rather than interpreting this in theological terms—if they obeyed the law rigorously enough they will be "saved"—Neil Elliott suggests that we read this in more obviously political terms. These Jews needed salvation from Roman persecution. One way to achieve that would be to become part of the Roman story by seeking Roman citizenship. Rather than assert their identity as followers of the God of Abraham, these Jews sought to save themselves by joining in the story of their conquerors.

Isn't that a little far-fetched?

Not at all, it is merely a repeat of what we have seen throughout Israel's history. At various points when push came to shove, Israel made alliances with her would-be oppressors. Rather than wait for God to act on her behalf, Israel chose to align herself with her enemies so that she might be saved.[13]

---

13. E.g., 1 Kgs 16:5–17:1; Isa 39; Hos 5:13; 7:11–13; 8:8–10.

This is precisely what Paul's fellow Jews are doing by putting their trust in Roman law to save them from suffering.

Actually, I am familiar with that part of Israel's history. What I meant was, isn't it far-fetched to think that Jews were trying to become Roman citizens?

Not at all. In 38 C.E. some of the Jews in Alexandria petitioned for Roman citizenship, with violent results.[14]

So he isn't upset that they have rejected Jesus?

Of course he is! But the way they have rejected Jesus isn't by trying to enter eternal life by an excessive trust in keeping the laws of Israel (a picture of Judaism that has been shown to be false); rather they have rejected Jesus by putting their trust in the laws of Rome as a way to escape suffering rather than in the God of Jesus who is with them in their suffering.

Well, you've got to admit that it is tempting when you are persecuted to try to secure your future any way you can.

Paul's whole point, however, is that this isn't how the future is secured or how salvation will come. Rome is the wrong place to put your faith. That is why he says in Rom 12:2 not to be conformed to this age, but to be transformed. Such transformation will enable this community to live in an entirely different way than Roman citizens live.

It is hard to imagine what such a transformation would have looked like in ancient Rome beyond keeping your mouth shut and your head down. If Paul had really wanted them to endure this suffering, as he says in Rom 8:17, how could the community in Rome have proclaimed this as "good news?"

That's a very good question. That is why Paul goes on to describe what this new community looks like if it is shaped by God's will. But if we are to understand the radical impact of that new community, we need first to understand Roman society. Do you know anything about patronage?

I know that in the Roman empire there were patrons who supported those of lower social class with money and by doing them favors, like helping with a court case.

In fact, the patronage system, with its promise of benefits from the patron in exchange for the honor and praise of the clients, functioned as a powerful means of cohesion and social control in Roman society.[15] It permeated not only personal relationships, but also larger societal interac-

---

14. See Elliott, *Arrogance of Nations*, 93–95, for a concise outline of the events.

15. In this section I have drawn on my article "If Your Enemy Is Hungry: Love and Subversive Politics in Romans 12–13," in *Character Ethics and the New Testament:*

tions. Subverting the system of status and honor, the building blocks of the patron/client relationship, Paul counsels the members of the community not to think of themselves more highly than they ought (12:3) This is counterintuitive in a society where one was to think as highly of oneself as possible. Moreover, Paul calls the community to love one another with mutual affection and to outdo one another in showing honor (12:10). To make sure they grasp how counter-imperial this showing of honor is to be, he adds, "Do not be haughty, but associate with the lowly," or, in a better translation, "walk with the oppressed"[16] (12:16). Rather than honoring those who already have status, they are to honor those who traditionally deserve no honor in Roman society. Throughout these verses, the contrast between the empire of Rome and the kingdom of the Messiah is unmistakable: one is built upon honor and privilege, the other raises up the oppressed and is built upon service.

But if the Christians refused to participate in this system, wouldn't that make it hard for them to function in society at large? It wasn't as if they could just decide to "opt out" of the system that shaped their whole society.

That is precisely what made it so difficult. Paul is calling this community to form an alternative body politic. This alternative community does not interact according to the honor/shame dynamic of the empire, it rejects patron/client relationships, and it practices a fundamentally different ethic towards enemies. Notice Rom 12:14: "Bless those who persecute you; bless and do not curse them."

I don't understand why you would call this a "body politic." This passage doesn't seem to be about political relationships at all. Paul is talking about the personal relationships within this community, isn't he?

That has been the great misunderstanding of these verses. In the ancient world, the line between private and public was not as clearly drawn as it is today. Even so, this passage seems to address both "public" and "private" life. So, for instance, this community is called to extend hospitality to strangers, those who wouldn't normally be welcomed into their midst (v. 13). They are to bless those who persecute them, a likely reference to the Roman authorities (v. 14). They are to walk with the oppressed, again

---

Moral Dimensions of Scripture (ed. Robert L. Brawley; Louisville: Westminster John Knox, 2007), 145.

16. Elliott indicates that throughout the LXX "oppressed" is a common translation for *tapeinoi*, the Greek word translated as "lowly" in Rom 12:16 (*Arrogance of Nations*, 152).

those they would be most likely to ignore (v. 16). But most telling of all, they are to offer food and drink to their enemies (v. 20).

Lest we be tempted to reduce this to an ethic of private life, we need to notice that the most obvious allusion for Paul's words here is a story from 2 Kgs 6:11–23, where Elisha had captured the Aramaean army and rather than allowing the Samarian king to kill them, he ordered food and drink for them and sent them on their way. The result of his actions was peace: the Aramaeans no longer came raiding into the land of Israel (2 Kgs 6:23). This is a decidedly political solution to a political problem.

In fact, these verses in Rom 12 seem to contrast the community of believers with the state described in 13:1–7. Rather than echoing the enthusiastic endorsement of Roman rule that would have been expected from those who swear allegiance to Rome, Paul asserts that the Roman authorities are subject to God (v. 1). He does not emphasize their legitimacy, as some contend, but rather their *subjection* to a God they don't even recognize. He continues by describing this state as one that rules by terror (v. 3), the sword (v. 4), and wrath (vv. 4–5). This is a state that demands fear (vv. 3–4).

But isn't that what the Romans boasted of? They were proud of their military might and the fear it inspired in others.

In general that is true, but not under Nero. Nero was proud of the fact that he didn't rule by force, proud that he had not conquered his empire by the sword. These verses are a slap in the face for a ruler who thought that he ruled by persuasion and reason. It is as if Paul is saying "by all means, obey the rulers" out of one side of his mouth, and out of the other is saying "because they'll crush you if you don't."

In fact, he is quite ambiguous as the passage goes on: "Pay to all what is owed them—taxes to whom taxes are owed, revenue to whom revenue is owed, fear to whom fear is owed, and honor to whom honor is owed" (13:7, author's translation). We have already seen that he has turned the question of honor on its head, so it is unclear whether these things are due to the Roman authorities or not (except, maybe, fear).

What is clear, however, is that Paul continues this language when he says, "Owe no one anything, except to love one another." This is what the Christians in the end owe to the Roman state.

But if he is undermining the state, why would he tell this community to love the state?

This is where the story of Jesus differs most strongly from that of Rome. Not only is this community to bear the suffering that Rome dishes out without fighting back, not only are they to pray for blessing, not curse, on the state as it brings that suffering, they are also to love that state.

In other words, they are to love their enemies.

Yes, and in so doing they undermine the story of Rome completely. What the empire expects is resistance that it can then crush with ever more violence. But Paul calls these followers of Jesus to rob that narrative of its power. They are part of the story of Jesus where enemies are loved. Paul puts it this way in Rom 5:8–10:

> But God proves his love for us in that while we were still sinners Christ died for us. Much more surely then, now that we have been justified by his blood, we will we be saved through him from the wrath of God. For if while we were enemies, we were reconciled to God through the death of this Son, much more surely, having been reconciled, will we be saved by his life.

So if we read Romans 12 alongside Romans 13, we see that it is actually political?

It is both public and personal. In Rome public structures shaped personal interactions, and personal interactions revealed allegiances to the state. That is why chapters 14 and 15 are concerned with matters that are deeply personal for the churches in Rome: how they negotiate differences in practice and status reveals their ultimate allegiance. Paul calls the community again to a way of interacting that challenges the honor/shame dynamic of the empire. In fact, he again reminds them that he proclaims the good news of a triumph that comes through suffering, death and resurrection, not violent control (15:16, 19, 20).

I can see why Paul is concerned with the allegiance of the community in Rome, and I can see why it matters that they live out of the good news of the triumph of God, not Caesar, but I don't understand what this had to do with his planned trip to Spain. He makes it clear in Rom 15:24–29 that Rome will only be a stop on his way to Spain.

It seems probable that Paul intended to make Rome the base for his mission to Spain. This was necessary because Greek and Latin were not commonly spoken on the Iberian peninsula, nor were there any Jewish communities where Paul could seek shelter or begin his teaching. He needed the believing community in Rome to help him find translators and provide contacts in Spain.

But none of this would work if that community had an imagination still under the sway of the story of Rome. In that story, Spain was considered to be populated by uncivilized barbarians (cf. Rom 1:14). According to the good news of Rome, those who live in Spain are losers.

So if the community in Rome is already being torn apart by a reluctance to welcome other "losers," there is little likelihood that they would want to support a mission to the barbarians of Spain.

Precisely. What is at stake is the ability of the believers in Rome to live this other gospel in their own communities so that they might become a catalyst for the spread of the good news of the triumph of God in Spain.

So the letter to the Romans does outline Paul's theology. But it does so in a culturally grounded, not abstract, way.

And it calls the believing community to participate in a new story, that of the triumph of God, whose Messiah died for his enemies, so that all people might bring praise.

No wonder they were considered a threat to the empire.

We can take that as a sign, I believe, that at least some of them were convinced by Paul to live out of this alternative story.

For Further Reading

Donfried, Karl P., ed. *The Romans Debate.* Rev. and exp. ed. Peabody, Mass.: Hendrickson, 1991. This collection of essays is the best introduction to the history of the debate about this letter.

Elliott, Neil. *The Arrogance of Nations: Reading Romans in the Shadow of Empire.* PCC. Minneapolis: Fortress, 2008. Elliott provides a detailed reading of Romans in light of both the Roman imperial context and contemporary imperial concerns.

Finger, Reta Haltemann. *Roman House Churches for Today: A Practical Guide for Small Groups.* 2nd ed. Grand Rapids: Eerdmans, 2007. This is an extremely accessible introduction to the social issues facing the Roman community at the heart of the empire.

Horsley, Richard A., ed. *Paul and Empire: Religion and Power in Roman Imperial Society.* Harrisburg, Pa.: Trinity Press International, 1997. This collection of contemporary historians writing about Roman religion and social relations is an excellent introduction to the Roman context of the Pauline epistles.

Jewett, Robert. *Romans*. Herm. Minneapolis: Fortress, 2007. The introduction to this comprehensive commentary on Romans is particularly helpful for gaining a sense of the letter as a whole.

Keesmaat, Sylvia C. "If Your Enemy is Hungry: Love and Subversive Politics in Romans 12–13." Pages 141–158 in *Character Ethics and the New Testament: Moral Dimensions of Scripture*. Edited by Robert L. Brawley. Louisville: Westminster John Knox, 2007. This essay outlines in detail an anti-imperial reading of Rom 12 and 13.

———. "The Psalms in Romans and Galatians." Pages 139–61 in *The Psalms in the New Testament*. Edited by Steve Moyise and Maarten J. J. Menken. New York: T&T Clark, 2004. This essay demonstrates how Paul's use of the Psalms in Romans undermines both the imperial story of Rome and the calls for vindication against enemies found in the Psalms themselves.

Price, S. R. F. *Rituals and Power: The Roman Imperial Cult in Asia Minor*. Cambridge: Cambridge University Press, 1984. Price describes the pervasiveness of the imperial cult in all areas of life throughout the empire.

Wengst, Klaus. *Pax Romana and the Peace of Jesus Christ*. Translated by John Bowden. London: SCM, 1987. This is a comprehensive introduction to the imperial context and the challenge of the gospel.

Wright, N. T. "The Letter to the Romans: Introduction, Commentary, and Reflections." *NIB* 10:393–770. Wright has produced a very readable commentary, brilliantly demonstrating both the theological and political implications of the letter.

Zanker, Paul. *The Power of Images in the Age of Augustus*. Translated by Alan Shapiro. Ann Arbor: University of Michigan Press, 1988. Zanker develops a riveting analysis of the way that imperial images captured the imagination of the people of the empire.

The Righteousness of God in Romans

A. Katherine Grieb

Is God reliable? Is God just? Can we put our whole trust in God? The moral integrity of God lies at the heart of Paul's argument in Romans. Paul's letter to the Christian house churches in Rome is a sustained argument for the righteousness or trustworthiness of God that is identified with and demonstrated by the faithfulness of Jesus Christ. In Romans, Christ's faithfulness is understood primarily as his willing obedience to suffer death on the cross for humanity's salvation. So the "righteousness of God" and the "faithfulness of Christ" are closely linked in Paul's thought. Since the heart of Romans (chs. 9–11) is Paul's lament for unbelieving Israel, the specific situation to which Paul applies his argument for "the righteousness of God" in Romans is that of God's covenant fidelity to Israel, even as salvation in Jesus Christ is being extended to the Gentiles. But well before Paul addresses this specific situation, he lays out his argument for God's righteousness in the early chapters of the letter by recalling God's gracious gift to sinners in the death and resurrection of Jesus Christ. This essay will list the passages where the phrase "the righteousness of God" appears, comment briefly on the importance of this issue for Christian believers, then make some preliminary ground-clearing comments about the Greek word groups concerned with "righteousness" and "faithfulness." Finally we will turn to a more detailed analysis of the key passages where Paul talks about the righteousness of God in Romans.

"The Righteousness of God" in Paul's Thought Prior to Romans

The phrase "the righteousness of God" (*dikaiosynē theou*) in Paul's letters is almost exclusively found in the letter to the Romans and there it plays an essential role in Paul's argument, since Romans is best read as an extended defense of the righteousness (or justice) of God. Before turning our attention to Romans, we might notice the one major exception to the general rule that Paul deals with the righteousness of God primarily in Romans. The only specific reference to "the righteousness of God" outside of Romans is found in 2 Cor 5:21 ("For our sake, [God] has made [Christ] to be sin who knew no sin, so that in him, we might become the righteousness of God").[1] Here Paul anticipates the argument he will make in Romans, that Christ died for the ungodly, for sinners. He describes the saving exchange by which Jesus Christ assumes humanity's sinfulness and dies for them, in order that by virtue of baptism into his death and resurrection, and subsequent new life in him, believers might be changed into his likeness.

Paul's bold claim in this verse is that human beings, imitating Christ's faithful obedience and his trust in God, can actually become, by the power of God, something of God's own righteousness. The logic by which Paul links the faithfulness of Christ and the justice or righteousness of God, hinted at here in 2 Cor 5:21, is more fully developed later on in Romans, where the issue of God's righteousness is linked specifically to God's dealings with Israel and with the Gentiles.

"THE RIGHTEOUSNESS OF GOD" IN ROMANS

When we turn to Romans, the weight of the phrase "the righteousness of God" in Paul's theology is evident from its first appearance in the letter's thesis statement (1:16–17, at 1:17). Here it functions programmatically to set the agenda for the rest of the letter and especially for chapters 9–11. Paul describes the gospel of which he is not ashamed as "the power of God for salvation" and insists that in this gospel "*the righteousness of God* is being revealed." The phrase reappears at 3:5 ("if our unrighteousness serves to show *the righteousness of God*, what shall we say, that God is unrighteous?") in the important context of 3:1–8 and 3:20. The same phrase appears again two more times at 3:21–26: once in 3:22 where "*the righteousness of God*" and "the faith or faithfulness of Jesus Christ" are closely linked and once in 3:25 where "*the righteousness of God*" has been called into question because, in God's mercy, former sins had not been punished. Finally, the phrase appears twice at 10:3, where Paul describes members of unbelieving Israel as "ignorant of '*the righteousness of God*'

---

1. Translations, unless otherwise indicated, are the author's. Here the insertions of "God" and "Christ" in place of pronouns are modifications of the NRSV.

and therefore seeking to establish their own righteousness, rather than submitting to '*the righteousness of God*.' " We will examine each of these briefly, but first it is necessary to understand (1) why this issue is so important for Paul, (2) something of the semantic range of the words "righteousness" and "faithfulness," and (3) a bit of the history of interpretation of the phrase "the righteousness of God" in Romans.

WHY DOES "THE RIGHTEOUSNESS OF GOD" MATTER SO MUCH TO PAUL?

Leander Keck reminds us that believing in God by itself is not enough. To use a human analogy, there is no great virtue in putting my trust in a con artist, for I will simply get swindled. Everything depends on the trustworthiness of the one in whom I put my trust or faith. So the question of the trustworthiness or "the moral integrity of God" is *the* most important question for the person entrusting his or her life to God. In Paul's understanding, the Christ event (Jesus' death on the cross and his resurrection from the dead) was the decisive revelation of God's moral integrity (righteousness) and also the exposure of the extent of human sinfulness. In the universal salvation that God accomplished in the death and resurrection of Jesus Christ, God's character as the "rectifier of the ungodly" (that is, the one who makes sinners righteous or, said another way, puts the ungodly back into right relationship with God) is made clear once and for all time.

MOVING FROM PAUL'S GREEK TO OUR ENGLISH TRANSLATIONS

In Rom 4:5 God is described as "the one who justifies/rectifies the ungodly." The difficulty of translating Paul's Greek verb into English points to the limitations of the English language with respect to the two key word groups that will dominate our discussion, those concerned with *dikaiosynē* (righteousness) and *pistis* (faith, faithfulness). In English, "righteousness" and "justice" are both used to translate the Greek noun *dikaiosynē*, even though they have different meanings in English. Similarly, we can use "righteous" or "just" as translations for the Greek adjective *dikaios*, but we lack a verb that corresponds entirely to the Greek *dikaioō* since "justify" picks up only part of the meaning. The basic idea behind the Greek verb is "to make right" or "to put in right relationship" (as in to "justify a margin"), but in English the primary meaning of the verb "justify" is to make excuses for something. The Old English term "rightwise" has been proposed to correct this deficiency, and the Jesuit poet Gerard Manley Hopkins spoke of how "the just man *justices*," but "rectify" may work better to convey the idea of "putting a relationship right again" since at its core *dikaiosynē* (justification, rectification) is about God's putting humanity back into right relationship with God.

The same sorts of problems arise with the Greek word group relating to faith and faithfulness. The noun *pistis* has a wide range of meanings, including "faith, trust, and belief" but also "faithfulness, trustworthiness, and credibility or believability." The adjective *pistos* can mean either "faithful, trustworthy, and credible" or "believing, trusting, having faith." Once again, the main difficulty translating from the Greek to the English occurs in the verb, *pisteuō*, which means "I believe" in the sense of "I have faith in" or "I put my trust in" (again, it is primarily a relational idea). But when many Christians read the word "believe," they tend to link it with the idea of assenting to a doctrine or asserting a truth. The matter is complicated by the fact that it can mean that and sometimes does mean that in Romans, but readers should keep in mind that the most basic meaning of the *pistis* word group for Paul in Romans is that "we put our faith in God who is faithful," or "we put our trust in God who is trustworthy and true."

An Important Shift in the Understanding of "the Righteousness of God" in Romans

There is one more grammatical complication to discuss before we return to our discussion of "the righteousness of God" in Romans. Ever since the Protestant Reformer Martin Luther, most interpreters of Romans had understood the expression "the righteousness of God" to be an *objective* genitive, that is, to refer to an "alien" imputed righteousness that individual Christians receive as a gift from God by believing in Jesus Christ. Ernst Käsemann provoked a controversy in 1961 when, following the interpretation of Adolf Schlatter twenty-five years earlier, he read a paper at Oxford suggesting that the expression "the righteousness of God" in the key passages in Romans is better read as a *subjective* genitive, meaning that it refers primarily to God's *own* righteousness, a "salvation-creating power" by which God "reaches out for the world" and reestablishes the rightful claim to the creation over which God is sovereign.[2] For Paul, says

---

2. Ernst Käsemann, "'The Righteousness of God' in Paul," in *New Testament Questions of Today* (Philadelphia: Fortress, 1969), 182.

Käsemann, the world's salvation consists of its being recaptured by God, who is its rightful sovereign.

Käsemann did not dispute God's gracious gift to sinners; indeed, he insisted that the primary work of God in Christ Jesus is the rectification of the ungodly (Rom 4:5); but he also insisted that with the gift comes the Giver: in Christ, humanity experiences God's salvation-creating power because "the gift itself has the character of power."[3] The relational character of the righteousness of God means that "Christ takes power over our life," transforming our existence in baptism, so that we become a new creation, which inevitably implies a change of lordship. The righteousness of God (*dikaiosynē theou*) in Paul, especially Romans, is at the same time God's covenant faithfulness to Israel and God's eschatological saving action towards the Gentiles. The righteousness of God is "a power which brings salvation to pass."[4] It is God's victory in the death and resurrection of Jesus Christ over the hostile powers of sin and death which have enslaved God's good creation, including human beings held captive to their power. The righteousness of God is "God's sovereignty over the world revealing itself eschatologically in Jesus."[5] Käsemann's insights have greatly influenced subsequent readings of Romans, even though some aspects of the evidence he used to support his argument, based in part on Qumran texts, have been amended by later scholars, as we shall see. Our task now is to revisit in more detail the key passages in Romans where the phrase "the righteousness of God" appears.

ROMANS 1:16–17: PAUL'S THESIS: IN THE GOSPEL, THE RIGHTEOUSNESS OF GOD IS REVEALED

> For I am not ashamed of the gospel; for it is the power of God for salvation to everyone who has faith, to the Jew first and also to the Greek [Gentile]; for in it the righteousness of God is revealed, from faithfulness to faithfulness, as it stands written [in Hab 2:4]: "the one who is righteous through faithfulness shall live." (my translation)

Almost every word in Paul's thematic statement is important to the rest of the letter, so it bears rereading as other parts of the letter are being studied.

---

3. Ibid., 170.
4. Ibid., 181.
5. Ibid., 180.

Writing his letters long before the four evangelists wrote their narratives of the life, death, and resurrection of Jesus, Paul may have been the first of the early Christians to use the word "gospel" to refer to the saving work of God in Christ. The term *euangelion* (gospel or good news) was already in use to announce the birth or arrival of the emperor and to announce victory from the battlefield. Paul seems to have redefined these familiar meanings of the word to suggest that Jesus Christ replaces the emperor for Christians and that God in Christ has won the victory over the powers of sin and death. All of this is indeed good news.

But Paul's insistence that he is not ashamed of the gospel prompts us to wonder: why might someone think Paul would be ashamed of the gospel? He may think his gospel has been misunderstood and there is strong evidence in Romans to suggest that Paul is eager to set the record straight on a few matters before he visits Rome. Or Paul may be defensive about his gospel because it looks as though God has abandoned the covenant promises made to Israel in favor of the inclusion of the Gentiles, an issue to which he will return in Rom 9–11. Or Paul may be drawing on an expression common in Israel's lament psalms and prophetic writings, expressing his confidence that God will not allow him to be put to shame by his enemies. Or Paul may be using a rhetorical device to say that he is actually proud of the gospel he preaches.

At any rate, he states clearly that the gospel is the power of God for salvation. It is not a message *about* God's power, but it *is* God's power. The gospel, namely the death and resurrection of Jesus Christ, is the event of God's saving power for everyone who puts their trust in God, which is to say, everyone who believes the promises of God about which Paul will say more later. The gospel is God's saving power for everyone who trusts God, "to the Jew first and also to the Greek," a formula that Paul will repeat (in 2:9–10) to argue both for the priority of God's promises to Israel and also for the impartiality (fairness) of God towards Gentiles as well as Jews. Both of these reflect "the righteousness of God."

In the gospel, the righteousness of God is revealed. This is God's justice towards Israel with whom God is in covenant relationship. It is also God's power to put things right for all God's creatures, Jew and Gentile. God's righteousness is God's "right dealing" and "impartiality" and, above all, it is God's action in Christ to "put things right" again between God and sinful humans. God's righteousness, says Paul is revealed "from faithfulness to faithfulness" or perhaps "from faithfulness through faithfulness." Either way, it picks up the pattern by which God's covenant faithfulness to

Israel is matched by the faithfulness of Jesus Christ (his obedient fidelity even to death on the cross), the saving event which has extended God's covenant promises to Gentiles. God is revealing God's own covenant faithfulness through the gospel, the world-changing event of God's power for salvation, the death and resurrection of Jesus Christ.

All of this was written down long before in the holy Scriptures of Israel. Paul assumes that the Scriptures are the key to the present situation because the same God who inspired writers like the prophet Habakkuk is guiding events now in Paul's churches. Habakkuk 2:4 is ambiguous as Paul quotes it. It states that "the righteous one shall live by faith or faithfulness" or "the one who is righteous by faith/faithfulness shall live." There are a number of possible meanings and Paul probably intended more than one of them: it could mean that Jesus, God's righteous one, will live again (be raised from the dead) because of his fidelity or that he will be raised because of his trust in God. It could mean that those who put their trust in God and Jesus will live by their faith in the God who has put them back in right relationship. It may refer to the resurrection of those who, like Jesus, put their trust in God. It may mean all of these things at once, but one point is clear: the gospel is the power of God for the salvation of humanity. The same God who made us also loved us enough that Christ died for us (5:8), and nothing in creation can separate us from the love of God in Christ Jesus (8:39).

Romans 3:1–8 and 3:20: God's Righteousness Contrasted to Human Unrighteousness

Paul must argue for the righteousness of God at the beginning of chapter 3 in Romans because he has just suggested that physical circumcision (one sign of the covenant between God and Israel) is negotiable, since real circumcision is a matter of the heart (2:29). Paul is not breaking new ground here (see Deut 10:16; Jer 4:4; 9:26; and Ezek 44:9 for circumcision of the heart as more important than circumcision of the flesh), but Paul's comment leaves room for someone to ask, "then what advantage is there to being a Jew?" Paul will take up that question in Rom 9–11, but here he simply answers, "much in every way!" and singles out the Scriptures, the "oracles of God," which are full of God's promises to Israel as his prime example. This leads him back to another discussion of the righteousness of God.

It is at this point in Paul's argument that we see the force of Käsemann's argument for the subjective genitive ("the righteousness of God" as

God's own righteousness rather than righteousness that has been imputed by God to believers) because of the structure of Paul's argument in Rom 3:1–8:

> 3:3 What if some [Jews] were *unfaithful*? Does their *faithlessness* destroy the *faithfulness* of God?
> 3:4 Even if every human being is *false*, let it be seen that God is *true*.
> 3:5 But if our *unrighteousness* shows the *righteousness* of God, what shall we say, that God is *unrighteous*?
> 3:7 But if through my *falseness* the *truthfulness* of God abounds to his glory....

In all of these verses Paul is clearly setting up a contrast between human unfaithfulness, untruthfulness, and unrighteousness, on the one hand, and God's faithfulness, truthfulness, and righteousness on the other. In fact, in this context, these words mean the same thing: they are three different ways of describing the integrity of God. "God is faithful to God's promises" is another way of saying "God spoke the truth when God made those promises." Human unfaithfulness implies playing false with God, while God's fidelity to humans is the way in which God is true to God's own self. All of these attributes point to the God who is reliable, dependable, faithful, and worthy of trust.

By contrast, Paul cites a chain (catena) of Bible verses in Rom 3:10–18 describing human wickedness. The effect of this rapid-fire machine-gun-like argument is summarized at 3:19: hearing this indictment from the Scriptures (law), humanity has nothing to say! Every mouth is stopped and the whole world is accountable (*hypodikos*, note the same root *dik-* that forms the group of words around "righteousness") to God. Paul concludes in 3:20 that since through the law comes knowledge of sin, "no human being will be rectified/ put right with God from God's point of view by works of the law." This is a loose citation of Psalm 143, which contains a number of references to the righteousness of God. The psalmist expects that the saving power of God's righteousness will reach out to save him (as Hays, paraphrasing Käsemann, explains).[6] Romans 3:20, then, provides

---

6. Richard B. Hays, "Psalm 143 as Testimony to the Righteousness of God," in *The Conversion of the Imagination: Paul as Interpreter of Israel's Scripture* (Grand Rapids: Eerdmans, 2005), 58–60.

not a contrast but a transition to the verses that follow, where Paul's language about the righteousness of God is at its most intense.

ROMANS 3:21–26: THE RIGHTEOUSNESS OF GOD MANIFESTED IN THE FAITHFULNESS OF CHRIST

Paul's rhetorical strategy in this section is to use three powerful word pictures (metaphors) to tell the story of God's righteousness, that is, God's saving work in Jesus Christ's death and resurrection. He reminds his hearers of the thesis sentence in Rom 1:16–17 as he repeats the phrase "the righteousness of God," now manifested apart from the law, although, of course, the law and the prophets testify to it, as we have already seen in Hab 2:4, Ps 143, and elsewhere. Paul repeats the phrase "the righteousness of God" and expands it along the lines of his earlier thesis statement by identifying "God's righteousness" with the faithfulness of Jesus Christ (his obedient and trusting death on the cross) for all who believe (another echo of the earlier thesis statement). Reminding us of the argument from 1:18 to 3:20 ("all have sinned and, like Adam, have forfeited the glory of God"), Paul is now poised to describe God's saving and powerful intervention.

God's righteousness (God's saving work in Christ) can be described in the first place as "justification" (rectification or putting things back in right relationship) using the metaphor of the law court. Paul stresses God's gracious gift: God is under no compulsion and has no legal duty towards the human creatures who have so wronged God. Paul looks back to the time of the fall of humanity described in Gen 3: ever since Adam and Eve our wrongdoing has caused us to be out of right relationship with God. The metaphorical image that Paul employs is that we are finally being held responsible for our crimes against God. Another way to see it is that we are finally being forced to pay off all our debts to God. Humanity is the condemned prisoner in the dock, already declared guilty, sentenced to death, and awaiting execution. But God loves us so much, says Paul, that God was willing to pay all of our fines, to serve all our time in prison, and even to die on our behalf, in order to restore us to the right relationship in love. The law court or "justification" model of atonement (at-one-ment, putting things back in right relationship) is powerful and has captured the imagination of Christians ever since Paul used it. But no analogy is perfect; no metaphor captures everything there is to say. Paul knew that telling the story of God's righteousness this way lays emphasis on the danger we were in, the wrongdoing and guilt that properly belonged to us, and

God's gracious gift in taking that wrongdoing from us, for us. But the metaphor does not say much about how we were set free or that we were cleansed from the effects of our sinfulness. To spell out those aspects of God's righteousness, Paul will need to use some other word pictures.

God's righteousness (God's salvation and restoration of humanity in Christ) can also be described employing economic language, the metaphors of "redemption" and "liberation from slavery." Here the verbal image behind Paul's language is the group of Hebrew slaves in bondage to Pharaoh, forced to build storehouse cities and tombs in Egypt, until God (Israel's "Redeemer") leads them out with a mighty arm and with signs and wonders. Note the stress on God's *power* to save. Redemption means "buying back" lost family members who have been enslaved, kidnapped, captured by pirates, taken as prisoners of war, or sometimes forced to sell themselves into slavery in order to pay off their debts. God was called the Redeemer of Israel with respect to the exodus from Egypt, not because any ransom money changed hands, but because the results were the same as if it had: God's people were free again. God loves us so much, says Paul, that God was willing to venture far away into Egypt to find lost human beings, to fight on their behalf against the tyrants of sin and death who oppressed them, and to bring them back to a place where they could worship God without fear. The redemption metaphor, like the justification metaphor, cannot say everything that needs to be said about Pauline soteriology (doctrine of salvation), but it does underline the helplessness of those enslaved to sin and death and the distortion of perspective that results from a long enslavement. The Israelites in the wilderness actually longed to return to Egypt, forgetting their cruel slavery and God's powerful deliverance.

Finally, Paul uses a third metaphor to describe the righteousness of God: God put Jesus Christ forward as "*hilastērion*," that is, as an atoning sacrifice for sin. If the first two metaphors in Rom 3:24 draw from the fields of Israel's law and economics, Paul's third word picture in 3:25 borrows from the cultic vocabulary of Israel. This is the boldest and most provocative metaphor of the three, not only because it insists that the saving death of Christ on the cross was God's own work (God put him forward), but also because the death of an executed criminal on a Roman (pagan) cross is conceptually so far removed from the sacred liturgical duties of Israel's high priest in the holy of holies in the temple of Jerusalem (the holiest place in the world) on the Day of Atonement, Yom Kippur (the holiest time in the world). The blood poured out there on the mercy seat, the golden cover of the ark of the covenant, is the means by which God

"covers" the sins of the people and cleanses them from all unrighteousness. God loves us so much, says Paul, that God's own self, God's own
Son was not spared, but was poured out as a sacrifice for sin, as the blood
by which the new covenant was cut and sealed. Paul reminds us in Rom
3 that through the saving power of God, demonstrated in Christ's death
and resurrection, we are made clean again and purified from every stain
or defilement that we imagine could separate us from the love of God.
God's holiness and righteousness are not compromised by God's merciful
forgiveness of sins. It is God's own atoning sacrifice that makes us whole,
that puts us back into right relationship with God once more.

In three different ways, each metaphorical image evoked by a single
Greek word, Paul has expressed as well as anyone could what is essentially indescribable: the depths of the love of God for the people of Israel
and, indeed, for all of humanity. The result of God's action in Christ is,
once more, the silencing of the world (3:19) and especially of any within
it who are tempted to boast of their own righteousness before God (3:27).
All such boasting is necessarily excluded in the face of God's "salvation-
creating power" that is seen in the costly death of Christ on the cross and
the stunning reversal of that death in resurrection. It is only in ignorance
of the righteousness of God that anyone could seek to establish their own
righteousness and refuse to submit to God's own righteousness. And yet,
as Paul sees it, that is exactly what has happened to Israel.

Romans 10:3: The Righteousness of God
in the Context of Romans 9–11 as a Whole

Romans 10:1–4 marks the second occasion in Paul's long and dense argument in Rom 9–11 where Paul interjects himself into the argument. (The
first was 9:1–5.) Here Paul insists his heart's desire and repeated prayer
for Israel is that they may be saved. Paul offers to testify on their behalf
that they have a zeal for God, even if their zeal is not informed by the
knowledge of God in Christ. This section may well reflect Paul's subsequent assessment of his own pre-Christian experience, since elsewhere in
his letters he claims that his zeal led him to persecute the church. Paul's
own experience, as he later reconstructed it, probably shaped his analysis
of the situation of unbelieving Israel.

> For being ignorant of the righteousness of God, and [therefore] trying
> to establish their own [righteousness], they have not submitted to the

righteousness of God. For Christ is actually the whole point of the law, so that [in Christ] there may be righteousness for everyone who has faith. (10:3–4, my translation)

These last two references to *dikaiosynē theou* (the righteousness of God) have brought us close to the beginning of this essay, where we looked very briefly at Paul's use of the phrase in 2 Cor 5:21. The only way that Paul can see human beings (who are naturally enslaved to sin and death) doing righteousness is if they are "in Christ," having submitted to his lordship in baptism and having become a new creation in him. Only then, in Christ, can Paul imagine anyone becoming the righteousness of God. Everything else is delusional, the product of misinformation and self-deception. The problem, as Paul sees it, is that faith in God, the ability to put one's trust in God's trustworthiness, is not something human beings can initiate; faith in God is a gift from God. Remembering, perhaps, what he now recalls as his own blindness and stubborn zeal for God, he is painfully aware that nothing but the "salvation-creating power" of God in Christ, that is, nothing but the righteousness of God, could have diverted him from his course of action. The rest of Rom 9–11 is Paul's attempt to think through the consequences of that realization. We see, finally, in 10:3–4 the way Paul's thesis statement leads theologically to the situation of unbelieving Israel that preoccupies him throughout this strange and wonderful letter.

SOME THOUGHTS BY WAY OF CONCLUSION

At this point we do well to recall what we noted in the thesis statement in Rom 1:16–17: for Paul the gospel is not a message *about* God's power, it *is* God's power. The gospel is the event of God's saving power both enacted and revealed in the death and resurrection of Jesus Christ. God's *dynamis*, the explosive world-changing power of God to save, is, at the same time, God's righteousness, from faithfulness to faithfulness. God's righteousness, truthfulness, and faithfulness are matched by the fidelity of Jesus Christ, and ultimately, since God's will *is* done, by the fidelity of those in Christ. The faithful obedient death of Jesus Christ was at once God's own action of covenant faithfulness to Israel and also the action of the Creator redeeming and restoring all humanity.

The righteousness of God is Paul's preoccupation throughout his letter to the house churches at Rome. For him, everything depends upon the integrity of God who keeps the covenant promises made to Israel. God remains deeply mindful of the priority of the people of God, and, at the same time, welcomes Gentiles into Israel, showing no partiality but granting salvation in Christ Jesus to all who believe. The human mind can hardly hold such a paradox together: we can hardly blame Paul for not expressing the apparent tension within God's own righteousness more clearly or for finally throwing up his hands to exclaim the unsearchability of God's judgments and the inscrutability of God's ways (11:33). But even in his inconclusive conclusions, Paul is clearer than most of us about one thing: the righteousness of God is at the center of it all.

For Further Reading

Cousar, Charles B. *A Theology of the Cross: The Death of Jesus in the Pauline Letters*. Minneapolis: Fortress, 1990. See esp. pp. 36–48. This book is one of the best general introductions to Paul's theology of the cross, filled with exegetical explanations and pastoral insights.

Grieb, A. Katherine. *The Story of Romans: A Narrative Defense of God's Righteousness*. Louisville: Westminster John Knox, 2002. My book argues that from start to finish Romans is a defense of God's righteousness. It is designed for readers of Romans in seminaries and parishes who wish to understand Paul's argument by means of the stories underneath it and apply it to our Christian life.

Hays, Richard B. "Psalm 143 as Testimony to the Righteousness of God." Pages 50–60 in *The Conversion of the Imagination: Paul as Interpreter of Israel's Scripture*. Grand Rapids: Eerdmans, 2005. This important article amends Käsemann's argument for "the righteousness of God" that had relied on Qumran texts. Hays shows that Ps 143, which is actually referenced in Rom 3:20, supports Käsemann's argument.

Käsemann, Ernst. " 'The Righteousness of God' in Paul." Pages 168–82 in *New Testament Questions of Today*. Philadelphia: Fortress, 1969. This is the essay that prompted a new theological understanding of "the righteousness of God" in Romans. He builds this understanding on Paul's thesis statement that the gospel is God's saving power in which God's righteousness is revealed.

Keck, Leander E. *Paul and His Letters*. 2nd ed. Philadelphia: Fortress, 1988. See esp. pp. 110–22. Leander Keck's introduction to Paul's letters and his theology is the single most helpful resource I know for understanding the logic of Paul's thought at all levels of education.

Stevenson, Peter K., and Stephen I. Wright. *Preaching the Atonement*. London: T&T Clark, 2005. See esp. pp. 105–19. Stevenson and Wright's book will be especially useful for preachers dealing with classic biblical texts on the atonement. The pages cited provide an introduction to Rom 3:21–26 and comment on a sermon of mine demonstrating one way to preach on that passage.

ATONEMENT IMAGES IN ROMANS

Joel B. Green

Generally speaking, theological language used in New Testament studies can be traced back to Greek usage, or sometimes Latin. The term *theology* itself, for example, is formed from the combination of two Greek words, *theos* ("god") and *logos* ("speech"); hence, "theology" refers generally to "speech about god" or even "god-talk." Unlike much of our theological vocabulary, though, the term *atonement* derives from sixteenth-century Middle English: *at-onement*. *Atonement*, then, broadly referred to the means by which two parties could be made "as one," that is, how they might be reconciled. Already in Middle English and subsequently, the sense of *atonement* is broader than its relation to the concept of reconciliation might suggest; today, it refers more broadly to *the saving significance of Jesus' death.*

William Tyndale coined the term for use in his English translation of the Bible, and it found its way into common English especially through the wide-ranging influence of the Authorized (or King James) Version (KJV) of the Old Testament (1611). In the New Testament of the KJV, however, the term was rare, appearing only once—in Rom 5:11: "And not only so, but we also joy in God through our Lord Jesus Christ, by whom we have now received the atonement." In the 1989 New Revised Standard Version (NRSV), the words *atonement* and *atoning* occur in the New Testament only twice each (Rom 3:25; Heb 2:17; 1 John 2:2; 4:10). Most recently, the Common English Bible (CEB) of the New Testament (2010) uses the term only once, in Acts 27:9, where it introduces a reference to "Atonement Day." Given how rarely the term appears in the New Testament, how important is it that we examine atonement images in Romans? Actually, very important. This is because of the centrality of Jesus' death to Paul's understanding of the gospel as this is presented in Romans.

This chapter will follow a simple outline. First, we will note the importance of the atonement for theologians who want to take Paul seriously. This will lead to some basic considerations about how best to take Paul on his own terms. Second, we will explore in some detail a text in Romans where the atonement occupies center stage in Paul's argument: Rom 3:21–26. This will lead, third, to a brief discussion of the nature and importance of "metaphor" for reading Paul on the atonement. Finally, we will examine something of the range of metaphors Paul introduces in his presentation of the atoning significance of Jesus' death.

READING THE ATONEMENT, READING PAUL

A close reading of Paul's letters supports two indisputable and intimately linked claims about the crucifixion of Jesus of Nazareth. The first is that Jesus' death at the hands of Roman justice, represented theologically in the motto "Christ crucified," is the means for comprehending the eternal purpose of God as this is known in Israel's Scriptures. The second is that the significance of Jesus' death is woven tightly into the fabric of God's purpose with the result that there are many ways of unpacking its significance as the basis of the divine offer of salvation. One of the twentieth century's leading Pauline scholars, Ernst Käsemann, observed that, for Paul, the cross is "the signature" of the resurrected Christ.[11] Emphatically put, no cross, no gospel.

How the cross is important for Paul is sometimes hard to grasp. This is because later reflection on the atonement sometimes gets in the way of how we read Paul. Over the last two millennia, theologians have identified and developed a wide range of theories for making sense of the saving significance of the cross of Christ. These include the following:

> *Christ the Conqueror*, which framed reflection on the cross and resurrection in terms of cosmic conflict, within which Jesus' death spells victory over sin and the powers of evil, including the devil (Irenaeus, ca. 130–200)
> *Satisfaction*, which understands the cross as "satisfying" the debt owed to God by a sinful humanity (Anselm, 1033–1109)

---

1. Ernst Käsemann, "The Saving Significance of Jesus' Death," in *Perspectives on Paul* (Philadelphia: Fortress, 1971), 32–59, here 56.

Moral Influence, which views Jesus' life and death as a demonstration of God's love capable of moving humans to repentance and love of God and neighbor (Abelard, 1079–1142)

These are often called the three "classical" theories of the atonement, but theologians have added many others as well as developed these three in different directions. We might find hints of one or another of these theories in Paul's letters, including Romans. However, it is important to recognize that none of these is derived from Paul alone, and none of them explains in a comprehensive way how Paul sketched the significance of Christ's work on the cross. It will not do to read the history of later theological reflection back onto Paul.

In addition, for Paul, the concept of "atonement" actually comprises a constellation of images. Each has its own integrity, and Paul is quite capable of arranging his atonement images in an assortment of constellations. Let me illustrate something of the variety of Paul's understanding of the atonement by noting his use of two quite different formulas:

The "dying formula"—for example, "But God proves his love for us in that while we still were sinners Christ died for us" (Rom 5:8 NRSV; see also, e.g., Rom 5:6; 1 Cor 15:3; 2 Cor 5:14)

The "giving up" of Jesus, whether as a divine act—for example, "[Jesus our Lord] was handed over to death for our trespasses and was raised for our justification" (Rom 4:25 NRSV; see also Rom 8:32); or as an act of Jesus' own self-giving—for example, "[the Lord Jesus Christ] gave himself for our sins to set us free from the present evil age" (Gal 1:3–4 NRSV; see also Gal 2:20)

These suggest the importance of interpreting Pauline texts in relation to the larger story he is telling, without trying too quickly to fit his atonement thought into a neat or narrow presentation. Unlike some ways of understanding the gospel in the contemporary West, Paul's gospel sets the cross of Christ within the larger story in which God's agenda to save God's people and, indeed, the entire cosmos is unveiled. The cross is the means by which God reveals God's own covenant faithfulness, through which the whole world becomes the beneficiary of God's restorative justice. How this gets worked out for Paul cannot be reduced to a single atonement image or model or theory.

PAUL ON THE ATONEMENT: ROMANS 3:21–26

Within the letter of Romans, 3:21–26 is a central text for understanding Paul's view of the atonement:

> But now, apart from law, the righteousness of God has been disclosed, and is attested by the law and the prophets, the righteousness of God through faith in Jesus Christ for all who believe. For there is no distinction, since all have sinned and fall short of the glory of God; they are now justified by his grace as a gift, through the redemption that is in Christ Jesus, whom God put forward as a sacrifice of atonement by his blood, effective through faith. He did this to show his righteousness, because in his divine forbearance he had passed over the sins previously committed; it was to prove at the present time that he himself is righteous and that he justifies the one who has faith in Jesus. (NRSV)

This short paragraph is tightly packed and how we understand it depends on how we make sense of its place in the argument Paul has been making.

One problem over which readers of Romans have struggled is how to make sense of Paul's Greek term *hilastērion*, which the NRSV translates as "sacrifice of atonement." The term refers to the means by which the goodwill of a god is recovered. What stands in the way of right relations with God? Some of Paul's interpreters think that the problem Jesus' death needed to overcome is God's wrath. For evidence, they point to Paul's references to divine anger in Rom 1:18; 2:5 (2x); 3:5 and on this basis urge that Paul had to show how God's personal anger against human sin was addressed. Their answer: Christ's death, his "sacrifice of atonement," was Christ's taking upon himself the penalty due the human race on account of their sin. This view is held by a number of interpreters, but there is very little to support this understanding of Paul's argument.

It is true that we can imagine some of Paul's first-century readers would have understood Paul's language in just this way. Among the Romans, the gods were like companions in the stuff of everyday life. City administration was organized in part to maintain good relations with the gods. Sacrifices were offered in recognition of the supremacy of the gods and in exchange for their favors. In the ancient Roman world it was not uncommon to pacify or appease a deity through worship and sacrifice. We can imagine, then, that Gentile converts to the church might have imagined that Jesus' death functioned in this way.

However, the God of Israel's Scriptures is not well-represented by a view like this one. Unlike the portrait of the ancient gods we find in Greek and Roman literature, Israel's Scriptures depict a God whose anger is neither whimsical nor irrational. Instead, they document a series of motivations behind expressions of God's wrath—especially idolatry and injustice. God's wrath is typically a response to Israel's failure to maintain the covenant, especially when Israel slipped into idolatrous practices. A good example is the account of the golden calf, when Israel formed an idol in the form of a calf:

> The LORD said to Moses, "Go down at once! Your people, whom you brought up out of the land of Egypt, have acted perversely; they have been quick to turn aside from the way that I commanded them; they have cast for themselves an image of a calf, and have worshiped it and sacrificed to it, and said, 'These are your gods, O Israel, who brought you up out of the land of Egypt!'" The LORD said to Moses, "I have seen this people, how stiff-necked they are. Now let me alone, so that my wrath may burn hot against them and I may consume them; and of you I will make a great nation." (Exod 32:7–10 NRSV)

In this instance the Lord "changed his mind about the disaster that he planned to bring on his people" (32:14 NRSV). This was the consequence of Moses's mediation, and especially Moses's calling to remembrance the Lord's promise to Abraham.

In Israel's Scriptures, God's wrath can also be motivated by opposition from foreign peoples against God's people. As a consequence we find images and accounts of God in the guise of the divine warrior acting on behalf of his chosen. For example,

> Your right hand, O LORD, glorious in power—your right hand, O LORD, shattered the enemy. In the greatness of your majesty you overthrew your adversaries; you sent out your fury, it consumed them like stubble. At the blast of your nostrils the waters piled up, the floods stood up in a heap; the deeps congealed in the heart of the sea. (Exod 15:6–8 NRSV)

Nevertheless, God's "personality," so to speak, is not one quickly or impulsively given to anger or retribution. Instead, we repeatedly read, God is "slow to anger and abounding in steadfast love" (e.g., Exod 34:6; Num 14:18). God's wrath is relationally based, not retributively motivated. It seeks to restore and protect God's people. What is more, God might avert his wrath in response to repentance, prayer, or mediation, but even this is a result of God's own, gracious change of mind. Never do we read in Israel's Scriptures that Israel's sacrificial system served as a means of averting or assuaging God's wrath.

This raises the question of how best to understand sacrifice in Israel's Scriptures and, then, in Paul's writing. Most of the sacrifices and sacrificial offerings discussed in the Scriptures had nothing to do with sin at all. For this reason, the most important for our purposes is the purification offering (e.g., Lev 4:1–6:7; 6:24–7:10; see Lev 16), the focus of which is on cleansing the effect of sin, one type of cultic impurity. These sacrifices had to do with "expiation" (sacrifice as the means by which God frees and cleanses people from the onus and blemish of sin) rather than "propitiation" (sacrifice as a means of averting God's wrath). The importance of forgiveness is highlighted in a text like Lev 19:22: "And the priest shall make atonement for him with the ram of guilt offering before the LORD for his sin that he committed; and the sin he committed shall be forgiven him" (NRSV). Sin has resulted in an estranged relationship between the sinner and God, and it is this separation that must be addressed. Serving as mediator, the priest resolves the broken relationship through a sacrifice. How is this so? First, basic to this legislation is the opposition of life and death—with death a great evil to be avoided, and with everything related to death (whether the corpse itself, bloody discharge, or disease) rendering people unclean and unfit to enter into God's presence. Second, the choice of an unblemished animal serves as an analogy for the election of Israel set apart for holy life in relationship to and service of God. Third, in the sacrificial rite, the laying of hands on the beast's head signals the importance of "identification" or "representation"—with sinners identifying themselves with the beast and the beast now representing sinners in their sin. Thus, the shedding of blood—with blood understood as the substance of life, sacred to God—signifies the offering of the lives of those for whom the sacrifice is made. In the end, "sin" pollutes, stains, and spoils; sacrifice wipes away sin and its effects.

Accordingly, a "sacrifice of atonement" resolves estrangement between God and humanity, but not by appeasing God's wrath. How, then, are we to understand the sacrificial death of Jesus? Different texts point in different directions. For example, Paul's reference to Jesus as "Passover lamb" in 1 Cor 5:7 calls to mind the Passover sacrifice so central to Israel's story. Celebrated annually, Passover both memorialized and reappropriated for generations of God's people God's election and great act of deliverance.

Read in relation to Paul's directive regarding the presence of an immoral person within the church ("Drive out the wicked person from among you," 1 Cor 5:1–13), his allusion to Passover marks the Corinthian believers as a community of persons set apart from the bondage of sin as the distinctive people of God. Again, the status of Jesus' death as a "sin offering" is clear in several Pauline texts. This is especially true of Rom 8:3 ("as a sin offering") and 2 Cor 5:21 ("God made Christ sin for us"), but also in references to the saving efficacy of Jesus' blood (Rom 3:25; 5:9; Eph 1:7; 2:13; Col 1:20), which must be understood symbolically in this way since the mode of Jesus' execution was not markedly bloody. In these instances, Paul speaks to the effectiveness of sacrifice in terms of exchange and representation: sin and death transferred to the sacrificial victim, its purity and life to those who receive the benefits of the sacrifice. Jesus' death wipes away sin and its effects.

What, then, are we to make of the meaning of the atonement in Rom 3:21–26? This paragraph is the heading for a subsection of the letter (3:21–4:25) in which Paul returns to the theme decisively broached in Rom 1:16–17: the gospel "is the power of God for salvation to everyone who has faith, to the Jew first and also to the Greek. For in it the righteousness of God is revealed through faith for faith." Here the apostle recalls his earlier emphases on *all* (whether Jew or Gentile), the response of faith, and the disclosure of God's righteousness. In preparation for this new section, Rom 3:21–23 summarizes the argument in 1:18–3:20 ("all have sinned and fallen short of God's glory") and signals an epochal shift (3:21: "but now"; see 3:26: "at the present time").

What is this shift in "the times"? *In the past*, human sin—defined in 1:18–23 as idolatry that suppresses the truth about God—had led to the manifestation of God's wrath, with God's wrath described as nothing other than an expression of God's righteousness. Accordingly, God's judgment is presently revealed against "all ungodliness and wickedness" (1:18) as God hands people over to experience the consequences of the sin they choose. *But now* God has revealed his righteousness "apart from the law" (3:21). This is the law that, on the one hand, segregated Jew and Gentile, and, on the other, was the basis on which the Jewish people were found guilty. The phrase "apart from the law" thus underscores again the common lot of Jew and Gentile in God's plan.

In this new time, how does God reveal God's righteousness? God does so in the faithfulness of Jesus Christ, which culminates in his death and its effects, the benefits of which are available to those who believe. Those who believe are now justified—that is, restored to right relations with God. They are included within the community of God's people now, in anticipation of the end-time judgment.

Accordingly, the problem to be overcome is not God's wrath as such, but rather the human assault on God's righteousness sketched in 1:18–3:20 and summarized in the conclusion found in 3:23, that all have sinned and fallen short of God's glory. God's wrath is God's judgment on ungodliness and wickedness, and it is this ungodliness and wickedness that must be addressed. Indeed, it is this ungodliness and wickedness that has been addressed by means of the faithfulness of Jesus Christ, which Paul understands as the revelation of God's own covenant faithfulness. The only possibility for humans to be restored to right status with God is God's own action. This emphasis comes to the fore in Rom 3:24–26: by his grace, as a gift, through a divine act of liberation (a term that reminds us of God's mighty act of delivering Israel from Egyptian slavery) in Christ. For Paul, then, God's righteousness is revealed for all (whether Jew or Gentile) who believe through the faithfulness of Jesus Christ, whose faithfulness unto death wipes away human hostility toward God.

Therefore, in the complex paragraph of Rom 3:21–26, Paul underscores that Jew and Gentile are on the same footing with regard both to sin and its resolution in restoration to right relations with God, that this being restored to right status with God is the result of God's gracious gift, that this gift is realized in the sacrificial death of Jesus Christ, and that liberation is appropriated in the same way for both Jew and Gentile, namely, through faith.

Metaphor and Atonement

One of the most important challenges in reading Rom 3:21–26 (and other texts concerned with the atonement in Paul) has to do with how we read metaphors. After reflecting for a moment on how metaphors work, we can see how sensitivity to metaphor makes a difference in understanding the nature of the atonement in Paul.

Metaphors reveal and conceal. On the one hand, this means that no one metaphor can capture the reality of the atonement. Metaphors from Israel's sacrificial system communicate something important about the death of Jesus, but they cannot say everything we need to say about the cross of Christ. On the other hand, this means that, in a given use of a metaphor, not all properties of the metaphor are necessarily embraced.

For example, Mark 10:45 ("For the Son of Man came not to be served but to serve and to give his life a ransom for many") employs the metaphor of ransom, but we would be foolish to push too far the nature of this business transaction. Who pays the ransom? To whom is it paid? These questions are not addressed by the text, either by this verse or by the larger narrative of Mark's Gospel. This may well be because, in Israel's exodus from Egyptian bondage, "ransom" is understood primarily as "release" (and not as "payment").

Given that all language is culturally embedded, it almost goes without saying that much of what we want to communicate is never explicitly verbalized. We need more than a dictionary since context, shared cultural background, shared histories, and so on contribute to our understanding of utterances. Accordingly, our ability to communicate with one another rests to a significant degree on our understanding more than the words that we speak. We need linguistic competence, but we also need what we might call contextual competence. A few sentences can illustrate:

> Are they going to make a go of it?
> They're only spinning their wheels.
> Where are we headed?
> We've gone our separate ways.

At one level, these utterances make no sense. At another level, they seem quite natural to us. This is because most of us are familiar with our tendency to conceptualize relationships as journeys. We know what these sentences mean even though they are highly metaphorical. These examples suggest the degree to which our utterances are grounded in everyday action in the world and rely on larger systems of thought.

These general comments on metaphor are important because they help us to see that metaphors for the atonement are implicit comparisons that rely on larger systems of thought grounded in life in the world. Getting those larger systems of thought right, then, is critical. We might refer to this as reading a metaphor according to the right frame.

To return to Romans, it makes a great deal of difference whether we read Paul's language in Rom 3:21–26 in terms of a Western law court or in terms of the world portrayed by Israel's Scriptures. In today's law courts in the West, the decisive issue would be "guilty versus innocent." In Israel's Scripture, the focus would fall on faithful adherence to the covenant relationship initiated and maintained by Yahweh. To illustrate the difference, we might consider the case of Tamar, who played the role of a prostitute as she tricked Judah into fathering her sons. In our law courts, we would likely determine that Tamar is guilty, whereas in Gen 38 she is portrayed as "more righteous" than Judah—because he failed to meet his covenantal obligations toward her.

Similarly, within a frame determined by a Western judicial system, it makes sense to think of Jesus' death as God's way of declaring sinners "not guilty"; this, then, would be the meaning of "justification." This way of thinking would be alien to Rom 3, however, because Paul works out his argument within a different legal frame. He is not concerned with the frame or system of Western justice, but with the frame of covenantal relations as these are portrayed in Israel's Scriptures. For Paul in Rom 3, then, God's righteousness is his covenant faithfulness, not his adherence to an abstract code of law that demands he punish those who break that law. And God's covenant faithfulness is revealed in the faithfulness of Jesus Christ, particularly in his death. Framed in this way, "justification" refers to God's embracing believers, Jew and Gentile, as members of God's own people. For those who believe, God does this on the basis of their sins having been wiped clean through the sacrificial death of Jesus.

Atonement Metaphors

Whatever else can be made of Paul's understanding of Jesus' death, his theology of the cross lacks any developed sense of divine retribution. Quite the contrary, according to a text like Rom 5:6–8, the death of Christ is the ultimate expression of the boundless love of God: "But God demonstrates his love for us in that while we were still sinners Christ died for us" (Rom 5:8).

Within its context, this affirmation in Rom 5 brings to the fore three crucial declarations that can broaden our perspective on Paul's theology of the cross. First, God's love for humanity is immeasurable. No human parallels help us to plumb its depths. Even though someone might dare to die on behalf of a righteous person (5:7), Christ died for "the ungodly" (5:6), for "sinners" (5:8), for God's "enemies" (5:10). Second, Paul's audience can be certain that their suffering (cf. 5:1–5) has significance because the suffering of Christ has proven to be so meaningful. The effectiveness of Jesus' death is framed in three ways—"we have been justified," "saved from the wrath of God," and "reconciled to God" (5:9–11). In the midst of human impotence, Christ took on the measure of human powerlessness and died in the place of humanity; as a result of his death, humans share in his life and find that human suffering has significance.

Third, in a crucial though perhaps unexpected turn of phrase (5:8), Paul says that God demonstrates God's love by means of what *Christ* did. We might have anticipated that God's love would be manifest best in God's own deed. This would certainly be the case if Paul were sketching an atonement theology centered on God's action toward Christ—that is, if God were the subject and Jesus the object of Jesus' crucifixion. Paul's way of putting things, however, ensures that we see God's attitude toward and action on behalf of the world in Christ's own action. That is, Paul affirms the oneness of purpose and activity of God and God's Son in the cross. Thus any atonement theology that assumes that in the cross God did something "to" Jesus stands in tension with Paul's clear affirmation in Rom 5.

The language Paul uses in Rom 5 presses in another direction, too, by suggesting something of the range of ways Paul can describe Jesus' death. Here he uses three types of language: (1) legal language (though, as have seen, this is a metaphor borrowed from covenantal relations and not from the Western judicial system): "we have been justified," (2) the language of end-time judgment: "saved from the wrath of God," and (3) the language of interpersonal relations: "reconciled to God" (5:9–11).

In Paul's writings, as in the New Testament more generally, the saving significance of the death of Jesus is represented chiefly (though not exclusively) by means of five constellations of images, five frames. These refer to central spheres of public life in the larger Greco-Roman world:

The court of law (e.g., justification)
Commercial dealings (e.g., redemption)
Personal relationships (e.g., reconciliation)
Worship (e.g., sacrifice)
The battleground (e.g., triumph over evil)

Each of these examples provides a window into a cluster of terms and concepts that relate to that particular sphere of public life.

For example, without using the actual term *sacrifice*, Paul can refer to Jesus as the "Passover lamb" (1 Cor 5:7) and as "firstfruits" (1 Cor 15:20, 23; cf. Lev 23; Deut 16), and he can refer to the handing over of Jesus in ways that recall the binding of Isaac (Rom 8:32; cf. Gen 22). Similarly, "reconciliation" can be represented by the specific language of reconciliation (Rom 5:10–11; 11:15; 1 Cor 7:11; 2 Cor 5:18–20; Eph 2:16; Col 1:20, 22), but also by the terminology of peace (Eph 2:14–18) and the many practices (e.g., Rom 16:16), pleas (e.g., Philemon), and testimonies (e.g., Gal 3:26–29) of reconciliation that dot the landscape of the wider Pauline corpus.

Why are there so many images? First, language for the atonement is metaphorical. Calling our language metaphorical does not detract from the concreteness of that language or the actions and experiences to which that language refers. It means rather that we conceive of the saving significance of Jesus' death in multiple ways through implicit comparison with real-world institutions and experiences.

Second, language for the atonement is pastoral. The language by which Paul portrays the effectiveness of Jesus' death depends in part on the needs he hopes to address. If people are lost, they need to be found. If they are oppressed by hostile powers, they need to be delivered. If they exist in a state of enmity, they need to be reconciled. And so on. Indeed, images of atonement are often used in the Pauline writings because of the specific needs of a local congregation. The image of reconciliation, for example, which comes very much to the fore in 2 Cor 5:14–6:13, helps Paul to lay bare the nexus between the Corinthians' relationship toward him and their status before God. In this context, reconciliation with God would work itself out also in reconciliation with Paul. This lies behind Paul's dual request: "Be reconciled to God!" and "Open wide your hearts [to us]!"

Third, we have to account for wider cultural considerations. If the offer of salvation is universal, and if that message is to be grasped in ever-expanding cultural circles, then that message must be articulated in culture-specific ways. Not surprisingly, then, Paul draws atonement images both from Israel's own Scriptures and religious life and the wider public discourse of Roman antiquity.

CONCLUSION

We can talk about the importance of the cross of Christ for Paul in a number of ways. He turns to the cross as a slogan identifying the church, as the means by which Christ identified himself with human shame and suffering, as a marker of genuine discipleship among Christ's followers, and more. Basic to all of these, however, is the way Paul identifies the cross of Christ as the means by which God grants salvation to the world. Even here, though, Paul exercises freedom in how he describes the saving significance of Jesus' death. Drawing on major themes in Israel's Scriptures as well as on public life in the Roman world, he seeks to communicate the significance of Jesus' death within God's overarching, saving purpose. He does not rely on one atonement image alone. Nor does he present one as the key to the rest. Taking seriously both the initiative of God on behalf of the cosmos and the diverse ways the human situation can be experienced and explained, Paul draws on diverse systems of thought grounded in everyday life in the world in order to draw out in diverse ways the meaning of the atonement.

FOR FURTHER READING

Baker, Mark D., and Joel B. Green. *Recovering the Scandal of the Cross: Atonement in New Testament and New Testament Contexts*. 2nd ed. Downers Grove, Ill.: InterVarsity Press, 2011. An examination of the pluriform models of the atonement in the New Testament and subsequent Christian theological tradition.

Brandos, David A. *Paul on the Cross: Reconstructing the Apostle's Story of Redemption*. Minneapolis: Fortress, 2006. A theology of the cross in Paul, arguing that Jesus' death is salvific because God responded to Jesus' faithfulness by raising him from the dead, so that God's promised redemption would be fulfilled through him.

Carroll, John T., and Joel B. Green. *The Death of Jesus in Early Christianity*. Peabody, Mass.: Hendrickson, 1995. Explores the variety of ways in which Jesus' death is portrayed in the New Testament.

Chapman, David W. *Ancient Jewish and Christian Perceptions of Crucifixion*. WUNT 2/244. Tübingen: Mohr Siebeck, 2008. Reexamines the evidence for how crucifixion was practiced and understood in Roman antiquity.

Cousar, Charles B. *A Theology of the Cross: The Death of Jesus in the Pauline Letters*. OBT. Minneapolis: Fortress, 1990. An exegetical and theological study of the cross in Paul, emphasizing God's role as the chief actor in the drama of salvation.

Finlan, Stephen. *The Background and Content of Paul's Cultic Atonement Metaphors*. AcadBib 19. Atlanta: Society of Biblical Literature, 2004. Examines the background and use in Paul of sacrificial images.

Fretheim, Terence E. "Theological Reflections on the Wrath of God in the Old Testament." *HBT* 24 (2002): 1–26. Important study for reflecting on the influence on Paul of OT perspectives on God's wrath.

Hooker, Morna D. *Not Ashamed of the Gospel: New Testament Interpretations of the Death of Christ*. Grand Rapids: Eerdmans, 1994. Explores the variety of ways in which Jesus' death is portrayed in the New Testament.

Janowski, Bernd, and Peter Stuhlmacher, eds. *The Suffering Servant: Isaiah 53 in Jewish and Christian Sources*. Grand Rapids: Eerdmans, 2004. A collection of specialized studies, some of which are focused on the importance of Isaiah's suffering servant for New Testament writers.

Travis, Stephen H. *Christ and the Judgment of God: The Limits of Divine Retribution in New Testament Thought*. 2nd ed. Peabody, Mass.: Hendrickson, 1986. Important study of divine wrath and judgment in the New Testament, arguing that New Testament writers focus less on retributive and more on relational aspects of divine judgment.

THE LAW IN ROMANS

Francis Watson

Paul uses the word *nomos* ("law") on seventy-two occasions in Romans, and in all but a few cases the reference is to the Torah, the law of Moses whose five books are foundational to Jewish Scripture. Thus the law was given through Moses (Rom 5:14), and before his time "there was no law" (5:13). The law was entrusted specifically to the Jewish people (2:17), or "Israel" (9:31), for whom it is a legitimate source of pride (2:24). Gentiles are basically ignorant of the law although they sometimes unknowingly observe it (2:14). The law is associated with wrath (4:13) and with sin or transgression (3:20; 4:15; 5:13; 7:7, 8). It is dissociated from the righteousness of God (3:21), promise (4:13–14), and grace (6:14, 15). Although its commandments are many, they can be summed up in a single negative or positive statement: "You shall not desire" (7:7), or, "You shall love your neighbor as yourself" (13:8–10).

Among the more important compound expressions are the following:

(1) *Works of law* (3:20, 28; abbreviated to "works," 9:32; 11:6). These "works" are simply the individual actions (or abstentions) prescribed by the law. Thus Moses is reminded by his father-in-law that his task is to show the people of Israel "the ways in which they shall walk and the works that they shall do" (Exod 18:20: Greek, *ta erga ha poiēsousin*; Hebrew, *ha-ma'aśeh 'ašer ya'aśûn*). Works of law are those practices that together constitute the distinctive Jewish way of life.[1]

---

1. "Works of law" should neither be understood too broadly, as "good works intended to gain merit with God" (Luther's view, powerfully restated in the twentieth century by Rudolf Bultmann), nor too narrowly, as circumcision and other "identity markers" differentiating Jews from Gentiles (the view of James D. G. Dunn, N. T. Wright, and the so-called "new perspective on Paul"). See Rudolf Bultmann, *Theology of the New Testament* (trans. Kendrick Grobel; 2 vols.; London: SCM, 1952–1955),

(2) *The law and the prophets* (3:21). This is the only Pauline occurrence of this familiar reference to Scripture as a whole (cf. Matt 5:17, 7:12; Luke 16:16; John 1:46; Acts 13:15, 24:14).

(3) *The law of God* (7:22, 25; 8:7). Although Paul elsewhere refers to "the law of Moses" (1 Cor 9:9), the authorship of the law rests ultimately not with Moses but with God. Since God is its author, the law is "holy" (7:12), "spiritual" (7:14), and "good" (7:16). In Romans Paul does not repeat his earlier speculation about angelic involvement in the law's origin (cf. Gal 3:19–20).

(4) The law of God is also *the law of my mind* (Rom 7:23), that is, the law my mind acknowledges. As such, it is opposed by *another law*, that is, *the law of sin which is in my members* (7:23), *the law of sin* (7:25), or *the law of sin and death* (8:2).

(5) *The impossibility of the law*, that is, what was impossible for the law (8:3). Weakened by the flesh, the law can only be put into effect through *the law of the Spirit of life in Christ Jesus* (8:2).

(6) *Righteousness by law* (10:5). This is said to be the sum total of what Moses "writes." Although the law is the law of God, the law's righteousness is emphatically not the righteousness of God.

Three related points stand out from this brief survey. First, Paul speaks of the law in connection both with Jews and with Christians. While there is a historically close relationship between the law and the Jewish people, the law remains a concern for Christians. Second, the law appears to have both a negative and a positive significance for Christians. Third, the sheer frequency of references to the law is remarkable: the seventy-two occurrences of *nomos* contrast strikingly with the eight or nine appearances of *euangelion*, "gospel."[2] Exploring the reasons for this discrepancy will help to clarify the role of the law within the letter as a whole. The best place to begin is where Paul does.

1:263–64; James D. G. Dunn, "The New Perspective on Paul," in *Jesus, Paul, and the Law: Studies in Mark and Galatians* (Louisville: Westminster John Knox, 1990), 183–214, 191–94; and, for the mediating position summarized above, my *Paul, Judaism, and the Gentiles: Beyond the New Perspective* (2nd ed.; Grand Rapids: Eerdmans, 2007), 19–21, 124–30, 229–31.

2. Rom 1:1, 9, 16; 2:16; 10:16; 11:28; 15:16, 19; (16:25?). The cognate verb occurs in 1:15; 10:15; 15:20.

Paul introduces himself to his Roman readers as "a slave of Jesus Christ, called to be an apostle, set apart for the gospel of God" (Rom 1:1).[3] This gospel has a particular individual as its theme, one whose human origin may be traced back to David and whose divine destiny is fulfilled in his powerful resurrection: Jesus Christ, the Son of God (1:3–4). So the gospel is "the gospel of his Son" (1:9), and Paul longs to proclaim it in Rome as he has done elsewhere (1:15). If his intention is to preach the gospel of Jesus Christ when present in person, we would expect this gospel and this theme to be equally central to what he now writes while still absent.

This expectation seems on the point of fulfillment as Paul announces in a programmatic statement that the gospel is "the power of God unto salvation for everyone who has faith," and that in it faith is revealed as the true righteousness, valid before God, in accordance with the prophetic testimony that "the righteous person will live by faith" (1:16–17). As in the opening statements, the gospel is still closely associated with God (cf. 1:1). Yet it is a little surprising that Paul now speaks of the gospel in more abstract terminology (salvation, faith, righteousness), which seems to *replace* the preceding personal references to Jesus as God's Son (cf. 1:3–4, 9). It is still more surprising that Paul makes so little further mention of Jesus until he reaches chapter 5, or of the gospel until he reaches chapter 10. It is of course true that faith is evoked by the gospel and oriented towards Jesus as the figure of whom the gospel speaks. The divine righteousness is said to be "through faith of Jesus Christ" (3:22); God justifies or makes righteous the person who is "of the faith of Jesus" (3:26). Since faith is the human response intended by the gospel, this faith has Jesus as its origin and its object.[4] Yet it is still striking that, after the christologically rich introduction to the letter (1:1–15), Paul makes so few explicit references to Jesus in these opening chapters.[5]

This christological reticence has led many of Paul's later readers to suppose that the theme of his gospel is *not* Jesus per se but "justification by faith," the theme announced in 1:16–17 and resumed in 3:21–4:25.

---

3. Translations here and throughout are my own, though they often echo the RSV.

4. The reference is probably not to Jesus' own faith, popular though that view is in some quarters. For a useful presentation of various positions on this issue (including my own), see Michael Bird and Preston M. Sprinkle, eds., *The Faith of Jesus Christ: Exegetical, Biblical, and Theological Studies* (Peabody, Mass.: Hendrickson, 2010).

5. This point is discussed in detail in my *Paul and the Hermeneutics of Faith* (London: T&T Clark, 2004), 33–76; see also *Paul, Judaism, and the Gentiles*, 192–258.

Jesus would then be the means by which this justification is attained, but the focus would now be on *ourselves*, as the ones who either do or do not receive the gift of righteousness or forgiveness promised to those who believe. This might be described as the *subjective* reading of Romans. It has been much criticized in recent years for its alleged "anthropocentrism," its "anti-Judaism," or its "Lutheran bias"—and not without good reason.[6] Yet it is important to note that this "subjective" reading responds to genuine features of Paul's text, and that its weaknesses cannot be identified until its strengths have been acknowledged.[7] These strengths may be seen in its recognition, first, that in Rom 1–4 Paul does indeed speak of the gospel in terms of righteousness by faith rather than (say) the resurrection of Jesus and, second, that he does so by way of a contrast with "the law" and its "works".

We are (so Paul argues) justified *by faith and not by works of law*. The negation is not simply incidental. Paul does not affirm that we are justified by faith and then add as a mere afterthought that this rules out an alternative possibility, justification by the law. Rather, the affirmation and the negation belong together. That is why Paul sometimes seems more concerned with the role and significance of the law than with the gospel itself. Righteousness is attained through one of two mutually exclusive possi-

6. See Krister Stendahl, *Paul among Jews and Gentiles and Other Essays* (London: SCM, 1977); E. P. Sanders, *Paul and Palestinian Judaism: A Comparison of Patterns of Religion* (London: SCM, 1977); Dunn, "The New Perspective on Paul"; Sidney G. Hall, *Christian Anti-Semitism and Paul's Theology* (Philadelphia: Fortress, 1993); John G. Gager, *Reinventing Paul* (New York: Oxford University Press, 2000); Richard B. Hays, *The Faith of Jesus Christ: The Narrative Substructure of Galatians 3:1–4:11* (2nd ed.; Grand Rapids: Eerdmans, 2002); Douglas Harink, *Paul among the Postliberals: Pauline Theology beyond Christendom and Modernity* (Grand Rapids: Brazos, 2003); Douglas A. Campbell, *The Quest for Paul's Gospel: A Suggested Strategy* (London: T&T Clark, 2005), and *The Deliverance of God: An Apocalyptic Rereading of Justification in Paul* (Grand Rapids: Eerdmans, 2009). One thing these otherwise diverse works have in common is their sharp opposition to what is taken to be the Paul of traditional Protestantism.

7. For important defenses of the "old" readings of Paul, see D. A. Carson, P. T. O'Brien, and M. A. Seifrid, eds., *Justification and Variegated Nomism: A Fresh Appraisal of Paul and Second Temple Judaism* (2 vols.; Tübingen: Mohr Siebeck; Grand Rapids: Baker, 2001–2004); Simon J. Gathercole, *Where Is Boasting? Early Jewish Soteriology and Paul's Response in Romans 1–5* (Grand Rapids: Eerdmans, 2002); Stephen Westerholm, *Perspectives Old and New on Paul: The "Lutheran" Paul and his Critics* (Grand Rapids: Eerdmans, 2004).

bilities, faith or law, and we do not grasp Paul's point if we play down the mutual exclusion.

Law First, Then Gospel?

In Rom 2–3, the twenty-eight occurrences of the term *nomos* ("law") are distributed evenly across three distinct passages (2:12–16, 17–25; 3:19–31). Each passage has its own rationale, and it is in the third that the characteristic Pauline emphases emerge most clearly.

In Rom 2:12–16, Paul is arguing against the claim that being Jewish and defining oneself over against Gentiles bestows a soteriological advantage. Although he refers in passing to his gospel (2:16), the basis of his argument is the general principle that God *cannot* be anything other than impartial (2:11). Accepting for the moment that God's dealings with humanity are indeed regulated by the law, Paul asserts that "those who sinned under the law will be judged by the law" (2:12), for God justifies those who *do* what the law requires (even if they are Gentiles) rather than those who merely *hear* the law as they attend synagogue every Sabbath (2:13–14). Taken out of context, Paul's statement that "the doers of the law will be justified" (2:13) seems a blatant contradiction of his later insistence that "by works of law shall no flesh be justified" (3:20). The earlier statement occurs in a context where Paul is arguing with imagined Jews on their own ground, exploiting the tension he sees between the claim to privileged status and divine impartiality.

The possible existence of law-observant Gentiles is also raised in the second passage, in the context of a vivid characterization of a fictitious figure who is not simply a disobedient hearer of the law but rather a disobedient *teacher* of it (2:17–29). This individual is a highly trained theologian who discourses impressively about how the law represents "the embodiment of knowledge and truth" (2:20), yet manages to overlook simple instructions such as "you shall not commit adultery" in his private life, outside the lecture hall (2:22). Here and throughout Rom 2, Paul himself seems to become once again a teacher of the law, addressing a prophetic critique to his own people.

In Rom 2, disobedience to the law is a contingent reality: it happens, regrettably often and even at the highest levels, but it need not do so. Perhaps obedience to the law also happens, even in places and among people where one least expects it? In Rom 3, however, disobedience to the law has become universal and inescapable. The law says, "You shall not commit adultery," and it is a matter of common knowledge that some people observe this commandment while others flout it. Yet, in the words of its later scriptural interpreters, the law also insists that "there is no one righteous, not even one" (3:10). In Paul's own language, "By works of law shall no flesh be justified before [God], for through law comes knowledge of sin" (3:20). On the face of it, it seems that the law was given to provide guidance for daily living, at least for those who accept its divine authority. Yet more fundamentally the law is not simply guidance but critique, unmasking, and exposure. Addressed initially to the Jewish people, the law is in reality the divine indictment of the entire human race. Thus the help and guidance it can provide are limited. It shows how far humanity has strayed from its calling to the pursuit of the good as the way to eternal life (cf. 2:7). While it does identify a range of acts that must (or must not) be carried out, it also negates its own prescriptions insofar as these were supposed to represent the divinely ordained path to life.

It is at just this point that Paul returns to his earlier claim that righteousness is "by faith" (3:21–22, cf. 1:17). No one is justified by works of law; yet by faith we are indeed justified. While the negation and the affirmation are closely linked, it is not yet clear how we are to understand that connection. Is the law seen here as a necessary preliminary to the announcement of righteousness by faith, in the sense that the law must first convince us of our guilt if the gospel's offer of forgiveness is to be received as a gracious divine gift? In Paul's unfolding argument, the negation (3:19–20) undeniably has priority over the affirmation (3:21–22). How far is this a matter of theological principle for him? Is he always and everywhere obliged to proclaim the negative role of the law as an essential preliminary and foundation for the announcement that righteousness is by faith?

The issue here is neatly summarized in E. P. Sanders's celebrated question: for Paul, does "plight" precede "solution," or does "solution" precede "plight"?[8] Is an awareness of one's own participation in universal human sinfulness a prerequisite for the credibility of the gospel, or is the gospel a prerequisite for awareness of sin? For Sanders, Paul's gospel is self-grounded: it announces a decisive and unprecedented divine action, but it does not preface that announcement by explaining on general grounds why it had to take the form it did take. Paul thinks *a posteriori*, from the

---

8. Sanders, *Paul and Palestinian Judaism*, 442–47.

accomplished divine act, rather than *a priori*, from the independently established conditions that made this act possible and necessary.

It would follow that the direction of the argument in Rom 3 (law first, then faith) does *not* represent the true direction of Paul's thought. Perhaps this argument was occasioned by contingent factors specific to the Roman situation? Along these lines Douglas Campbell has recently presented an elaborate and impressively coherent rereading of Rom 1–4, arguing that as Paul writes to the Romans a very particular problem is uppermost in his mind.[9] Paul has reason to believe that his readers will shortly be exposed to the gospel proclaimed by "the Teacher" (cf. 2:17–24; 16:17–20). This is probably the same figure who, along with others, created such disruption among the churches in Galatia by insisting that Gentile allegiance to Christ necessitated full submission to the law. For Campbell, Rom 1:18–3:20 is intended not as the indictment of sinful humanity but as the statement and refutation of the Teacher's gospel. Since the Roman Christians are as unfamiliar with the Teacher as they are with Paul, the rival gospels must *both* be presented. And so, in Rom 1:18–32, Paul does not speak in his own voice but presents the Teacher's characteristic arguments.[10] The eschatology of Rom 2 may similarly be attributed to the Teacher, a hard-line advocate of retributive justice; but it is Paul who neatly exploits the tension between this commitment and the commitment to the elect status of Israel.[11] In 3:9–20, the Teacher is the main target of the scriptural catena, which he may have constructed himself.[12] Thus Rom 1:18–3:20 as a whole is emphatically *not* a preliminary "vestibule," requiring one to pass through the sphere of the law in order to arrive at the Pauline gospel. According to Campbell, the problems posed by this section of Paul's argument can be resolved by simply attributing it to the Teacher and to Paul's engagement with him.

Campbell's argument is unpersuasive for a number of reasons. There is no indication in the text that the Teacher of 2:17–24 is Christian, or that he is *en route* from Galatia to Rome, or that it is his position rather than Paul's that is spelled out in 1:18–32, or that he is the intended target

---

9. Campbell, *Deliverance of God*, 519–600; note the summary presentation, 590–93. For an overview of this volume, see my review, *EC* 1 (2010): 179–85.

10. Campbell, *Deliverance of God*, 542–47.

11. Ibid., 547–71.

12. Ibid., 579–87.

of the indictment of the whole human race in 3:9–20.[13] More broadly, the attempt to show that Paul argues "from solution to plight" founders on the evidence of what Paul actually says.

For Campbell, Pauline statements in which a reference to the human predicament (sin, law, death) precedes a reference to the divine saving action (Christ, grace, life) are deeply problematic if they are taken to imply that a rationally grounded, non-theological account of the human predicament must frame the understanding of the divine saving act itself.[14] On that view, access to the gospel would be mediated by a "natural theology" in which the Torah itself is assimilated to an ethical and religious knowledge available to the unaided light of reason. Underlying Campbell's identification and rejection of this position is a Barthian concern to assert the absolutely self-grounded nature of the gospel.[15] The coming of Christ, then, represents a new creation transcendent over everything that already exists.

---

13. Romans 1:18–32 is the key to Campbell's hypothesis and perhaps its weakest point. Acknowledging that this section does not explicitly present itself as a false gospel that is to be refuted, Campbell suggests that "the initial auditors of Romans could have detected such a strategy relatively easily through a plethora of nonverbal signals" (*Deliverance of God*, 530). The strategy is thus dependent on Phoebe, who is to deliver and present Paul's letter to the Roman communities (cf. 16:1–2): Paul "presumably would have given Phoebe explicit instructions in how to perform it" (532). But it would be difficult for a single actor, ancient or modern, to perform Rom 1:17, 18 in such a way as to communicate the change of speaker supposed to occur here. Phoebe surely needs a colleague to act out the negative role of the Teacher?

14. Campbell has in view here a popular evangelical understanding of the gospel in which "premises already in place" (concerning the reality of God, sin and guilt, and so on) are allowed to "dictate to a large degree the nature of the solution that is being offered" (*Deliverance of God*, 23; the relevant premises are listed on p. 17). It is wrongly assumed that modern Pauline scholarship remains trapped in that popular evangelical account.

15. See Karl Barth's essay, "Gospel and Law," in *God, Grace and Gospel* (trans. James Strathearn McNab; Edinburgh: Oliver & Boyd, 1959), 1–27. Barth argues that "if the law also is God's Word, and if it is grace that God's Word sounds forth and is audible, and if grace means nothing else than Jesus Christ, then it is perverse to try to derive God's law from some entity or event other than the event in which the will of God becomes visible to us as grace" (8, slightly abbreviated). In consequence, Barth asserts elsewhere that the scriptural citations in Rom 3:11–18 are "spoken by Jesus Christ as the one to whom the OT witnesses and who witnesses to himself in the OT through the voice of the fathers" (*A Shorter Commentary on Romans* [trans. D. H. van Daalen; London: SCM, 1959], 41). Paul's view is that Scripture (including the law)

According to Rom 3:20, however, "knowledge of sin" comes not through Christ's death but "through the law." There is no indication here that Paul is merely refuting an opponent's argument by showing it to be internally incoherent, or that he himself is uncommitted to this claim. Paul as a Christian retains his pre-Christian conviction that "sin" is identified as such through the law, although this conviction is drastically modified when relocated within a new Christian frame of reference. Yet this new perspective does not invariably *replace* former commitments with new ones. Thus in Romans sin and law are still repeatedly correlated:

> All who have sinned under the law will be judged by the law. (2:12)
> Where there is no law there is no transgression. (4:15)
> Sin is not counted where there is no law. (5:13)
> Law came in to increase the trespass. (5:20)
> Sin will have no dominion over you, since you are not under law. (6:14)
> If it had not been for the law, I should not have known sin. (7:7)
> The mind set on the flesh is hostile to God; it does not submit to God's law, indeed it cannot. (8:7)

The correlation between sin and law is asserted both where the law is still assumed to be valid (2:12; 7:7, 8:7) and where its role seems to lie in the past (3:20–22; 4:15; 5:20; 6:14). It is striking that in most of these passages sin and law appear to *precede* grace. Grace does not enter some neutral sphere but a world in which sin, law, and death are already operative:

> Through the law comes knowledge of sin. But now the righteousness of God has been manifested apart from law, although the law and the prophets bear witness to it. (3:20–21)
> For the law brings wrath, but where there is no law there is no transgression. (4:15)
> Law came in to increase the trespass, but where sin increased grace abounded all the more (5:20)
> Sin will have no dominion over you, since you are not under law but under grace. (6:14)

---

bears witness to what has taken place in Jesus, but he does not normally claim that Jesus himself speaks in Scripture (though cf. Rom 15:3).

This twofold sequence (law/sin and grace) can also take a threefold form in which sin and death are associated initially with Adam and subsequently with Moses, before giving way to righteousness and grace with the coming of Christ (5:12–15).[16] It is this Adam/Moses/Christ sequence that reveals the true source of Paul's insistence that sin and law precede grace. He derives this view not from "natural theology" but, simply and straightforwardly, from *Scripture*. Whether or not there is or can be a natural knowledge of God and God's will, knowledge of the significance of Adam and Moses within the divine economy can only be scripturally derived. As a Jew, Paul knows of these figures before he becomes aware of Jesus. As a Christian, his understanding of their significance is transformed as he attempts to correlate them with what has now taken place in Jesus Christ. Yet the Pauline gospel does not unilaterally impose itself on Scripture, but is itself scripturally shaped. In the Adam/Moses/Christ triad, each member is affected by the presence of the other two. If Adam becomes a "type" of Christ (5:14), Christ himself is understood in Adamic categories as one whose single act determines the destiny of the entire human race. Only as Moses makes the reign of death fully explicit does it become clear that in Jesus Christ grace has abounded all the more (5:20).

SCRIPTURE, LAW, AND FAITH

The Pauline gospel, then, is *not* self-grounded in the sense of being essentially independent of the scriptural testimony. If it were so, Scripture would simply be redundant. Yet the very first thing that Paul says about the gospel in this letter is that it "was promised beforehand by [God's] prophets in the holy Scriptures" (1:2). The gospel of which Paul is not ashamed, in which the righteousness of God is revealed as by and for faith, corresponds precisely to the prophetic assertion that "the person who is righteous by faith will live" (1:16–17, citing Hab 2:4). The divine mystery is disclosed not only in "the *kerygma* [preaching or proclamation] of Jesus Christ" but also "through the prophetic writings" (16:26). In Scripture, the gospel announces itself in advance, just as it announces itself in the living proclamation of the apostle. The only gospel that Paul knows is a scripturally mediated one. The prophetic writings precede and prepare for

---

16. The law-gospel sequence of Rom 3:19–21 thus establishes a pattern. If there is no necessary connection here, as Campbell argues (*Deliverance of God*, 520–29), Rom 5:20 is difficult to understand.

the gospel just as the law does; indeed, it could not be otherwise, as the prophetic writings comprise the law itself as well as the prophets (cf. 3:21). Law must precede gospel because Scripture does so, and the law is Scripture. For Paul as for the author to the Hebrews, God speaks in Scripture "in many and various ways" (Heb 1:1), and one way in which God speaks through the law is to declare all people—Jews as well as Gentiles—guilty before his judgment seat. "No one is righteous, not even one" (Rom 3:10): this is indirect testimony to the divine saving action because the concept of a saving action is meaningless if there is no prior predicament to be saved *from*. Yet both the predicament and the saving action are attested in the scriptural testimony, consisting as it does of the "words of God" (3:2). If the arguments of Rom 1–2 are to some degree based on non-scriptural ground, it is for that very reason that their conclusions fall far short of the scriptural testimony.[17]

According to Rom 3:21, the law and the prophets bear witness to the righteousness of God, which is through faith.[18] The law does so indirectly, by showing that the righteousness of which it speaks—in the form of a way of life wholly shaped by its prescriptions and prohibitions—does not actually exist. No one is righteous. Not even one. The prophets bear witness more directly, by speaking of a righteousness that is not the righteousness of the law. The person who is *righteous by faith* will live: the whole prophetic testimony is summed up in this laconic citation from the prophet Habakkuk, just six words in Paul's Greek version and five in the original Hebrew. A simple pattern comes to light: the righteousness that is right relation with God is associated with faith rather than law, for law is to be associated not with righteousness but with its opposite, sin. Paul's aim in Rom 1–3 is to construct a scripturally grounded account of salvation in which the human relation to God is defined by faith rather than the practice of the law. This scriptural focus also accounts for Rom 4, in which the only

---

17. Romans 1:18–3:20 should therefore not be seen as a single argument but as three distinct though related units (1:18–32; 2:1–29; 3:1–20). On this see my *Paul, Judaism, and the Gentiles*, 218–19.

18. See my *Paul, Judaism, and the Gentiles*, 234–38, for critique of Käsemann's influential but untenable view that "righteousness of God" refers to divine saving action rather than to the status divinely bestowed on the one who believes (E. Käsemann, "'The Righteousness of God' in Paul," in *New Testament Questions of Today* [Philadelphia: Fortress, 1969], 168–82). Käsemann implausibly detaches the "righteousness of God" from its context within a scripturally informed discourse on faith, on the grounds that it represents a fixed expression inherited from Judaism.

other scriptural passage to connect righteousness and faith (Gen 15:6) is interpreted at length, in its context within the Genesis narrative.[19] And this focus accounts for the *christological reticence* of Rom 1–4 as a whole. So far as possible, Paul here confines himself to scriptural terrain in order to show that the partial disjunction between law and faith is not his own invention but is based in explicit statements of Scripture. Paul's celebrated doctrine of justification by faith and not works of law is nothing more or less than an extended paraphrase of his two key scriptural texts, Hab 2:4 and Gen 15:6, understood as proposing a radical alternative to the righteousness of the law.[20] In the case of the Genesis text, Paul can exploit the fact that Abraham "believed God, and it was reckoned to him as righteousness" not only before the coming of the law (4:13–15) but also before he himself submitted to the law-like commandment that he be circumcised (4:9–12). Naturally, the two scriptural righteousness-by-faith texts can hardly provide a *full* account of a salvation independent of the law. By choosing to work within their limitations, Paul has unwittingly led many of his readers to suppose that his primary concern is with the subjective appropriation of salvation at the expense of its objective basis in God's act in Christ. Yet this is a false dichotomy that misunderstands the limited and specific purpose of this section, which is to demonstrate that Scripture attests something other than a righteousness based in the observance of the law.

What is often overlooked is that this claim of Paul's is not only controversial but also utterly counterintuitive. For most early readers of Scripture, the Sinai event dominates the Pentateuch and remains foundational for the narrative and prophetic texts that follow. At Sinai, God reveals the commandments which are henceforth to shape the relationship between himself and the elect people, whether they obey them or disobey. That is why, in developing his scriptural account of a salvation based on faith rather than law, Paul must repeatedly oppose and negate a Sinai-centered reading of Scripture:

> By works of law humankind shall *not* be justified before him. (3:20)
> Where then is boasting? *It is excluded.* On what basis? Works? *No,*
> but on the basis of faith. For we hold that a person is justified by
> faith, *without* works of law. (3:27–28)

---

19. See my *Paul and the Hermeneutics of Faith*, 168–219.

20. The fundamental importance of these texts is rightly noted by Albert Schweitzer, *The Mysticism of Paul the Apostle* (London: Black, 1931), 209.

If Abraham was justified by works, he has cause to boast—*but not* before God. (4:2)

Not through the law was the promise to Abraham or his seed, that he should be heir of the world, *but* through the righteousness of faith. (4:13)

In these chapters of Romans, an interpretative argument is enacted in which one reading of Scripture as a whole is pitted against another. At the heart of this argument is the Torah. Given that Scripture is not *only* Torah, is it to be understood as *primarily* Torah, or is the role of Torah subsidiary to something else?

Precisely in that subsidiary role, Torah remains important for Paul. "Do we nullify the law by this faith? Absolutely not! Rather, we uphold the law" (3:31). Thus, later in the letter, Paul can be entirely positive about the law and its place within the Christian life, in contexts where its subsidiary status in relation to the gospel is clear (cf. 8:1–8; 13:8–10). Where he uses more negative language, contrasting life under law with life under grace (6:14–15) and speaking of the need to be liberated from the law (7:1–6), it is the assumed primacy of the law that is in view. If the relationship between humanity and God is definitively encoded in the Torah, what need is there for Christ?[21]

CONCLUSION

Exegetical debates occur within social contexts, and this one is no exception. It is often wrongly assumed that Paul addresses Romans exclusively to Gentiles—on the basis of a misinterpretation of 11:13, where "I am speaking to you Gentiles" refers only to the immediate context and not to the letter as a whole. In the greetings in chapter 16, three individuals are explicitly identified as Jews: Andronicus, Junia, and Herodion (16:7, 11).

---

21. On this reading, Rom 1–4 should not be seen as a model for all communication of the gospel, as Martin Luther assumed. Explaining Paul's strategy in these chapters of the letter, Luther writes, "It is right for a preacher of the gospel in the first place by revelation of the law and of sin to rebuke and to constitute as sin everything that is not the living fruit of the Spirit and of faith in Christ, and to become humble and ask for help. This is therefore what St Paul does" ("Preface to Romans" [1522], in *Word and Sacrament I* [ed. E. Theodore Bachmann; vol. 35 of *Luther's Works*; Philadelphia: Fortress, 1960], 372).

"Those who belong to the family of Aristobulus" (16:10) were presumably Jewish if the reference is to a member of the Herodian royal family. There is evidence elsewhere that Aquila and presumably Prisca were Jewish (16:3; cf. Acts 18:2). In Rom 14:1–15:13, Paul's concern for those who are "weak" in faith seems to relate to Roman Christians who continue to practice a relatively conservative Torah-observance at points that are not mandatory for Pauline Gentile Christians. It is this mixed composition of the Roman Christian community that accounts for Paul's even-handed insistence that the message of salvation is intended "for the Jew first and also for the Greek" (1:16), an emphasis that runs throughout the letter (cf. 2:9–10; 3:9, 29–30; 4:9–12; 9:24–25; 10:11–13; 11:1–24; 15:7–13). Paul writes as he does in order to provide a theological basis for the common life of the diverse Christian groups within the metropolis—which may currently be more or less independent of each other.

If this common life is to become a reality, Gentile Christians must learn to respect and revere the law, acknowledging its roles both in preparing for the gospel and in articulating and reinforcing Christian ethical values, resisting the temptation to distance the God of the gospel from the God of the Jews. Christians of Jewish origin or outlook must learn that the Torah's significance lies in its subsidiary status in relation to a gospel which places them on a level with Gentiles under the judgment and mercy of God. In this letter, Paul engages with the law in the context of a utopian program for the future of the Roman community.

For Further Reading

Campbell, Douglas A. *The Deliverance of God: An Apocalyptic Rereading of Justification in Paul.* Grand Rapids: Eerdmans, 2009. In the course of this monumental fourteen-hundred-page study, Campbell argues that Romans is directed specifically against a teaching that demands Gentile observance of the Torah regulations followed by observant Jews; examples of this teaching are embedded within the text of Romans itself, notably in chapters 1 and 2. Campbell's wider agenda is to promote an "apocalyptic" reading of Paul in which topics such as justification and the law are of only incidental significance.

Dunn, James D. G. "The New Perspective on Paul." Pages 183–214 in *Jesus, Paul, and the Law: Studies in Mark and Galatians.* Louisville: Westminster John Knox, 1990. In this highly influential article, Dunn outlines an account of Paul's view of the law that departs fundamentally from older interpretations inherited from the Reformation period. Dunn sees "works of the law" as "boundary markers" that set Jews apart from Gentiles (specifically, circumcision, the Sabbath, and observance of Jewish dietary regulations).

Käsemann, Ernst. "'The Righteousness of God' in Paul." Pages 168–82 in *New Testament Questions of Today*. Philadelphia: Fortress, 1969. Käsemann contends that "the righteousness of God" refers to the salvation-giving power of God rather than to a status that God confers upon believers. This essay continues to be influential in shaping discussion of this crucial Pauline expression.

Sanders, E. P. *Paul and Palestinian Judaism: A Comparison of Patterns of Religion*. London: SCM, 1977. This celebrated and ground-breaking work argued that first-century Palestinian Judaism in its various forms is best characterized in terms of "covenantal nomism," and that older pejorative language about "works righteousness" is entirely misleading. Paul opposed Judaism not because it promoted works righteousness but because he held that salvation is attained exclusively through Christ.

Watson, Francis. *Paul, Judaism, and the Gentiles: Beyond the New Perspective*. 2nd ed. Grand Rapids: Eerdmans, 2007. In an extensively rewritten version of an earlier work dating back to 1986, I emphasize the social dimension of Paul's antitheses of faith and works, grace and law, often overlooked in more theoretically oriented approaches. I argue that these antitheses have to do with Paul's conviction that the new communities focused on the gospel of Christ are, and should be, quite distinct from synagogue communities focused on the law of Moses.

———. *Paul and the Hermeneutics of Faith*. New York: T&T Clark, 2004. This work considers some of the same Pauline material as the one listed above, from a different yet complementary perspective. Its concern is with Paul as a reader of Scripture—one who reads alongside other contemporary Jews whose works have survived, and who encounters some of the same interpretative challenges as they do. It is argued here that Paul's view of the law should be seen as his reading of a text—that is, the text of the Torah, especially of Exodus through Deuteronomy.

"Promised through His Prophets in the Holy Scriptures": The Role of Scripture in the Letter to the Romans

Rodrigo J. Morales

At the beginning of the letter to the Romans, Paul writes of the gospel he proclaims that "[God] promised [it] beforehand through his prophets in the holy scriptures" (Rom 1:2). True to this opening, the letter brims with quotations of and allusions to the Scriptures of Israel, texts that help to make up what Christians today refer to as the "Old Testament."[1] More than any other of his letters, Romans refers again and again to texts from the Psalms, from the Prophets (especially Isaiah), and from the Torah (the first five books of the Bible). As with so many features of Romans, Paul's use of Scripture has generated much debate. This essay will first discuss a few contemporary approaches to Paul's use of Scripture and then selectively examine citations in Rom 1–4, 9–11, and 15:7–13.

Paul and Scripture: Three Views

Recent years have seen a proliferation of studies on Paul and Scripture. The

---

1. Finding the right term to refer to the biblical texts with which Paul interacts is a difficult one. The term "Old Testament," by which Christians have traditionally referred to these writings, is anachronistic, having developed over a century after Paul's death. "Hebrew Bible," a term preferred by many scholars, is inaccurate since more often than not Paul relies on what scholars commonly refer to as the "Septuagint," the Greek translation of the Old Testament (more on this below). For the sake of simplicity, in this essay I will use the familiar term "Old Testament." Unless otherwise noted, all citations are taken from the NRSV. I should also note that in this essay the term "Scripture" refers to the writings of the Old Testament, rather than the entirety of the Christian Bible.

questions are numerous and complex. To what extent does Paul intend to evoke the broader context of the passages he cites and to which he alludes? Did Paul read Scripture "correctly"? That is, does he use Scripture in accord with the "original" sense of the texts? And how well would his audience have understood his quotations and allusions? Was Paul influenced by other interpretations of Scripture current in his day? Scholars have offered a variety of answers to these questions. In this section we will briefly outline three prominent approaches to the issues.

One of the most influential studies in the field is Richard Hays's *Echoes of Scripture in the Letters of Paul*.[2] Drawing on literary criticism, Hays sets forth an approach that attends to Paul's place in a literary tradition, that of Israel's Scriptures. Like the prophets before him, Paul reappropriates the language of earlier biblical texts to address problems in his own day. For Hays, making sense of Paul's use of Scripture is a twofold task: first, one must identify the citation or allusion; then, one must explain what purpose the biblical reference serves. One key to the second part of this task is a literary device called "metalepsis," which relates to allusions. Allusions work by making reference to a parent text. Often when an author alludes to a text, the unstated elements of the text are as important as the words cited. Thus, in order to understand Paul's use of Scripture, Hays proposes that the interpreter consider the broader context of the passages Paul alludes to, looking for resonances between the two texts beyond the explicit verbal agreements.

Christopher Stanley has criticized Hays for paying insufficient attention to the competence of Paul's readers.[3] According to Stanley, these readers would have lacked the literary skills to follow Paul's arguments, at least as construed by Hays. Paul's audiences would not have known Scripture well enough to catch the broader context of his allusions. Moreover, with limited access to the Scriptures, these readers could not have looked up his references. In light of these factors, Stanley suggests rhetoric as the key to understanding Paul's use of Scripture. Interpreters should consider the way Paul frames his citations of Scripture rather than the broader context of the passages to make sense of what Paul is doing. Stanley also takes into

---

2. Richard B. Hays, *Echoes of Scripture in the Letters of Paul* (New Haven: Yale University Press, 1989).

3. His most recent book-length treatment of the topic is Christopher D. Stanley, *Arguing with Scripture: The Rhetoric of Quotations in the Letters of Paul* (New York: T&T Clark, 2004).

account the different levels of biblical literacy among Paul's audience, suggesting how an "informed audience," a "competent audience," and a "minimal audience" would have understood Paul's biblical quotations.

In *Paul and the Hermeneutics of Faith* Francis Watson argues that Paul understands the Torah as a continuous narrative.[4] Paul does not cite isolated verses as prooftexts but rather tries to make sense of the narrative shape of the Torah. According to Watson, this is not a smooth reading of the text. Paul notices and exploits tensions within the Torah, playing off one text against another to construct a method of interpreting Scripture. Ultimately Paul's method depends upon the gospel: "Scriptural dissonance is both uncovered by the gospel and resolved by it, since its theological function is to testify to the gospel."[5]

None of these three approaches is without its shortcomings. Watson has been criticized for overemphasizing the independent role of Scripture in Paul's theology. There is an unresolved tension in his work between an insistence that Paul respects the integrity of Scripture and an affirmation that he rereads Scripture in light of Christ. Stanley may be correct to suggest that Hays overestimates the reading proficiency of Paul's readers. On the other hand, the fact remains that Paul himself was steeped in Scripture and on many occasions almost certainly intended to evoke the broader context of the passages he cites. As we will see, the cumulative evidence suggests that, whether or not the Romans fully understood Paul's allusions, the apostle gravitated toward certain texts because of wider resonances between those passages and his argument.

SCRIPTURE IN ROMANS

The distribution of scriptural citations in Romans is uneven. Explicit citations are concentrated in the first and third major sections of the letter (Rom 1–4 and 9–11), as well as in a brief recapitulation toward the end of the epistle (Rom 15:7–13). Though he refers to biblical figures such as Adam and Moses and often uses biblical language, Paul quotes Scripture sparingly in Rom 5–8. Similarly, most of Rom 12–15 evinces a biblical minimalism with few scriptural citations.

---

4. Francis Watson, *Paul and the Hermeneutics of Faith* (New York: T&T Clark, 2004).

5. Ibid., 24.

The constraints of this essay preclude a full discussion of the many uses of Scripture in Romans. In the rest of the chapter, we will look at representative samples from three of the major sections of the epistle, focusing for the most part on explicit citations. I will then suggest some conclusions about the role of Scripture in the letter as a whole. The nature of Paul's scriptural citations and their distribution suggest at least a two-fold purpose. First, Paul appeals to Scripture to articulate the relationship between Jews and Gentiles, evidenced both in Rom 1–4 and in Rom 15:7–13. Second, Paul wrestles with Scripture in order to make sense of God's purposes for ethnic Israel.

"To the Jew first, and also to the Greek"

The first scriptural citation in the letter appears at Rom 1:17, a quotation from the book of the prophet Habakkuk. Many modern scholars consider Rom 1:16–17 to serve as a kind of thesis statement for the letter, though some have argued based on ancient letter structure that the thesis is to be found earlier, in Rom 1:1–7.[6] Even if this latter interpretation is correct—and there is much to commend it—most scholars agree that Rom 1:16–17 plays a significant role in laying out some of the central concerns of the letter. Indeed, these verses set the tone for much of what follows: "For I am not ashamed of the gospel; it is the power of God for salvation to everyone who has faith, to the Jew first and also to the Greek. For in it the righteousness of God is revealed through faith for faith; as it is written, "The one who is righteous will live by faith." In the first fifteen verses of the letter the term "gospel," which literally means "good news," appears no less than three times: Paul is a servant "set apart for the gospel of God" (1:1); Paul serves God by "announcing the gospel" (1:9); and Paul desires to "proclaim the gospel to you also who are in Rome" (1:15).[7] Moreover, Paul asserts that the gospel was "promised beforehand through [God's] prophets in the holy scriptures" (1:2). Thus, it should come as no surprise to see Paul open the letter with an appeal to Scripture.

The careful reader will notice that Paul's citation differs from the one found in most translations of the Old Testament. In contrast to Paul's for-

---

6. See J. R. Daniel Kirk, *Unlocking Romans: Resurrection and the Justification of God* (Grand Rapids: Eerdmans, 2008), 33–39.

7. Many translations repeat the term "gospel" in Rom 1:3, but the word does not appear a second time in the Greek text.

mulation, a standard translation of Hab 2:4 reads, "The righteous live by their faith." Discrepancies between Paul's references to Scripture and the source text are common and can be explained in various ways. Often the differences arise from Paul's reliance on the Septuagint. This term, abbreviated by the initials LXX, refers to the translation of the Old Testament from Hebrew to Greek, a project that spanned several centuries beginning around the third century B.C.E. The Greek translations of the Old Testament have different nuances than the Hebrew original, sometimes simply because of differences between the two languages, other times as a result of deliberate modification on the part of the author.

In the case of Hab 2:4, an appeal to the Greek text does not resolve the discrepancy, since Paul's citation also differs from the LXX. There we read "The righteous one will live by *my* faith." In contrast to the Hebrew text on which most translations of the Old Testament are based, the Greek tradition emphasizes God's faith or, more accurately, fidelity.[8] But Paul's citation lacks any possessive pronoun whatsoever. What are we to make of this? Although it is possible that Paul drew on a manuscript no longer available to us, it is more likely that he has deliberately altered the citation to suit his purposes. One plausible explanation is that Paul dropped the possessive pronoun in order to make a double reference to both God's fidelity and the faith of the believer. Both themes play an important role in the letter (God's fidelity: Rom 3:3; 11:1; the faith of the believer: 3:30; 5:1), and the double reference would fit with the phrase "from faith to faith" (a better rendering of the Greek than the NRSV's "through faith for faith") in 1:17. By leaving out the pronoun, Paul suits the quotation to his dual purpose.

The broader context of the Habakkuk citation supports the suggestion that Paul has in mind not only human faith but also God's fidelity. Indeed, the fundamental themes of Habakkuk overlap considerably with those of Romans. Habakkuk begins with a series of complaints about the injustices threatening Israel. In the midst of attacks by Israel's enemies, how can the people trust in God? The answer comes in the verse Paul cites: "The righteous shall live by their faith" (Hab 2:4). Despite appearances to the contrary, God has not abandoned his people. Habakkuk calls on Israel

---

8. Most modern translations of the Old Testament are based on a complete manuscript dating to roughly the ninth century C.E. Because of the relative lateness of this manuscript, it is often difficult to determine whether it represents the text that would have been available to the New Testament writers or to the translators of the LXX.

to be patient and trust that God will fulfill his promises. The parallels with Romans, though not exact, are nevertheless significant. Whereas in Habakkuk's day the issue was Israel's suffering at the hands of a foreign oppressor, in Paul's day the issue is Israel's seeming rejection of the gospel. The basic question, however, remains the same: "Has God rejected his people?" (cf. Rom 11:1). Paul's answer, as Habakkuk's, is a resounding "No!" and a call for patience and trust in God. Despite appearances to the contrary, God remains faithful to his chosen people.

In Rom 3 Paul anticipates potential objections to his argument that hinge on two interrelated questions: (1) is there any benefit to being a Jew? and (2) has God remained faithful to his covenant with Israel? In answer to these questions, Paul appeals to Ps 51:4. The surface meaning of this verse fits Paul's argument: Scripture affirms God's justice in condemning human sin. The words of the citation, however, are just the tip of the iceberg. Psalm 51 is a song of repentance in which the psalmist acknowledges his sin and asks for God's mercy. The testimony of Scripture rings in the background of Paul's affirmation of God's justice, reminding the attentive reader that Scripture testifies also to human sin.

This emphasis on sin continues in Rom 3:10–18, a chain of scriptural citations drawn primarily from the Psalms. At first glance this litany seems like an intemperate, almost misanthropic rant. Paul's basic point is simple and is summarized in his paraphrase of Eccl 7:20: "There is no one who is righteous, not even one" (Rom 3:10). A closer reading, however, reveals the care with which Paul has selected these citations. As with Ps 51, the broader context of most of these citations evokes key themes in Romans.[9] Following the introduction drawn from Ecclesiastes, Paul cites Ps 14:2–3. The majority of the psalm is taken up with castigating the wicked for their evil ways, but it ends with a plea for God to deliver Israel and to "restore the fortunes of his people" (Ps 14:7). Psalm 5 describes the throats of the wicked as an "open grave" and accuses them of using their tongues to practice deceit. Immediately preceding the verse Paul quotes, the psalmist prays, "Lead me, O LORD, in *your righteousness* because of my enemies; make your way straight before me" (Ps 5:8; cf. Rom 1:17). The next two quotations, taken from Pss 140 and 10, include pleas for God to act to bring about his kingdom. An accusation from Isa 59 follows. The broader

---

9. See N. T. Wright, "The Letter to the Romans: Introduction, Commentary, and Reflections," *NIB* 10:393–770, here 457–58.

context of the passage laments the lack of justice in Israel (Isa 59:9: "Therefore justice is far from us, and righteousness does not reach us") and confesses Israel's sins (59:12: "For our transgressions before you are many, and our sins testify against us"). In response to Israel's plight God takes it upon himself to deliver Israel: "[The Lord] saw that there was no one, and was appalled that there was no one to intervene; so his own arm brought him victory, and *his righteousness* upheld him. He put on *righteousness* like a breastplate, and a helmet of *salvation* on his head" (Isa 59:16–17). Once again the theme of God's righteousness subtly echoes in the background. The litany ends with a citation of Ps 36:1. By this point it should come as no surprise to find yet another reference to God's righteousness and fidelity in the broader context of the psalm: "Your steadfast love [LXX 'mercy'], O Lord, extends to the heavens, your *faithfulness* [cf. Rom 3:3] to the clouds. Your *righteousness* is like the mighty mountains, your judgments are like the great deep; you save humans and animals alike, O LORD" (Ps 36:5–6). Were these connections to be found in only one or two of Paul's citations, we might dismiss them as coincidence. That each of the texts in the chain resonates with broader themes in the letter suggests that Paul cites these in particular to emphasize not only human sin, but also, more subtly, God's righteousness and fidelity.

At the end of this litany Paul explains its purpose: "Now we know that whatever the law says, it speaks to those who are under the law, so that every mouth may be silenced, and the whole world may be held accountable to God" (Rom 3:19). The Jews, as stewards of the "oracles of God" (cf. Rom 3:2), are just as guilty of wickedness as the Gentiles. Paul ends this part of the discussion with a paraphrase of Ps 143:2: "For 'no human being will be justified in his sight' by deeds prescribed by the law, for through the law comes the knowledge of sin" (Rom 3:20). Once again, we will miss Paul's deeper point if we focus only on the surface meaning of the citation. The psalm continues the primary theme of the chapter: all human beings, Jew and Gentile alike, are sinful. Beneath the surface, however, we see once again the counterpoint to this theme. In Ps 143, the psalmist acknowledges human sinfulness as part of a plea to God to act based on his own righteousness: "Hear my prayer, O LORD; give ear to my supplications in *your faithfulness*; answer me in *your righteousness*" (Ps 143:1). The psalm ends with a similar appeal, again based on God's righteousness: "For your name's sake, O LORD, preserve my life. In *your righteousness* bring me out of trouble. In your steadfast love cut off my enemies, and destroy all my adversaries" (Ps 143:11–12). Over and over again Paul's indictment of humanity is tempered, not because humanity is righteous, but because of God's own righteousness. Despite the ubiquity of sin, Paul holds out hope that God in his faithfulness and righteousness will ultimately deliver his people.

In Rom 4 Paul offers a more extended explication of Scripture focused on the figure of Abraham. Most translations of Rom 4:1 obscure the central thrust of the chapter. The NRSV, for example, renders the verse, "What then are we to say was gained by Abraham, our ancestor according to the flesh?" Though such a rendering of the text is possible, Hays argues for the following translation based on a different punctuation of the Greek (the earliest manuscripts of the New Testament had no punctuation): "What then shall we say? Have we found Abraham to be our forefather according to the flesh?"[10] The rest of the discussion makes it clear that Paul's answer is a resounding "No!" The chapter thus has less to do with the question of "works" than with how one becomes a descendant of Abraham. Such a reading continues the line of thought begun toward the end of Rom 3, where Paul asks whether God is God of the Jews only, or also of Gentiles (Rom 3:29–30). Similarly, when Paul goes on to ask whether Abraham was "justified by works" (Rom 4:2), he has in mind not good works in general, but rather the works of the Jewish law (cf. Rom 3:28–30). Just as Rom 1–3 focused on the equal culpability of Jew and Gentile, Rom 4 explicates the equal status of Jew and Gentile in Christ as descendants of Abraham.

If Paul and his readers have not found Abraham to be their father according to the flesh, then in what sense is Abraham their father? Paul answers by appealing to the story of Abraham in Gen 15. The discussion revolves around Gen 15:6, portions of which recur throughout the chapter (Rom 4:3, 5, 9, 22). Paul's basic point is clear: it is by sharing in Abraham's faith that anyone, Jew or Gentile, is "reckoned righteous," that is, becomes a part of Abraham's family (4:11–12, 14, 16–17) and has one's sins forgiven (4:7–8). Paul combines the Genesis citation with Ps 32:1–2 using a common Jewish interpretive principle called *gezera shawah*. According to this principle biblical texts are joined by means of a catchword, in this case the word "reckon" ("it was *reckoned* to him as righteousness," "blessed is the one against whom the Lord will not *reckon* sin"). Paul thus enlists David to fill out his understanding of "righteousness."

---

10. See Richard B. Hays, "Abraham as Father of Jews and Gentiles," in *The Conversion of the Imagination: Paul as Interpreter of Israel's Scriptures* (Grand Rapids: Eerdmans, 2005), 61–84, esp. 63–69.

As Paul continues to expound the Abraham story, he seems less interested in the manner in which Abraham was reckoned righteous than in the timing. In the broader context of the Genesis narrative, the passage Paul quotes appears well before Abraham received the commandment of circumcision (Rom 4:9–12). This narrative detail is no coincidence for Paul. From it he draws the conclusion that Abraham was to serve both as a model for and as the father of all who believe, Jew and Gentile alike.

Genesis 15:6 is not the only part of the Abraham narrative to which Paul appeals. In the latter half of Rom 4, he continues to develop the idea that those who share Abraham's faith are to be counted as his heirs. In addition to the example of Abraham's faith, Paul also points to one of the promises God made to Abraham: "for he is the father of all of us, as it is written, 'I have made you the father of *many nations*'" (Rom 4:16–17; cf. Gen 17:5). Just as Scripture testifies that all have sinned (Rom 3:19–20, 23), so also it promises Abraham a family of many nations, including both Jews and Gentiles.

One more feature of Paul's retelling of the Abraham story bears comment. Paul describes Abraham's faith in terms decidedly shaped by the death and resurrection of Christ: "the God in whom [Abraham] believed, who gives life to the dead and calls into existence the things that do not exist" (Rom 4:17). Indeed, Paul recasts the entire Abraham story in light of the resurrection.[11] Abraham perseveres in his faith despite the fact that his body was "already dead" (Rom 4:19; most translations render the phrase "as good as dead," but the Greek literally reads "dead"). Moreover, he is not swayed by the "barrenness [literally 'deadness'] of Sarah's womb" (Rom 4:19). By repeatedly using categories of death and resurrection in his references to the Abraham story, Paul emphasizes that the God in whom Abraham believed is the one who raises the dead. It is for this reason that Abraham is the father and serves as the example of those who share his faith: "Now the words, 'it was reckoned to him,' were written not for his sake alone, but for ours also. It will be reckoned to us who believe in him who raised Jesus our Lord from the dead, who was handed over to death for our trespasses and raised for our justification" (Rom 4:23–25; cf. 4:16). Paul thus forges a bond between Abraham and Christians based on their resurrection faith.

---

11. See Kirk, *Unlocking Romans*, 56–83.

"Has God abandoned his people?"

Due to space limits, we must skip ahead to Rom 9–11. This section of Romans is one of the densest in Paul's writings and contains roughly one quarter of the Scripture citations in his letters. The reason for this concentration of texts is fairly obvious, even if the argument is not. Paul here wrestles with the question of why many of his fellow Jews have rejected the gospel. He draws on Scripture both to explain the problem and to make sense of God's promises to Israel. Following an introduction in which Paul expresses his anguish over Israel's unbelief (Rom 9:1–5), Rom 9–11 may be divided into three broad subsections: (1) 9:6–29: God's Election; (2) 9:30–10:21: Israel's Unbelief; (3) 11:1–36: Israel's Ultimate Fate.

Paul lays out the thesis of the first subsection in Rom 9:6–7: "It is not as though the word of God had failed. For not all Israelites truly belong to Israel, and not all of Abraham's children are his true descendants; but 'It is through Isaac that descendants shall be named for you.'" Citing Gen 21:12, part of the story of Abraham's dismissal of Hagar and Ishmael, Paul makes a simple point. Physical descent from Abraham does not guarantee inclusion in God's covenant; rather, membership is based on God's promise. Even though Ishmael was a natural descendant of Abraham, he was not counted among the chosen people. By contrast, Isaac was born as a result of God's promise, as Genesis testifies (Gen 18:10, 14 in Rom 9:9). Paul shows a similar logic at work in Isaac's two children, Jacob and Esau. Just as God freely chose Isaac over his (half) brother Ishmael, so he chose Jacob over Esau "before they had been born or had done anything good or bad" (Rom 9:11). What makes Paul's argument shocking is that he categorizes unbelieving Jews, the bearers of the promise, with the physical descendants of Abraham whom God rejected in the Old Testament.

This emphasis on God's election raises the objection that God acts capriciously (Rom 9:14). Paul addresses this charge by citing a text from Exod 33 in which God reveals his name to Moses. On the surface, this citation seems to confirm rather than to refute the charge of caprice: "I will have mercy on whom I have mercy, and I will have compassion on whom I have compassion" (Exod 33:19 in Rom 9:15). The broader context of the citation, however, tells a different story. God's self-description appears shortly after Moses's intercession on behalf of Israel following the people's act of idolatry. God responds to Moses's intercession by showing mercy to Israel. The statement is not a simple descriptor of what God is like, but rather is a part of a story of God's fidelity to Israel.

Continuing this line of thought, Paul draws on an image common in the prophetic literature, that of the potter and the clay (Rom 9:19–21). A surface reading of the imagery again might elicit the charge of caprice: because God is the potter, he can do whatever he wants. A closer look at how the prophets use the imagery, though, reveals a different picture. One of the most well-known uses of this image occurs in Jer 18:1–11. In that story God leads the prophet to a potter's house and shows him how the potter reworks a spoiled vessel into something better. The punch line follows: "Can I not do with you, O house of Israel, just as this potter has done? says the LORD. Just like the clay in the potter's hand, so are you in my hand, O house of Israel" (Jer 18:6). The end of the passage makes it clear that the imagery holds out the prospects of both judgment and mercy: "Now, therefore, say to the people of Judah and the inhabitants of Jerusalem: Thus says the LORD: Look, I am a potter shaping evil against you and devising a plan against you. Turn now, all of you from your evil way, and amend your ways and your doings" (Jer 18:11). By using this image Paul does not simply condemn Israel to destruction; rather, he holds out hope for repentance.

Toward the end of the first subsection Paul cites three prophetic texts to interpret the phenomenon of believing Gentiles and unbelieving Jews. The first text is actually a combination of two different verses from Hosea, 1:10 and 2:23. In their original context these verses refer to the restoration of Israel after her punishment by God, but Paul applies them to the Gentiles based on the key phrase "not my people." The Gentiles, as outsiders to God's covenant with Israel, were not God's people, but now, Paul argues, they have been incorporated into God's people. Paul then introduces the theme of a remnant within Israel with two citations from Isaiah (Isa 10:22–23; 1:9), a theme to which he returns in Rom 11.

In Rom 9:30–10:21 Paul continues to wrestle with the problem of Israel's unbelief. Early in this section he lays out his interpretive principle: "For Christ is the end of the law" (Rom 10:4). Like the English word "end," the Greek word *telos* can have two connotations, "termination" and "goal." Based on the broader argument of the passage, the primary connotation here is the latter. For Paul, Israel's Scriptures point to Christ. This principle leads Paul to offer a provocative reinterpretation of Deut 30:12–14 in Rom 10:6–8. The text originally referred to the commandment God gave Israel before entering the promised land, but Paul systematically reinterprets the passage to refer to Christ's incarnation, his resurrection, and Paul's proclamation of the gospel. Taking up the language of Deut 30:14, Paul formulates the conditions for salvation: "If you confess with your lips that Jesus is Lord and believe in your heart that God raised him from the dead, you will be saved" (Rom 10:9).

Paul further explicates these twin acts of confessing and believing by citing two more prophetic texts.[12] He first cites Isa 28:16 for a second time (cf. Rom 9:33), but with a slight modification not noticeable in most English translations. Paul adds the Greek word *pas* ("all"/"every") to suggest that everyone who believes in Christ "will not be put to shame," a point he makes explicit in his explanatory comment: "For there is no distinction between Jew and Greek; the same Lord is Lord of *all* and is generous to *all* who call on him" (Rom 10:12). The imagery of calling on the Lord leads Paul to the prophet Joel to underscore the point once more: "For, '*Everyone* who calls on the name of the Lord shall be saved'" (Rom 10:13, citing Joel 2:32). All of this flows from Paul's interpretive principle, "Christ is the goal [*telos*] of the law" (Rom 10:4).

In Rom 10:14–21 Paul draws once more on the prophet Isaiah to explain his ministry. It is a short step from arguing that Scripture foretells the events of Christ's death and resurrection to seeing the activity of Christian missionaries as part of that prophecy. Paul applies Isa 52:7 to his mission to proclaim the gospel, while appealing to Isa 53:1 to help explain Israel's unbelief. The end of this section (Rom 10:18–21) might lead one to think that the apostle has abandoned all hope for his people. Quoting texts from the Psalms, Deuteronomy, and Isaiah, he seems to indict Israel by contrasting their lack of faith with the Gentiles' reception of the gospel. But Paul's argument does not end at Rom 10:21.

At the beginning of Rom 11 Paul returns to the remnant theme. In response to the possible objection that God has abandoned his people, Paul appeals to the story of Elijah as an analogy to the apostle's own day. Just as in Elijah's day God preserved a remnant within Israel of those who had not become idolaters, so in Paul's day he and some of his fellow Jews, the faithful remnant, have come to faith in Christ.

Paul appeals to other biblical texts to explain the hardening that has come upon "the rest" of Israel (Rom 11:7). The first citation loosely combines Isa 29:10 and Deut 29:4, two texts that speak of Israel's stubbornness. Paul also cites Ps 69. Most likely he gravitates toward this psalm because

---

12. See J. Ross Wagner, *Heralds of the Good News: Isaiah and Paul in Concert in the Letter to the Romans* (NovTSup 101; Leiden: Brill, 2002), 168–70.

of the language it shares with the previous mixed citation, but it is possible that the common association of this psalm with Jesus' crucifixion among early Christians (e.g., Matt 27:48) also influenced the selection.

In Rom 11:25–32 Paul once again draws on Isaiah to explain Israel's mysterious hardness of heart. This section has been the subject of much debate, and no single interpretation has been found that can account for all the data. Several features of the text indicate that Paul is still wrestling with the question of unbelieving Israel. He begins with a reference to the partial "hardening" of Israel (11:25), he refers to them as "beloved for the sake of their ancestors" (11:28), he affirms that "the gifts and the calling of God are irrevocable" (11:29), and he holds out hope for mercy on them: "so they have now been disobedient in order that, by the mercy shown to you, they too may now receive mercy" (11:31). It is in this broader context that we must interpret Paul's mixed citation of Isa 59:20–21 and Isa 27:9 (Rom 11:26–27).

Taking Isa 59:20–21 first, we should recall that Paul cites another verse from this chapter earlier in Romans (Isa 59:7 in Rom 3:15–17). Much of Isa 59 recounts Israel's sins, twice noting the lack of justice and righteousness among the people (Isa 59:9, 14). Between these two verses the people confess their many sins and the distress these sins have caused Israel. Then, the prophet announces that God will act on his own to rescue Israel because of his own righteousness (Isa 59:16). At the end of the oracle appear the words Paul quotes: "And he will come to Zion as Redeemer, to those in Jacob who turn from transgression, says the LORD. And as for me, this is my covenant with them" (Isa 59:20–21a). Puzzlingly, at this point Paul cuts off the quotation and inserts a verse from Isa 27. It is impossible to explain with any certainty why Paul leaves off the end of Isa 59:21, but the verse he uses to modify the quotation makes perfect sense given that it shares many themes with Rom 11.

The common theme of the removal of Israel's sins explains why Paul gravitates toward Isa 27 (Isa 59:20: "to those in Jacob who turn from transgression"; Isa 27:9: "Therefore by this the guilt of Jacob will be expiated"). The broader context of Isa 27 also shares with Rom 11 the imagery of Israel as a vine. The chapter begins with a reference to Israel as a vineyard, echoing an earlier use of the image in Isa 5. God then holds out two alternatives to Israel: "If it gives me thorns and briers, I will march to battle against it. I will burn it up. Or else let it cling to me for protection, let it make peace with me, let it make peace with me" (Isa 27:4–5). Later the prophet asks whether God's punishment of Israel is temporary or permanent: "Has he struck them down as he struck down those who struck them? Or have they been killed as their killers were killed?" (Isa 27:7; cf. Rom 11:1). In answer the prophet holds out hope for Israel: "By expulsion, by exile you struggled against them; with his fierce blast he removed them in the day of the east wind. Therefore by this the guilt of Jacob will be expiated." (Isa 27:8–9a). The parallels with Paul's argument are clear: though Israel has stumbled and justly received punishment, God will ultimately cleanse Israel of her sins and redeem her. Paul thus grounds his hope for his fellow Jews in Israel's Scriptures.

"Let all the peoples praise him"

Paul closes the body of the letter with one final chain of scriptural texts (Rom 15:7–13), introducing them by recapitulating one of his main purposes in writing, namely the reconciliation of Jews and Gentiles in Christ: "Welcome one another, therefore, just as Christ has welcomed you, for the glory of God" (Rom 15:7). Following the pattern established at the beginning of the letter ("to the Jew first and also to the Greek"), Paul summarizes Jesus' ministry to both Jew and Gentile: "For I tell you that Christ has become a servant of the circumcised [i.e., Jews] on behalf of the truth of God in order that he might confirm the promises to the patriarchs, and in order that the Gentiles might glorify God for his mercy" (Rom 15:8–9a). There follows a string of scriptural citations linked by the catchword "Gentiles." Each of these citations envisions the Gentiles joining Israel, and the texts represent each of the three major divisions of the Old Testament in Paul's day: the Law (Deut 32:43 [Lxx]), the Prophets (Isa 11:10), and the Writings (Ps 18:49; 117:1).

As with the chain of quotations in Rom 3:10–18, the broader context of several of Paul's citations here influenced his selection of texts. Both of the psalms (Ps 18:49; 116:1) resonate with broader themes in the immediate context of the letter. Psalm 17:50 (Lxx) notes that God "deals *mercifully* with David his anointed, and his seed, forever." Psalm 116:2 bases the call to worship on God's "mercy" and "truth." While it is possible that these resonances are coincidental, it is more likely that Paul deliberately chose these verses because they support his affirmation of God's "truth" and "mercy" in Rom 15:8–9.

It is fitting that Paul ends the chain with a passage from Isaiah, given the prominent role Isaiah plays throughout the letter. Once again, this selection subtly recapitulates some of Paul's main themes. The broader context of the passage promises redemption for Israel, drawing on the remnant theme: "On that day the Lord will extend his hand yet a second time to recover the *remnant* that is left of his people.... He will raise a signal for the nations, and will assemble the outcasts of Israel, and gather the dispersed of Judah from the four corners of the earth" (Isa 11:11–12). Paul thus ends the body of the text with one more intimation of hope for Israel.

Conclusion

With its reference to the "root of Jesse" (i.e., David), Paul's citation in Rom 15:12 forms a second bookend around the body of the letter, recalling the opening of the letter. There he affirms that the gospel was "promised beforehand by the prophets" and that Jesus is descended from David. Between these two bookends Paul leads the reader through a complex and multifaceted argument about the relationship between Jews and Gentiles in Christ and God's faithfulness to his people Israel. Though not the only issues Paul addresses, these are significant issues, and Paul frequently uses Scripture to make sense of them. Thus, in gaining a better understanding of Paul's use of Scripture, one will go a long way toward making sense of Romans as a whole.

For Further Reading

Hays, Richard B. *The Conversion of the Imagination: Paul as Interpreter of Israel's Scripture*. Grand Rapids: Eerdmans, 2005. A collection of scholarly essays including several offering more detail on specific issues in Romans.

———. *Echoes of Scripture in the Letters of Paul*. New Haven: Yale University Press, 1989. This book has had an enormous influence on the discussion of Paul's use of Scripture. The first chapter outlines the basic approach and criteria for determining an allusion to Scripture; the second offers an insightful reading of the function of biblical references in Romans.

Keesmaat, Sylvia C. *Paul and His Story: (Re)Interpreting the Exodus Tradition*. JSNTSup 181. Sheffield: Sheffield Academic Press, 1999. This study of the exodus tradition in Romans and Galatians builds on the methodological approaches of Hays and Wright. Keesmaat offers an intriguing reading of Rom 8, suggesting that Paul reappropriates the exodus tradition to make sense of the Romans' own situation. Particularly helpful for seeing how Scripture can function in Paul's argument without explicit citation.

Kirk, J. R. Daniel. *Unlocking Romans: Resurrection and the Justification of God*. Grand Rapids: Eerdmans, 2008. A recent study arguing that resurrection is the key to understanding Romans. Among other things, Kirk emphasizes the implications of Jesus' resurrection for Paul's reading and use of Scripture.

Moyise, Steve. *Paul and Scripture: Studying the New Testament Use of the Old Testament*. Grand Rapids: Baker, 2010. This useful and accessible primer includes chapters on Paul and various biblical figures and corpora. Also surveys several recent approaches to the topic.

Porter, Stanley E. and Christopher D. Stanley, eds. *As It Is Written: Studying Paul's Use of Scripture*. SBLSymS 50. Atlanta: Society of Biblical Literature, 2008. Provides a helpful snapshot of the current state of English-speaking scholarship on the topic, with several essays directly related to Romans.

Stanley, Christopher D. *Arguing with Scripture: The Rhetoric of Quotations in the Letters of Paul*. New York: T&T Clark, 2004. Stanley offers the most trenchant critique of Hays's approach to Paul and Scripture. Includes chapters on rhetoric, literary criticism, Paul's audiences, and Paul's quotations, as well as case studies on 1 and 2 Corinthians, Galatians, and Romans.

Wagner, J. Ross. *Heralds of the Good News: Isaiah and Paul in Concert in the Letter to the Romans*. NovTSup 101. Leiden: Brill, 2002. A detailed technical study of Paul's use of Isaiah in Romans, with a special emphasis on Rom 9–11. Insightful and illuminating, but not for the faint of heart.

Watson, Francis. *Paul and the Hermeneutics of Faith*. New York: T&T Clark, 2004. Puts Paul in conversation with other Second Temple Jewish interpreters of the Torah and argues that Paul read the Torah as a narrative whole.

Wright, N. T. "The Letter to the Romans: Introduction, Commentary, and Reflections." *NIB* 10:393-770. A pastoral commentary on Romans that pays careful attention to Paul's use of Scripture, especially the context of Paul's citations and allusions and the narrative shape of the Old Testament story.

Adam and Christ

James D. G. Dunn

At first glance an essay on "Adam and Christ" in Paul's letter to the Romans does not seem to allow much scope for discussion. Adam, after all, is mentioned in only one verse (Rom 5:14). That verse, of course, deserves close attention, especially its somewhat enigmatic reference to Adam as "a/the type of the one to come." And, as we shall see, the context and following *contrast* that the chapter makes between Adam and Christ, and between the effects of what they did (5:15–21), certainly call for a careful discussion of "Adam and Christ." But to confine discussion to Romans misses the more explicit and intriguing contrast between Adam and Christ in 1 Cor 15:22, 45, not to mention the controversial point made in 1 Tim 2:13–14.[1] So an essay on "Adam and Christ" in Romans will hardly allow consideration of the larger issue of Paul's "Adam Christology."

Nevertheless, Romans does give a good deal more scope for a larger discussion of Paul's understanding of the role and significance of Adam than the single passage—Rom 5:12–21. For it is possible that Paul had Adam, or the Adam story of Gen 2–3, in mind when he dictated other passages in Romans—particularly 1:18–32, 3:23, 7:7–13, and 8:19–22.[2] If

---

1. There is also the very controversial issue of whether Phil 2:6–11 is in any degree shaped by an allusion to the Adam story of Gen 3.

2. I have set out the case for seeing allusions to Adam in these passages in my *Romans 1–8* (WBC 38A; Dallas: Word, 1988); also *Christology in the Making* (2nd ed.; London: SCM, 1989; Grand Rapids: Eerdmans, 1996), 101–5; also *The Theology of Paul the Apostle* (Grand Rapids: Eerdmans, 1998), 90–101—all with supportive bibliography, including particularly A. J. M. Wedderburn, "Adam in Paul's Letter to the Romans," in *Studia Biblica 1978, III: Papers on Paul and Other New Testament Authors* (ed. E. A. Livingstone; Sheffield: JSOT Press, 1980), 413–30. Here I focus more on the christological significance of these references.

these passages do express an Adam theology and/or Adam Christology,[3] then Romans in fact provides the major source for Paul's view of "Adam and Christ," and a comprehensive discussion of these passages will perhaps provide the heart of Paul's views on the subject, if not a complete picture.

One issue should perhaps be clarified at the beginning: did Paul regard Adam as a historical figure? The most obvious answer, as most agree, is that Paul did of course regard Adam as a historical figure, did regard the narrative of Gen 2–3 as a historical account. For Paul, Adam was a historical figure, in the same sense that Jesus was a historical figure. This certainly seems to be the implication of Rom 5:12–14, where the entries of sin and death into the world are spoken of as events that could be recorded in history, and are regarded as events like the giving of the law at Sinai. Adam to Moses was a period of history. Typology need not imply that the "type" is a historical figure; Jonah in the belly of the sea-monster could be a type of Christ (Matt 12:38–42/Luke 11:29–32) without it following that Jonah was a historical character. But to speak of Adam as a "type" of Christ in the context of Rom 5:12–14 is presumably an example of historical characters and events prefiguring a character of equivalent (eschatological) significance.[4]

At the same time, however, Paul was clearly aware that "Adam" was a proper name derived from the Hebrew meaning "*man*" (*adam*). This is implied in the contrast between the "one man/human being" Adam and the "one man/human being" Christ in 5:12, 15, 19. Paul was no doubt aware of the transition in the Genesis narrative from "the man" (*ha-adam*) (Gen 2:7–4:1) to the proper name "Adam" in Gen 4:25.[5] Whether that transition denoted some awareness of a transition from a beginnings myth to real history is unimportant. What matters more is the awareness thus attested, and probably by Paul's use of the Genesis story, that what was in view was not so much a human individual as such, but man, that is, humankind.

---

3. The case for seeing allusions to Adam in all these passages is much contested and probably a minority view in New Testament scholarship; see, e.g., the hesitation of Gordon D. Fee, *Pauline Christology: An Exegetical-Theological Study* (Peabody, Mass.: Hendrickson, 2007), 272, 513–14, 517, 523.

4. The classic treatment is Leonhard Goppelt, *Typos: The Typological Interpretation of the Old Testament in the New* (trans. Donald H. Madvig; Grand Rapids: Eerdmans, 1982).

5. Joseph A. Fitzmyer maintains that "Paul has historicized the symbolic Adam of Genesis" (*Romans* [AB 33; New York: Doubleday, 1993], 407–8).

"Adam" stood for humankind as a whole. Adam was significant as the representative "man." That is presumably why Paul drew upon the Adam stories, because by speaking of "Adam" Paul could speak of the plight of humankind as a whole. Adam was a type of Christ in that Christ could also be characterized as a representative "man," representing a different kind of humanity from Adam, his action as epochal in its consequences for humankind as Adam's. We will return to the full significance of Rom 5 below, but the lesson which we have already learned may be significant in discussing the other Romans passages. For if Paul's Adam-theology was a way of speaking of the plight of *humankind* generally, then it may well be the case that other passages that speak of the human plight may be more influenced by Paul's use of the Genesis Adam narratives than appears on the surface.

ROMANS 1:18–32

The argument that Rom 1:18–32 draws on the Adam narratives of Genesis is largely based on the observation just made. For Adam is not mentioned in the passage, and there is little or no allusion to the Gen 2–3 stories. And this is quite sufficient for many commentators to deny that Rom 1:18–32 should be counted as expressive of Paul's Adam theology.[6] However, there are several factors that suggest that Paul had in mind the same context as the Genesis Adam narratives and was alluding to features of these narratives in what was his initial analysis of the human plight.

The first is the creation context: Paul refers to the knowledge of God given to human beings through what God had created (Rom 1:19–21). The evocation of the Genesis narrative, of the man given stewardship over what had been created (Gen 2:15) and dependent on God so far as knowing what to do was concerned (2:16–17), lies close to hand. That Paul speaks not of Adam but of human beings in general (Rom 1:18) is less important, since, as just noted, Adam can stand for humankind (*ha-adam*).

The second is the analysis of human failure: human beings failed to give God the glory and thanks due to him (1:21). Given that Adam =

---

6. Fitzmyer, *Romans*, 274, 283. But Robert Jewett (*Romans* [Herm; Minneapolis: Fortress, 2007]) is sympathetic to the case made by Morna D. Hooker, "Adam in Romans 1," *NTS* 6 (1959–1960): 297–306: "The persistence of the plural verbal forms and the aorist tense in this verse [1:28] indicate that the story of Adam's fall remains in the background" (Jewett, *Romans*, 182, 184, 186).

humankind, it would be surprising if such a statement did not have in mind the failure of Adam and Eve to obey the explicit command of God not to eat of the fruit of the tree of the knowledge of good and evil (Gen 2:17; 3:3). Adam and Eve failed to give God his due glory and their gratitude by failing to acknowledge their dependency on God, their inability to stand completely on their own feet.

The third is the consequence of that failure: far from being like God/gods, knowing good and evil for themselves, without needing God, they became subject to the divinely decreed punishment of death (Gen 2:17); that is, in terms of the Genesis narrative, they were expelled from the garden and prevented from eating from the other named tree, the tree of life (2:9, 16; 3:22–24). This was what Paul presumably had in mind when in his analysis of the human plight he characterized human failure as, "claiming to be wise, they became fools"; "their foolish minds were darkened" (Rom 1:21–22). This was an apt paraphrase of Gen 3: humankind thought to become as God/gods (Gen 3:5) but simply confirmed the mortality of their all too human existence, a mortality now in consequence allowed to play out in death (1:32).[7] They had exchanged the truth of God for the lie told them by the serpent (1:25). In so drawing on Gen 3, Paul would have been echoing Jewish theology's regular use of the Genesis account to explain the human condition and corruptibility.[8]

It is quite true that Paul's analysis of the human condition goes on to expound human folly in terms of idolatry: "they changed the glory of the incorruptible God for the likeness of the image of corruptible man, and of birds, and of beasts and of reptiles" (Rom 1:23). The echo here is more of Ps 106:20's reference to *Israel's* own failure in committing the idolatry of the golden calf. But probably Paul was simply following the regular path of Jewish polemic against Gentile idolatry, seen as the most typical and self-delusory example of the (other) nations' failure to know God, that is, the God of Israel.[9] And it should not be forgotten that the golden calf episode, following so closely upon the exodus and the giving of the covenant at

---

7. Cf. Jewett, *Romans*, 190–91.

8. Wis 2:23–24; Jub. 3:28–32; L.A.E.; 2 Bar. 54:17–19.

9. Notably Isa 44:9–20; Wis 11:15; 12:24; 13:10, 13–14; 14:8; 15:18–19 (see further my *Romans 1–8*, 161). That Rom 1:18–2:4 evidences influence of and a number of allusions to the Wisdom of Solomon is generally recognized. See already William Sanday and Arthur C. Headlam, *A Critical and Exegetical Commentary on the Epistle to the Romans* (5th ed.; ICC; Edinburgh: T&T Clark, 1902), 51–52.

Sinai, could be regarded within the Judaism of the day as Israel's own first sin, equivalent to that of Adam.[10]

It should be stressed that the interpretation of Rom 1:18–32 does not depend on allusion to the Genesis Adam narratives. It is simply that recognition of such allusion sets Paul's analysis of the human plight more fully into the tradition of Jewish thought on the same theme and, probably more to the point, helps fill out what Paul had in mind in his talk of human folly. The crippling lust of humankind is to be done with a God whom they cannot control (like an idol), the God on whom they have to depend for the knowledge that they need to direct their lives and communities. But the consequence is not ability to stand on their own feet, independent of God, but dependence on different non-gods—not greater wisdom, but darkened counsel and an attitude that puts self-concern at its center and that corrupts community.

ROMANS 3:23

"All have sinned and lack the glory of God."[11] Any allusion here to the story of Adam's "fall" or loss is not so obvious from the perspective of Christian scholarship. For the tradition within Christian theology has been to understand Adam's fall in terms of his losing or distorting the image of God (referring to the first creation account, Gen 1:27—male and female created in the image of God). This however was not how Jewish theology understood Adam's punishment. And Paul was probably of the same view, since he could speak of man as "the image and glory of God" (1 Cor 11:7; similarly Jas 3:9). A clearer expression of Jewish theology was of Adam being deprived of God's *glory*, seen explicitly in Apoc. Mos. 21:6: Adam accusing Eve, "You have deprived me of the glory of God" (similarly 10:2).[12] The hope for the age to come could then be expressed in terms of the restoration or enhancement of the original glory.[13]

It is this line of theological reasoning that, notwithstanding 1 Cor 11:7, Paul seems to follow in Rom 3:23: "All lack, are deficient, or fall short of the glory of God." That is, they suffer from the defect Adam brought upon

---

10. See Wedderburn, "Adam," 414–15.

11. Translations are the author's own unless noted otherwise.

12. See further Robin Scroggs, *The Last Adam: A Study in Pauline Anthropology* (Philadelphia: Fortress, 1966), 26, 48–49.

13. Apoc. Mos. 39:2–3; 1 En. 50:1; 4 Ezra 7:122–25; 2 Bar. 51:1, 3; 54:15, 21.

the human race—the turning away from God, the failure to give God the glory due to him (1:21), and the resultant failure of humankind to reflect that glory to any adequate degree.[14] This would also help explain why Paul expresses the divinely intended outcome of the process of salvation in terms of participating (once again or still more fully) in the glory of God.[15] The value of being able to link Rom 3:23 into Paul's soteriology (that is, his understanding of salvation) in this way is that it highlights a further aspect of that soteriology—he sees salvation as a completion of God's purpose in the creation of humankind, as outlined in an Old Testament expression of Adam theology: to crown humankind with glory and honor (Ps 8:5).[16]

ROMANS 5:12–21

The most intriguing feature of this most explicit Romans exposition of Adam Christology is not the issue of whether Paul thought of Adam as a historical figure. It is the fact that he could sum up the plight of humankind by speaking of "one man" (Adam) and of the action of that one man. What mattered in Rom 5 was the consequence of Adam's, that is, humankind's decisions and actions. What happened to him as a result of his failure in Gen 3 was what had happened to humankind as a whole.[17]

Paul uses various terms to speak of that one act: he "sinned, missed the mark, erred, did wrong" (*hamartanein*); he committed "transgression" (*parabasis*), that is, he overstepped the boundary or norm set by God (5:14); he committed a "trespass" (*paraptōma*), that is, he violated the standards set by God (5:15–18, 20); he was disobedient (*parakoē*), that is, refused to listen, was unwilling to hear, and so disobeyed (5:19).[18] These descriptions are all drawn from the Adam story of Gen 3. The point is,

---

14. Fitzmyer thinks a reference to Adam here is "eisegetical" (*Romans*, 347). Jewett also cautions against seeing too direct a reference (*Romans*, 280 and n.104). Thomas S. Schreiner, however, sees "no reason to doubt that Paul reflects on Adam's loss of glory here" (*Romans* [BECNT; Grand Rapids: Baker, 1998], 187). Similarly Eduard Lohse, *Der Brief an die Römer* (KEK; Göttingen: Vandenhoeck, 2003), 131.

15. Rom 5:2; 8:18, 21; 9:23; 1 Cor 2:7; 15:43; 2 Cor 3:18; 4:17; etc.

16. Cf. Douglas J. Moo, *The Epistle to the Romans* (NICNT; Grand Rapids: Eerdmans, 1996), 226–27.

17. On the tricky question of interpreting 5:12b (and "original sin"), see particularly Fitzmyer, *Romans*, 408–10, 413–17; cf. Moo's wrestling with the issue (*Romans*, 320–28).

18. In each case I draw upon the fuller meaning indicated by BDAG.

however, that they not only illustrate the "impiety and unrighteousness" of humankind—the larger terms which headline Paul's indictment in Rom 1:18—they also indicate the *root* of that "impiety and unrighteousness." At the heart of human failure is a missing of the mark, an ignoring of norms and standards set by God, a refusing to listen to those who speak for and from God.

The Adam story also gives a way of understanding how that failure came about, and still comes about. For though Adam's action can also be described as "sin" (*hamartia*—5:13), the more striking reference is to "*Sin*" as a personified power: it entered the world (5:12); it now rules in death (5:21). "Sin," then, is Paul's word for a power or force to which humankind is subservient, a force that causes humans to sin, transgress, and disobey. How this "power" operates and how human beings experience it is a subject Paul will return to in Rom 7.

As with other thinkers in Second Temple Judaism, Paul found in the Adam story the reason why *death* was part of human experience.[19] Like Sin, Death can be thought of as a cosmic power. Through Adam's trespass Death too entered the world, and human beings became subject to it (5:12, 14, 17). Since Death came "through sin" (5:12), it remains unclear whether Paul thought that an unsinful Adam would never have died—presumably not, since he had had access to the tree of life. But Paul was concerned only with the stark reality of the human condition: death does rule over humankind (all die), and it is experienced as the victory of Sin (5:21).

Paul was clearly aware that Adam's sin as a historical event, and Adam as representing humankind, could not easily be held together. The simple equation, Adam's paradigmatic sin results in death, could not simply be transferred into the observation that humankind sins and therefore dies. The hesitation of 5:13–14 shows Paul's awareness of this awkwardness: death ruled even before sin could properly be reckoned to be sin. Similarly, in 5:19, the assertion that "through the disobedience of the one man, the many were made sinners," may be no more than Paul attempting to integrate the two Adams (the historical Adam and humankind) into the one picture. The fact is that *all are* sinners, and the Adam story provides a means of analyzing their condition as sinners.

---

19. Jewett justifiably links subsequent references to death in Romans to 5:12 (e.g., *Romans*, 409, 423, 426, 472, 480, 491).

The important point is that all this feeds into Paul's Adam Christology. His understanding of what Christ has achieved is precisely the counteraction that rights the wrong of Adam, or rather, which more than rights that wrong. The thought is the same as in 3:23: Adam not only falls short of the glory he originally had as God's creation, but he falls short also of the glory that would have been his without his failing as he did. The point is hammered home by a sequence of contrasts: not "trespass," but much more "free gift" (*charisma*), "grace" (*charis*), and "gift in grace" (5:15); sin resulting in condemnation, but free gift resulting in justification (5:16); trespass resulting in the rule of death, but much more the abundance of grace and the gift of righteousness resulting in the rule of life (5:17–18).

The point for Paul was that as the story of Adam could be told as the story of humankind in general, so the story of Jesus could be told as the story of those who believed in Christ. In coming to faith in Christ, in committing themselves to Christ through baptism in his name, they had made a transition from a life in Adam to a life in Christ, a transition from a life ruled by the power of Sin and its unavoidable partner Death to a life ruled by grace through righteousness that leads to eternal life (5:21).[20] As Adam's disobedience had "made" the many sinners, so Christ's obedience had "made" the many righteous (5:19). As the phrase "made sinners" did not exempt the many from personal responsibility and guilt (see 5:14, but Paul will also return to this issue in his next Adam passage), so the "made righteous" presupposed the hearing and commitment of faith.

The point is, then, that however awkwardly Paul holds together the two references of Adam (the historical figure and humankind), the Adam-Christ parallel sheds much light: (1) on the root cause of humankind's plight and subjection to the corrupting power of Sin and its final outcome in Death—the failure to observe the norms and standards set by God, the unwillingness to hear and obey God's commands, and (2) on the more than counteractive effect of Christ in demonstrating the outcome of a life marked by grace and obedience and in making such a life possible. It is important that the two aspects are not separated from each other: Paul uses the Adam story primarily as a way of illuminating his soteriology.[21]

---

20. It is very plausible to read Paul's subsequent "old man"/"new man" antithesis implied in Rom 6:6 as reflecting the same Adam/Christ contrast (e.g., Moo, *Romans*, 374–76).

21. I echo Frank J. Matera's comment on 1 Cor 15 in *New Testament Christology* (Louisville: Westminster John Knox, 1999), 98.

ROMANS 7:7–13

Next to Rom 5, this is probably the passage that most clearly reflects the influence of Gen 3. Christ does not appear as such. But as already made clear in Rom 5, a very fruitful way to understand the work of Christ and its significance is by telling the story of the human condition from which Christ delivers individuals.

Here Paul explains more clearly how Rom 5:19a works in real life, or how the story of Adam's trespass and disobedience can serve as the story of Everyman. More to the point, he takes up what he had left as something of a puzzle in Rom 5, the role of the law. He had made clear that sin is not counted apart from the law (5:13), which was fair enough, even though slightly confusing in regard to the rule of death prior to the giving of the law (5:14). But more puzzling, and potentially much more offensive to his Jewish audiences, had been the assertion that "the law came in to increase the trespass" (5:20). What was that about? And in 7:5 Paul had attributed the operation of sinful passions to the law. This was obviously a deliberate tactic, since it invited the conclusion that Paul regarded the law itself as sin (7:7). But in fact, as his exposition goes on to explain, he had only set up the issue in order to clarify it, and to show that he was not attacking the law. What follows is in effect a defense of the law, or rather a recognition of the law's weakness as a counter to the power of sin and death (7:7–13).[22] This was Paul's way of leading up to his explanation of the significance of what God had achieved in sending his Son: God has done through his Son what the law could not do (8:3), which included as its end result the now effective fulfillment of what the law required; what the law had been unable to do the Spirit was able to accomplish in those who were led by the Spirit (8:4). The point is, this clarification of the law's weakness, and so also clarification of how Christ has overcome that weakness, is achieved by, once again, turning to the Adam story.

Paul does this by reverting to first-person terms, "I" and "me."[23] He narrates how sin gained its hold on the "I." The fact that he reverts to the

---

22. See my *Theology of Paul*, 156–58, with bibliography.

23. The debate on the "I" of Rom 7:7–25 is unending. See the full treatments of Jan Lambrecht, *The Wretched "I" and Its Liberation: Paul in Romans 7 and 8* (Leuven: Peeters, 1992); Brian J. Dodd, *Paul's Paradigmatic "I": Personal Example as Literary Strategy* (JSNTSup 177; Sheffield: Sheffield Academic Press, 1999), 221–34. I continue to find it difficult to conclude that Paul could write in terms of such existential anguish

idea of Sin as a personal power in itself indicates that Paul had reverted to the storyline of Rom 5:12–21. The "I" had not known sin except through the law. In explicit terms "I" would not have known covetousness were it not for the law that said "You shall not covet" (7:7). It was this same power, the power of Sin, which used that commandment to stir up covetousness. "Apart from the law sin is dead. And I was alive once in the absence of the law, but when the commandment came sin came to life, and I died" (7:8–10). That Paul had in mind the Adam story is probably sufficiently confirmed by the echo of Gen 3:13 in Rom 7:11: "for sin seizing its opportunity through the commandment deceived me and through it killed me." The echo is of Eve's sad complaint, "The serpent deceived me, and I ate" (Gen 3:13).[24]

The echo of the Adam story is not diminished by the fact that Paul here cites the tenth commandment ("You shall not covet"). For covetousness was quite widely conceived to be the root sin[25] and so could be given its place in the story of the root sin quite acceptably. And, in point of fact, the sin of Eve (and Adam) could be characterized quite fairly in terms of covetousness—deceived by the serpent's reassurance that if she/they ate, they would be as God/the gods (Gen 3:5). It could also be the case that, as in Rom 1:23, Paul was meshing together the primary sin of Adam and the primary sin of Israel, since his analysis could equally apply to the entry of the law into the life of Israel.[26] This would also echo the train of Paul's indictment in chapters 1–3—humankind indicted as a whole but Paul then taking pains to explicitly include his fellow Jews in the indictment—

(7:14–24) without it including some expression of his own experience. See also Schreiner, *Romans*, 359–65 and Jewett, *Romans*, 441–45. That the command to Adam (not to eat of the tree of the knowledge of good and evil) already embodied or at least expressed the law of God was probably taken for granted in Jewish thought (see, e.g., my *Romans 1–8*, 379–80; Peter Stuhlmacher, *Paul's Letter to the Romans* [trans. Scott J. Hafemann; Louisville: Westminster John Knox, 1994], 106–7).

24. Fitzmyer regards an allusion to Adam as again "eisegetical," even though he acknowledges the likelihood of an allusion to Gen 3:13 in Rom 7:11 (cf. 2 Cor 11:3) (*Romans*, 464, 468; cf. 474). Jewett also thinks an allusion to the Genesis account likely (*Romans*, 452). Cf. Matera, *Christology*, 114. Often quoted is the provocative claim of Ernst Käsemann, *Commentary on Romans* (ed. and trans. Geoffrey W. Bromiley; Grand Rapids: Eerdmans, 1980): "There is nothing in the passage which does not fit Adam, and everything fits Adam alone" (196). Stuhlmacher agrees (*Romans*, 106).

25. Documentation in my *Romans 1–8*, 380.

26. See particularly Moo, *Romans*, 426–31 and on Rom 7:11 (440).

"*all* under sin" (3:9). So here the "I" could be used to speak of humankind in more than one way.

But the Adam story was particularly valuable for explaining how Sin exerts its power—by making what is good a means of temptation, the prohibition inciting the very curiosity and appetite for what it warned against. It is what Paul refers to in 8:3 as the weakness of the law—well able to point the right way, but unable to help flesh so readily deceived by sin and captivated by the forbidden fruit to follow that right way.

The value of reading Rom 7 in this way, then, is that the analysis of humankind's Adamic weakness highlights the way in which the second Adam counters that weakness and enables the beneficiaries to live that right way (8:3–4). The very likeness of sinful (Adamic) flesh was assumed and dealt with on the cross (8:3).[27] The law that, abused by sin, became an instrument of death, was transformed by the power of the Spirit into the law of the Spirit of life (8:2), delivering from the deadly effects of thinking only in terms of (satisfying) the flesh (8:6). The analysis of Christ's mission ("God sent his Son"), of Christ's death ("condemned sin in the flesh"), and of the outcome of his resurrection (the Spirit of life—cf. 1 Cor 15:45) is all sketched out on the template provided by Adam.

ROMANS 8:20–21

This is the last Romans passage on which the Adam story sheds some light. One of the clues is evident in Paul's assertion that "creation was subjected to futility (*mataiotēs*)" (Rom 8:20). For this clearly echoes his earlier description of failed humanity in chapter 1—"though they knew God they did not glorify him or give him thanks"; in consequence, "they became futile (*emataiōthēsan*) in their thinking" (1:21). These are the only two passages in Romans in which Paul uses the concept of "futility." This is the "futility" that was the consequence of humankind's/Adam's failure to honor God (by obeying him) and failure to give the Creator the glory and thanks due to him from the creature. In context the "futility" is obviously another way of referring to "the slavery of corruption" from which creation longs to be free (8:21–23). The implication once again is that the

---

27. Romans 8:3 is a tricky verse to grasp in its full significance; see my *Romans 1–8*, 421–22; Moo, *Romans*, 479–81; Lohse, *Römer*, 231–32; Jewett, *Romans*, 483–84.

consequence of human self-seeking has been a subjection to physical (and moral) corruption, decay, and death.

Here, however, the thought is that not only humankind is subject to such decay, but also creation as a whole. This too is an obvious deduction to draw from the Adam story in Gen 3. For there not only are Adam and Eve, and the serpent, punished (Gen 3:14–19), but also the ground is cursed (3:17–18).[28] And the punishment is put in terms of mortal decay ("to dust you shall return," 3:19), but also of exclusion from access to the tree of life (3:22–24). Adam as the crown of creation, for whom creation was prepared as an appropriate setting, brings down creation with him in his fall; for fallen humankind, a fallen creation. Paul's added note that the subjection of creation to this futility of decay was "not willingly, but on account of him who did the subjecting" (Rom 8:20)[29] shows a sensitivity to the possible charge that the inclusion of creation in the consequences of humankind's failure was not entirely fair to creation. But the logic is that creation is the only appropriate home for humankind; an unfallen creation would be no place for fallen humanity. And Paul does add that all this was done "in hope" (8:20), strongly suggesting that Paul viewed the consequences of humankind's turning away from God as always temporary in the total purpose of God. The subjection of humanity and all creation to decay was always in the sure hope of the future (eschatological, that is, final) deliverance of which Paul speaks in 8:21–23—when the redemption of the body will be accompanied by the redemption of creation, once again to provide the appropriate setting for now-resurrected humanity.

As the close parallel with 1 Cor 15:42–50 confirms, the underlying thought is once again of what Christ has accomplished by his own life, death, and resurrection. Once again it is the Adam story that helps Paul fill out the true nature of the human condition and its subjection to mortality in order to explain more clearly what Christ achieved, as attested by the gospel. It is not just that Jesus' action is an equivalent to Adam's in epochal terms (Rom 5:12). It is also that the consequence of Adam's trespass and disobedience, as a description of the reality of the human condition (the weakness of its flesh and domination by the self-seeking power of Sin, its subjection to decay and death) is also a description of what Christ delivered humankind from by his life, death, and resurrection.

---

28. Stuhlmacher, *Romans*, 134; Schreiner, *Romans*, 436; Jewett, *Romans*, 513–14.

29. Fitzmyer acknowledges a possible reference to Adam here, although he fails to note the link between 8:21 and 1:21 in the motif of "futility" (*Romans*, 507–8).

When we speak of "Adam and Christ," then, or of "Adam Christology," it is not simply that Adam is being seen as a type of Christ or that the status and significance of Christ himself for Paul is illuminated by the parallel with Adam and the Adamic features of what Christ did. In Romans what is more significant is the light that the Adam story sheds on the plight of humankind, its lostness of direction, its lack of glory, its sinfulness, its subjection to the power and weakness of self-seeking flesh, its belonging to a creation in decay. And still more, the light that it sheds on what the second Adam has accomplished on humankind's behalf, its renewed sense of direction, its hope of glory, its experience of grace, its readiness to respond to the Spirit, its assurance of complete redemption for the body also. In short, Adam Christology is not the most important aspect of Paul's Christology, but the Adam story provided Paul with a helpful and insightful way to illuminate what Christ had achieved and what the gospel offered.

For Further Reading

Dodd, Brian. *Paul's Paradigmatic "I": Personal Example as Literary Strategy.* JSNTSup 177. Sheffield: Sheffield Academic Press, 1999. Dodd focuses attention on the way Paul presents himself as an example, including ways in which this self-portrayal is similar to what popular philosophers of the first century did. He gives particular attention to the rhetorical function of Paul's descriptions of himself and sees Rom 7 as one of the places in which Paul talks about his own experience.

Dunn, James D. G. *Christology in the Making.* 2nd ed. London: SCM, 1989; Grand Rapids: Eerdmans, 1996. Dunn sees references to Adam and an Adam Christology in Rom 1, 3, 7, and 8 and not just 5 (and 1 Cor 15). He argues that Adam and Wisdom Christology do not necessarily imply Jesus' personal preexistence.

———. *The Theology of Paul the Apostle.* Grand Rapids: Eerdmans, 1998. This work provides a comprehensive account of Paul's theology that works from the template of Romans. The chapter entitled "Jesus the Man" includes a discussion of Adam Christology and integrates it with the several other ways in which Paul speaks of Christ.

Fee, Gordon D. *Pauline Christology: An Exegetical-Theological Study.* Peabody, Mass.: Hendrickson, 2007. Fee sees fewer connections between

Christ and Adam than I do. But he acknowledges some connections, particularly in relation to discussion of "new creation" and "image of God." See especially chapter 13.

Hooker, Morna D. "Adam in Romans 1." *NTS* 6 (1959–60): 297–306. Hooker sees Adam as no more than a background character in Rom 1. Thus, she does not see Adam Christology as central to the theology of Romans.

Lambrecht, Jan. *The Wretched "I" and Its Liberation: Paul in Romans 7 and 8*. Leuven: Peeters, 1992. Writing in a fairly accessible style, Lambrecht argues that the "I" of Rom 7 refers primarily to Paul's life before he became a Christian. Thus, when Paul speaks of the sin that lives within he is not speaking of a continuing struggle in his life.

Matera, Frank J. *New Testament Christology*. Louisville: Westminster John Knox, 1999. In this comprehensive and fairly accessible study, Matera examines the way Christ is understood in every New Testament writing except Philemon. He finds Adam Christology as one way in which Paul gives expression to his soteriology.

Scroggs, Robin. *The Last Adam: A Study in Pauline Anthropology*. Philadelphia: Fortress, 1966. Scroggs argues that Adam Christology gives coherence to Paul's theology. He sees Paul working from categories taken from contemporaneous Jewish writers, but departing from them in seeing Christ as the realization of true humanity and as the one who mediates that humanity to others.

Wedderburn, A. J. M. "Adam in Paul's Letter to the Romans." Pages 413–30 in *Studia Biblica 1978, III: Papers on Paul and Other New Testament Authors*. Edited by E. A. Livingstone. JSNTSup 3. Sheffield: JSOT Press, 1980. Wedderburn sets out in detail the case for seeing allusions to Adam in Romans and provides a basis for recognizing the development of an Adam Christology in this letter.

THE SPIRIT BRINGS CHRIST'S LIFE TO LIFE

L. Ann Jervis

The Spirit appears prominently in Romans, particularly in the central part of the letter—chapters 5–8. I happen to think that this is not accidental. As I read Romans, these chapters are central not only because they are in the middle of Paul's letter but also because they contain what for him was central to his gospel. Paul understood himself to be the apostle to the Gentiles (1:5), and he regarded the Romans as among his apostolic charges (1:6). Of course, when Paul writes to "all God's beloved at Rome" (1:7), they are already believers in Jesus Christ, having been converted by someone else. His purpose in writing to them is not, then, to convert them. It is, rather, to fulfill his obligation towards them. The Christian community at Rome had a significant number of Gentiles and so, as apostle to the Gentiles, Paul believes that he must preach the gospel also to them.[1] While there are likely many reasons why Paul wrote this remarkable letter to the Roman believers, among the most significant is that he considered it his duty to bring about the obedience of faith among them, as among the rest of the Gentiles (1:5–6).[2] Paul seems to have considered that until Gentiles (even those who had been converted by someone else) were exposed to his gospel for Gentiles, they had not come fully into the faith.

It is clear as I read Romans in the context of Paul's other letters that the apostle was convinced that *his* gospel for Gentiles allowed for their sanctification "by the Holy Spirit" (15:16). Paul believed that what set his

---

1. While there are Jews among the Roman believers to whom Paul writes (ch. 14 gives evidence of this), there are also Gentiles (1:6, 13; 11:13–32). As I read the letter Paul envisions the Gentiles in the front row of his audience, although he expects the Jews to be listening in as well.

2. See my *The Purpose of Romans: A Comparative Letter Structure Investigation* (JSNTSup 55; Sheffield: JSOT Press, 1991).

gospel for Gentiles apart was that when Gentiles received it they also came into knowledge of the life of the Spirit. It is clear from other of his letters that the Spirit is vital to and inseparable from the gospel Paul preaches.[3] The fact that, in distinction from how it figures in other of his letters, Paul barely mentions the Spirit until the fifth chapter of Romans suggests that his hearers (being converted by someone other than himself) do not know the critical connection between the gospel of Jesus Christ's death and resurrection and the Spirit.

In the first four chapters of Romans Paul gives his description of the gospel that he and the Roman believers share.[4] After doing this (and thereby holding the attention of this audience whose first loyalty would not have been to him), Paul introduces an intense discussion of the Spirit. At Rom 5 it becomes clear that Paul desires that those who already know that God's Messiah is the risen Jesus Christ should also know the Spirit's presence.

Paul was convinced that his gospel to the Gentiles allows Gentiles to know the Spirit.[5] The good news that the risen Jesus is God's Messiah (1:2–4), the good news that the righteousness of God has been manifested apart from the law and the prophets (3:21), the good news that God makes righteous those who have the faith of Jesus (3:26) and thereby justifies the ungodly (4:5), and that this happens when people "believe in him who raised Jesus our Lord from the dead, who was put to death for our trespasses and raised for our justification" (4:24)—this good news is even greater than the Roman believers imagine. In chapter 5 Paul begins to focus on filling out and expanding the Roman believers' understandings and expectations. Paul begins to tell them about the Spirit (the majority

---

3. Notice that in letters written to churches founded initially by Paul, such as those at Corinth, Thessalonica, Galatia, and Philippi, Paul *assumes* that his hearers connect the Spirit with the gospel and with reception of the gospel. For example, 1 Cor 1:4–7; 1 Thess 1:4–6; Gal 3:2; Phil 2:1.

4. Romans 1–4, introduced by a summary of the gospel that is anomalous in Paul—"the gospel concerning his Son, who was descended from David according to the flesh" (1:3)—is best read as Paul's presentation of the faith that he knows is largely shared by Roman believers. These believers were almost certainly converted by Jewish Christians who presented the gospel in Jewish categories. At ch. 5 Paul begins to add to and expand upon this gospel message.

5. There are indications that Paul considered that Jews (whether believers in Jesus' resurrection or not) would not need to be made aware of the Spirit; he writes that Jews have things of the spirit (15:27). It appears that Paul thought that when Gentiles know the Spirit they are sharing in what is of the Jews.

of references to the Spirit in Romans are found in chs. 5–8). His focus on the Spirit, begun in chapter 5, reaches it climax at the center point of the letter—chapter 8.

When we think about the Spirit in Romans, then, we are focusing on what Paul thought made his work for God on behalf of the Gentiles most distinctive.

WHAT MAKES AWARENESS OF THE SPIRIT SO CRITICAL?

Paul clearly thought that knowledge of who the Spirit is and what the Spirit does was essential for the Roman believers. Paul wants "God's beloved at Rome" to recognize that, by having accepted the good news as he describes it in Rom 1–4, they should know themselves now to be living in a particular location.

Paul describes that location at the beginning of chapter 5—believers are in a place of peace with God (5:1), which means that they are in a location where they have access to grace (5:2)—they are now close to God: "reconciled to God by the death of his Son" (5:10).

This new territory in which believers in Jesus Christ live is the territory of Christ Jesus and of the Spirit. So Paul speaks of believers being "in Christ Jesus" (8:1) and "in the Spirit" (8:9). Both Jesus Christ and the Spirit shape the environment of believers' lives, for once people believe that God raised Jesus from the dead their existence is changed. They now live in a new world—the world of Jesus Christ and the Spirit.[6]

Paul says many things about how Jesus Christ shapes believers' world—one of the most arresting and profound being that believers "suffer with him in order that we may also be glorified with him" (8:17).[7] In this essay, however, we are focused on the Spirit, although we will find that to speak of being in the Spirit is at once to speak of being in Jesus Christ.

---

6. This is rightly understood by Eduard Schweizer, who writes that to be in the Spirit is synonymous with being in Christ: "Both denote the existence of the believer. If he lives in the sphere of the work of Christ as the One who was crucified and raised again for him, he also lives in the sphere of the work of the Spirit, who reveals Christ and imparts salvation to him" ("πνεῦμα, πνευματικός," TDNT 6:427). It is, however, important in this regard to take into account, as Gordon Fee does, that nowhere does Paul equate the risen Christ with the Spirit (God's Empowering Presence: The Holy Spirit in the Letters of Paul [Peabody, Mass.: Hendrickson, 1994], 836).

7. All translations are mine.

Paul wants the Roman believers to be aware that they are "in the Spirit" and that the Spirit changes their world and their lives. Being in the territory and way of life of the Spirit is also to be in Christ Jesus. As Paul writes, "The law of the Spirit of life *in Christ Jesus* has set me free from the law of sin and death" (8:2). The word "law" refers here to the Spirit's intention or guiding principle. The Spirit's intention is to liberate individuals from the "law," that is, the intention of sin and death. The intention of sin and death is, of course, to produce more sin and death. The intention of the Spirit of life is to liberate individuals from sin and death. The Spirit's intention is life. The structure for existence in Christ Jesus is, then, one that, by the intention of the Spirit, breaks the hold that sin and death have on people. That is why Paul can write that "now there is no condemnation for those who are *in Christ Jesus*" (8:1).

Paul wants the Roman believers to be aware that the Spirit shapes their existence so that God's kingdom is actualized; that is, he wants them to recognize that the Spirit is the generating source, the organizing force, of God's kingdom: "the kingdom of God is … righteousness and peace and joy *in the Holy Spirit*" (14:17). The Spirit makes available the reality of God's way of life.

The Spirit creates a territory, an environment in which people can live along with the Spirit—the Spirit of God and of Christ. The Spirit sets up house (*oikei*—8:9) among those who are "in Christ Jesus" (8:1) and by doing so those people are "in the Spirit" (8:9).

The environment of the Spirit in which believers live shapes them. Believers begin to take on the characteristics of God. This is the case because the environment of the Spirit is the environment of God (and of Jesus Christ). As we will see, Paul describes the Spirit as simply the Spirit and also as the Spirit of God and the Spirit of Christ. When he talks about what it means to be "in the Spirit," then, he is talking about what it means to be "in Christ" and so to be reconciled to God. Among the characteristics of God that believers take on are love and hope. God's love is poured into believers' hearts by the Spirit (5:5),[8] and the Spirit empowers believers to share one of God's distinguishing characteristics—hope: "may the *God*

---

8. The phrase "God's love" in Rom 5:5 can be understood to mean either God's love for us or our love for God. Here I am focusing on the first meaning. This first meaning is never separated, however, from our love for God, since believers are able to love God only because God loves them into such love.

of hope fill you with all joy and peace in believing, so that by the power of the Holy Spirit you may abound in *hope*" (15:13).

It should be noted that being "in the Spirit" is not an occasional or necessarily ecstatic or extraordinary experience. Being "in the Spirit" is a stable way of life for believers.[9] Paul believes that God's Spirit has taken up residence among those humans who are "in Christ Jesus." There is an inextricable connection between the presence of the resident Spirit and being "in Christ Jesus," or, as Paul also puts it, belonging to Christ. Having the Spirit of Christ means that individuals belong to Christ, and such belonging happens because the Spirit of God dwells among those who are "in Christ Jesus": "you are in the Spirit since the Spirit of God dwells in you. Anyone who does not have the Spirit of Christ does not belong to him" (8:9). The Spirit creates an environment or way of life in which people live. The Spirit dwells among them and allows people to live "in Christ Jesus"— to belong to Christ.

Therefore, when Paul speaks of the gift of the Spirit (5:5) and of receiving the Spirit (8:15), he is not speaking of charismatic gifts such as speaking in tongues or prophecy. He is rather describing the presence and activity of the Spirit—something of which it appears he thinks the Roman believers may be unaware. Part of Paul's project in his fulsome discussion of the Spirit beginning at chapter 5 is to awaken the Roman believers to the gift they may not know they have received—the gift of living "in the new life of the Spirit" (7:6).

WHAT IS THE SPIRIT?

Paul thinks that humans have spirits; he refers to his own spirit (1:9) and to the collective spirit of believers (8:16). Once in Romans Paul distinguishes the spirits of humans from our bodies (8:10). The Spirit about which we are here concerned is a being separate and distinct from the human spirit, although the human spirit can relate to the Spirit (8:16). When we speak about the Spirit in Romans we are speaking about a divine entity.

As we have already seen, Paul understands the Spirit to be of God and of Christ. The Spirit is in the closest relationship to God and Christ. Paul describes the Spirit as being "of Christ" (8:9) once, and three or four times

---

9. So Leander E. Keck, referring to 8:9: "To be 'in the Spirit' does not refer to an exceptional, ecstatic state (as in Rev. 1:10); in our passage, it refers to the normal state of the believer" (*Romans* [ANTC; Nashville: Abingdon, 2005], 203).

as being "of God" (8:9; 8:14; also 8:11, and perhaps 15:19).[10] It should be noted, however, that the Spirit brings its own identity to the relationship it has with God and Christ.

The Spirit has its own intention or mind. The word Paul uses is *phronēma*. *Phronēma*, which is often translated as "mind," refers to what is essential to a being, what makes a being functional and able to think for itself—able to act in accordance with its integrity. Paul says that the Spirit has *phronēma*, and that that *phronēma* is life and peace: "the *phronēma* of the Spirit is life and peace" (8:6). The Spirit, then, values, intends, and desires life and peace.

The Spirit directs and enables a particular way of life—a way of life that is immensely pleasing to God. Those who walk "according to the Spirit" fulfill the law's just requirement (8:4). That is, the Spirit is a guide to living as God wants humans to live. If people accept the guidance of the Spirit, the Spirit shapes their values and intentions and desires. The Spirit's *phronēma* may direct the *phronēma* of human beings. Paul uses the verb related to the noun *phronēma* when he writes that "those who live according to the Spirit 'set their minds' (*phronousin*) on the things of the Spirit" (8:5). The Spirit is an entity who can draw human values, intentions, and desires into sympathetic concord with itself. The Spirit desires and is able to share its basic orientation with humans. Furthermore, the Spirit is a being who has "things." Paul writes that those who live according to the Spirit set their minds on "the things" of the Spirit (8:5). These "things" include life and peace (8:6). The Spirit is a being who seeks to create, through human beings, the things of itself.

Paul speaks personally of how the law of the Spirit of life has set him free from the law of sin and death (8:2).[11] It should be noted, however, that while individual believers benefit from the life and peace which result from setting one's mind on the things of the Spirit there are also broader consequences in view. First, while the Spirit affects the individual it also affects corporate life. In Rom 8 Paul primarily uses plural pronouns. He speaks mainly about how the Spirit affects a group of people. This can be hard to recognize in an English translation. However, in chapter 8, which focuses on the Spirit, the Greek word for "you" is almost always in the

---

10. The manuscripts for Rom 15:19 vary over whether it should read "in the power of the Spirit" or "in the power of the Spirit of God."

11. The manuscript tradition has both "me" and "you" (singular). Consequently, Paul could have written either "set me free" or "set you [singular] free".

plural. So, when Paul writes, for instance, "you are in the Spirit if the Spirit of God dwells in you" (8:9), he is referring to a group of people. "The things of the Spirit," which are life and peace, are, then, not simply evident in the contented lives of individual Christians. Life and peace from the Spirit will be evident in community. Perhaps one of the verses where the corporate influence of the Spirit is clearest is 8:16: "the Spirit bears witness with our spirit [note the singular] that we are children of God." Here Paul speaks of the spirit of a community of people being in conversation with the Spirit.

The life and peace that exist because a group of people set their minds on the Spirit will characterize their life together and so will be part of transforming the world. The life and peace that exist because people set their minds on the Spirit is a form of life and peace that they do not create on their own. It is not based on a particular form of governance or a particular ideology. It is rooted in the Spirit. The Spirit creates a place of peace and joy and righteousness in this world and in this time—the Spirit creates the kingdom of God. The kingdom of God is now and is present and it is rooted in the Holy Spirit: "the kingdom of God is ... righteousness and peace and joy *in* the Holy Spirit" (14:17).

The Spirit is a being who enables people to overcome destructive and death-dealing inclinations and actions. The Spirit is a being who helps people free themselves from an orientation towards death and find the life that is there waiting for them: "If by the Spirit you put to death the deeds of the body you will live" (8:13). While the life that results from working with the Spirit to put to death the deeds of the body is resurrection life (eternal life), such life may begin now. With the agency of the Spirit believers may start now to live the life that they will live forever. While life in the Spirit now does not offer all that God promises—that must wait until Christ's return—it does offer in the present the taste of God's life.

It is clear that for Paul the Spirit is focused on life. Another way this understanding is evidenced is when Paul describes the Spirit as intimately connected to God and to Christ. Paul speaks of the Spirit as the Spirit of God (8:9, 14) and in this context describes God as "the one who raised Jesus from the dead" (8:11). The Spirit of God, who brought Jesus from death to life, is a being who is characterized by life and who creates life, even out of death. This fact is seen particularly in the Spirit's intimate association with Christ's resurrection. Paul writes that Jesus was declared "Son of God in power according to the Spirit of holiness by resurrection from the dead" (1:4). That is, at the resurrection Jesus was appointed by the Spirit as Son of God in power. "The resurrection was the moment of

Christ's enthronement as Son of God in power *by God's Spirit*."[12] The Spirit was an essential player in Christ's resurrection and so the resurrection of others will be accomplished also by the Spirit (8:11). The Spirit is for and about life, even bringing life out of death.[13]

Paul speaks of the "law" of the Spirit of life (8:2). This "law" is not, of course, the Mosaic law, but, as a wise scholar has written, "the dynamic 'principle' of the new life, creating vitality and separating humans from sin and death."[14] The Spirit, being of God, is all about life. The Spirit, being of God, intends and is able to create life. And so Paul speaks of the Spirit as the Spirit of life.

The Spirit is a being who not only creates life but also a closer connection between God and human beings. These two aspects of the Spirit's identity are related, since God is the source of life. To be more connected to God is to be more alive. The aspect of the Spirit's being that is concerned with connecting people with God is described by Paul in the phrase "Spirit of adoption" (8:15).[15] The Greek word for "adoption" (*huiothesia*) has the noun "son" (*huios*) in it, and so it is sometimes translated as "sonship." In the ancient Mediterranean world to be taken into a family as a son was to be offered privilege and security. Paul describes the Spirit as an entity which enables the transfer of people into a secure and close relationship with God. Not only does the Spirit enable this, but the Spirit is then the being in whom such humans exist.

The Spirit, as I emphasized above, is an entity in which people may live—an environment. It is *in* the Spirit that humans are able to cry out in

---

12. Frank J. Matera, *Romans* (PCNT; Grand Rapids: Baker, 2010), 22 (italics mine).

13. Augustine meditated on the profound relationship of the Spirit and resurrection life and also drew a connection to the Spirit's role as creator: "In the morning I shall stand and shall see my God, ... who also will quicken our mortal bodies by the Spirit that dwells in us, because in mercy he was moving over our lightless and restless inner deep" (*Conf.* 13.14.15, in LCC [ed. and trans. Albert C. Outler; Philadelphia: Westminster, 1955], 308, cited from Eugene F. Rogers Jr., *After the Spirit: A Constructive Pneumatology from Resources Outside the Modern West* [Grand Rapids: Eerdmans, 2005], 84).

14. Joseph A. Fitzmyer, *Romans* (AB; New York: Doubleday, 1993), 482–83.

15. Paul may use the phrase "spirit of adoption" when presenting his gospel for Gentiles to Gentiles because, unlike Jews, Gentiles are not those "to whom belong the sonship" (9:4). The word "sonship" in 9:4 is the same word Paul uses in 8:15. I am grateful to Rogers for this observation (*After the Spirit*, 89).

intimacy and immediacy to God. It is in the environment of the Spirit that humans can connect in an especially close way with God. In fact, they can use the same name for God that Jesus did. As James D. G. Dunn writes, in reference to Rom 8:15, "This experience [of crying 'Abba! Father!'] reproduces what had hitherto been the unprecedented and unique spiritual experience of Jesus himself."[16] In the Spirit other humans may relate to God as did the human Jesus.

Furthermore, the Spirit is a being capable of working along with the spirits of humans. The Spirit does not overwhelm humans so that they lose their identity or their capacity to understand their own lives. Rather, the Spirit respects the human spirit and so it underscores what the human spirit itself recognizes—that once people's lives are defined by the environment of the Spirit of adoption they know themselves to be God's children. The Spirit, Paul writes, "bears witness with our spirit that we are children of God" (8:16).

As the Spirit dwells among them, believers in Jesus Christ live their lives in the environment of the Spirit. Paul speaks of the Spirit of God making its home among believers. "You are in the Spirit, since the Spirit of God dwells in you" (8:9).[17] In the Greek of Rom 8:9 "since" is the word *eiper*, often translated "if in fact." This word should not be read to indicate a condition that might not exist.[18] Rather, Paul is describing what is—the Spirit of God *does* dwell among them.[19] The Spirit of God, then, is a being who is able and willing to live among human beings.

Paul also speaks of the Spirit as the Spirit of Christ. When he does so he describes the Spirit as an entity which can be "had" by individual people. The Spirit is a being which allows itself to belong to individual humans. The result of this offering is that those humans belong to Christ: "anyone who does not have the Spirit of Christ does not belong to him" (8:9).[20] The Spirit is an absolutely essential player in the relationship between a person and Christ.

---

16. James D. G. Dunn, "1 Corinthians 15:45—Last Adam, Life-Giving Spirit," in *Christ and Spirit in the New Testament* (ed. Barnabas Lindars and Stephen S. Smalley; Cambridge: Cambridge University Press, 1973), 127–42, here 133.

17. Note that "you" here is plural.

18. Contra James D. G. Dunn, *Romans* (WBC 38A; Dallas: Word, 1988), 428.

19. So Keck, *Romans*, 203.

20. This is one of the rare passages where Paul speaks of individuals rather than a community being in relation to the Spirit.

Given the utter and complete involvement of the Spirit with God and with Christ it is no wonder that the primary way Paul describes the Spirit is as a being that is holy. Paul speaks once of the Spirit as the Spirit of holiness (1:4) and five times describes the Spirit as holy (5:5; 9:1; 14:17; 15:13; 15:16).

The Spirit is a being characterized by holiness—that way of being that is pure and completely free from corruption and sin. Such holiness is powerful. Paul connects the Spirit's holiness with the Spirit's power to change people's lives and the reality in which human beings live. When describing how the Spirit pours God's love into believers' hearts, Paul speaks of the Spirit as holy (5:5). When describing how the Spirit is capable of making Gentiles into godly people, Paul speaks of the Spirit as holy (15:16).[21] When writing of the Spirit's power to create hope in believers, Paul uses the adjective holy: "so that by the power of the Holy Spirit you may abound in hope" (15:13). When explaining the nature of the kingdom of God and how it is a reality grounded in the Spirit constructed on the vital energies of righteousness and peace and joy, Paul describes the Spirit as holy (14:17).

The Spirit is holy and so it transforms those whom it touches, by filling hearts with God's love and love for God (5:5), by making Gentiles into godly/sanctified people, and by instilling hope. The Spirit is holy and so where the Spirit is there are the holy characteristics of righteousness and peace and joy. The Spirit's holiness is, then, not a holiness that results in the Spirit keeping itself apart from that which is not holy. Rather, the Spirit's holiness results in its touching and transforming the unholy. The power of the Spirit's holiness changes people and their environment so that people can live more closely connected to God and with the good and life-giving energies of love and sanctity and hope, and in an environment of righteousness and peace and joy.

---

21. In Rom 15:16 Paul speaks of his commitment that the offering of the Gentiles may be "sanctified in the Holy Spirit." The idea of sanctification emphasizes a moral life in accordance with God's will (see "ἁγιασμός," *TDNT* 1:113).

The Spirit and God and Christ

Independence of the Spirit

In Romans the Spirit is primarily spoken of as a being with its own intention and activity. While, as mentioned above, there are a few times when Paul makes plain that he considers the Spirit to be entirely connected to God and to Christ, the Spirit mostly appears in Romans as an independent character. It is the Spirit itself who Paul says bears witness with our spirit that we are children of God (8:16). It is the Spirit itself who intercedes for us with sighs too deep for words (8:26). The word "itself" is a translation of the Greek *to auto*, which appears in both of these verses, and which emphasizes the activity of the Spirit and the Spirit alone. As mentioned above, Paul speaks of the Spirit having its own aim or way of thinking (*phronēma*) (8:6, 27).

Yet, while the Spirit is independent it is at the same time in complete accord with God. The *phronēma* (mind) of the Spirit is consonant and in step with God's will: "the one who searches people's hearts [i.e., God] knows what is the mind [*phronēma*] of the Spirit because the Spirit intercedes for the saints according to the will of God" (8:27).

God's Use of the Spirit

Not only are God and the Spirit of one mind, but the Spirit implements God's designs. In this sense the Spirit is God's power. The promise that God will make our mortal bodies alive is a promise that will be made reality by means of the Spirit (Rom 8:11).

Christ's Relationship to the Spirit

The relationship of Christ to the Spirit is intensely close. As we have seen, Paul can speak of the Spirit of Christ (8:9). And Paul can speak of Christ and the Spirit in parallel, as if being in Christ is also to be in the Spirit (see 9:1).

Believers' Relationship to the Spirit

Those who are "in Christ Jesus" are at the same time in the territory of the Spirit, and so their lives follow the design of the Spirit. Paul speaks of believers as those who "walk ... according to the Spirit ... who live according to the Spirit" (8:4–5).

Believers—those who are "in Christ Jesus" (see 8:1)—have the Spirit as their guide (8:14). In the lives of believers the Spirit is the active partner who offers a particular kind of existence. The new form of existence, this living "in the Spirit," occurs when the Spirit of God dwells among believers (8:9): "you are in the Spirit since the Spirit of God dwells among you." Those who live in this existence have a particular identity—they are "children of God." Believers recognize this about themselves with the aid of the Spirit who bears witness "with our spirit that we are children of God" (8:16).

Given the state of reality in the time before Christ's return—a state that Paul describes as one of suffering and of groaning for release (8:18–23)—Paul does not promise that being "in the Spirit" makes life easy. Paul acknowledges that those who have the Spirit have only the "firstfruits" and that they still wait for the release of their bodies from the difficulties every body knows (8:23). Believers' critical relationship with the Spirit does not shield them from suffering (see 8:17).

The activity of the Spirit does not overwhelm and take over the lives of believers. Rather, those who are "in Christ Jesus" must themselves participate in making vital the Spirit's activity in their lives. So Paul finds it necessary to command his Roman addressees to "be aglow with the Spirit" (12:11). Even though they are "in the Spirit," believers do not always find the power and life of the Spirit irresistible. The Spirit's relationship to believers is not overpowering, rather, it is up to believers themselves to "be aglow with the Spirit." Presumably the glow of the Spirit will manifest itself in the "things of the Spirit," such as life and peace (8:6) and love (15:30).

It is up to believers to access the Spirit so that they can have and know true life—life not dominated by an orientation towards death. Paul writes, "If by the Spirit you put to death the deeds of the body you will live" (8:13). "The deeds of the body" is a phrase that describes actions that lead to death. For Paul bodies are "dead because of sin" (8:10), and it is only when bodies exist with the Spirit of God in them and among them (8:11) that they are oriented towards life. However, it takes more than the Spirit's agency in creating a new environment and being present in it. It also takes believers working with the Spirit. Believers can be freed from a way of life concentrated on death only when they make use of the Spirit's presence and ability to help them do so.

What the Spirit Does

The Spirit Changes People So That They Fit "in Christ Jesus"

The change that the Spirit intends and enables in and for people is one that allows them to fit within the place that, as believers, they already are, that is, in Christ Jesus. What the Spirit intends and enables is for people to live "in Christ," to live as people who recognize and experience that the power of sin and death has been extinguished. As Christ condemned sin (8:3) and died to sin (6:10) and now lives to God (6:10), so, with the help of the Spirit, can others.

The change that the Spirit works transforms people into beings whose lives take on the shape of Christ's life. "All who are led by the Spirit of God are sons of God" (8:14), that is, "fellow heirs with Christ" (8:17). The outcome of cooperation with the Spirit's direction will be that the children of God (8:16) may choose to suffer with Christ so that they may be glorified with him: "if children, then heirs, heirs of God and fellow heirs with Christ, provided we suffer with him in order that we may be glorified with him" (8:17). The outcome of cooperation with the Spirit's direction is that people live "in Christ" in a manner that fits such a location.

While there are changes that Paul admits cannot and will not take place in the present state of affairs because this is the time before Christ's return, there are remarkable transformations which the Spirit creates now. Those who are "in Christ" and consequently "in the Spirit" must wait for the completion of their adoption as children, which is the liberation of their bodies (8:23).[22] Nevertheless, they can also know the firstfruits of that full flowering in the present. Though they must wait to share the same experience Christ now knows, that is, being raised from the dead, and though they live in hope that with the help of the Spirit God will "give life to [their] mortal bodies" (8:11), now they can live a transformed existence, one of life and peace (8:6).

Life and peace are available because the Spirit enables people to fulfill what Paul calls the "just requirement of the law" (8:4). The righteous requirement of the law is that humans live in harmony with the desires

---

22. "Redemption of bodies" refers, as Charles E. B. Cranfield puts it so well, to "the final resurrection of our bodies at the Parousia, our complete and final liberation" (*A Critical and Exegetical Commentary on the Epistle to the Romans* [2 vols.; ICC; Edinburgh: T&T Clark, 1975–1979], 1:419).

of God—their loving creator. When humans do so, they know what God most wishes for us—life and peace.

This new way of living is corporate; it is not solely individual. While the Spirit does liberate individuals for the new life (8:2), the evidence of that new life is not only seen individually. It is seen also, and even primarily, in community. The "just requirement of the law" is fulfilled among believers; it is "fulfilled in *us*" (8:4).

Those who are "in the Spirit," who live "according to the Spirit," know the kingdom of God. That kingdom is a way of life in Spirit-grounded communities of peace and righteousness. Paul writes that "the kingdom of God is not food and drink but righteousness and peace and joy in the Holy Spirit" (14:17) in the midst of his directions regarding how Gentile Roman believers are to behave towards their fellow believers who are Jews. Paul directs those who do not follow food laws or a particular calendar (Gentiles) not to pass judgment or despise or cause difficulties for those fellow believers who do (Jews). The kingdom of God, Paul says, is energized not by such concerns but by righteousness and peace and joy. The source of righteousness and peace and joy is the Holy Spirit.

This transformed way of living together, the onus of which is on the Gentiles who are Paul's front-row audience in Romans, is based on transformed lives. It is based on lives that are in the process of becoming holy. Paul sees the goal of his preaching to be the "sanctification" of the Gentiles (15:16). The apostle knows himself to have a commission from God to preach Jesus Christ to the Gentiles (1:5). The consequence of this preaching will be that "the Gentiles are acceptable, sanctified by the Holy Spirit" (15:16). "Sanctification" refers to progress towards a good and fine morality, towards behavior that fits with being "in Christ."[23] Paul expects and hopes that the result of his charges (the Gentiles) receiving his gospel will be the transformation of their lives. This transformation is not self-produced—it comes by means of the Spirit. The Spirit changes unholy lives into sanctified ones.

All of these Spirit-enabled changes allow people to be shaped by their place "in Christ Jesus"; they allow people to "be conformed to the image of [God's] Son" (8:29).

---

23. Otto Procksch writes, "The term [*hagiosmos*] is always distinguished from [*hagios*] and [*hagiadzein*] by the emphasis on the moral element ... if atonement is the basis of the Christian life, [*hagiasmos*] is the moral form which develops out of it and without which there can be no vision of Christ" (*TDNT* 1:113).

THE SPIRIT CHANGES THE WAY PEOPLE CONNECT TO GOD

The Spirit changes the way people connect to God. The Spirit allows for a relationship of love between humans and God. "God's love has been poured into our hearts through the Holy Spirit which has been given to us" (5:5). As mentioned earlier, the phrase "God's love" should be read as both God's love for us and our love for God. The Spirit makes possible a loving connection between God and humanity.

The relationship that the Spirit facilitates is so close that those who have received the Spirit cry out to God "Abba! Father!" This cry takes place in the Spirit. Now they can reach out to God knowing God to be a parent: "you received a spirit of adoption *in which* we cry out, 'Abba! Father!'" (8:15).

Paul points to the Spirit-enabled change in people's connection to God particularly in regard to prayer: "The Spirit helps us in our weakness; for we do not know how to pray as we ought, but the Spirit himself intercedes for us with sighs too deep for words" (8:26). Praying as "we ought" (8:26) is not praying so that God understands, for God searches people's hearts (8:27). The Spirit is not a mediator between God and humanity so that God understands people's desires and concerns; God does not need the Spirit for this. The Spirit is not a bridge between God and humanity in the sense of taking people's prayers to God in a way that God can accept. Rather, the Spirit functions to change the way people pray.

The Spirit helps believers communicate with God in the most fitting way. The Spirit does this not by making believers into puppets or giving believers particular words to say. Rather the Spirit gives "not words." The Greek translated by the phrase "sighs too deep for words" is literally "wordless groaning." The Spirit gives to pray-ers not words but urgings and concerns that connect to God's own desires and cares.

Paul uses the word "groan" earlier in the same passage when he describes the current state of affairs. He points to the fact that this time is a time of waiting and of unfinished business: "we know that the whole creation has been groaning in travail together until now; and not only the creation, but we ourselves, who have the first fruits of the Spirit groan inwardly as we wait for adoption as children, the redemption of our bodies" (8:22–23). When Paul goes on to speak of the Spirit allowing believers to groan wordlessly, he is describing the Spirit as the being who changes the prayers (and so the deepest desires) of people so that they are aligned with what is in God's time. Now is the time of groaning and waiting in eager expectation of liberation. That liberation includes the redemption of people's bodies from decay and death ("redemption of our bodies"), and the freedom of all creation from its current subjection to futility (8:20): "the creation itself will be set free from its bondage to decay and attain the glorious liberty of the children of God" (8:21). The Spirit helps believers to pray in accordance with reality as it is, and to start to desire fervently what matters most to God—the liberation of all creation.

Spirit-aided prayer allows believers to strain toward what God wants. It is prayer that transforms believers so that their prayers become "according to God," that is, in accordance with God's will. "The one who searches people's hearts knows what is the mind of the Spirit, because he intercedes for the saints according to the will of God" (8:27).

The Spirit Changes People's Self-Understanding

The Spirit not only changes who people are but who people understand themselves to be. The Spirit allows people to recognize the essence of their new identities. For those who are "in Christ Jesus" (8:1), their identity is precisely that; they are those who are "in Christ Jesus." Another way Paul describes this identity is that such people are "those who walk … according to the Spirit" (8:5), "are in the Spirit" (8:9), "are children of God, and if children, heirs, heirs of God and fellow heirs of Christ" (8:16, 17).

The Spirit enables people to know that this is who they are, so that when people experience the wonder of crying out to God as "Abba! Father!" through the Spirit, people know what this means: "it is the Spirit himself bearing witness with our spirit that we are children of God" (8:16). The Spirit does not simply change who people are, but allows people to understand who they have become. Those "in Christ Jesus" have become part of the family of God—"heirs of God and fellow heirs of Christ"—and the Spirit allows people to recognize this about themselves. This is especially significant since the identity of those "in Christ Jesus" is hidden in this present time in which all creation groans towards release: "the creation waits with eager longing for the revealing of the sons of God" (8:19). In the time of waiting, when believers' identity is hidden, the Spirit reveals to believers themselves who they are.

Conclusion

Paul, apostle to the Gentiles, thinks that awareness of the Spirit is essential for those Gentiles who are "in Christ Jesus." Paul is convinced that the

Spirit is the environment in which believers in Jesus Christ live, and Paul thinks it is critical that they be aware of this. The lives of believers take on the shape of Christ's life—that being the goal of believers' lives (8:29)—as they become aware of the presence and activity of the Spirit. The Spirit transforms people who are living "in Christ Jesus" so that their lives take on the shape of the one in whom they live.

The Spirit brings the life of Christ to life in the lives of believers. This life is not only Christ's resurrection life, which for believers will be a future event, but also a present mode of life (available because of Christ's resurrection). This present mode of life is unbounded by sin and death. This mode of life is the life of Christ—in whom God defeated the power of sin and death (8:3): "death no longer has dominion over him; the death he died he died to sin, once for all, but the life he lives he lives to God" (6:9–10).

Paul's direction to believers to live as Christ does—"so also you must consider yourselves dead to sin and alive to God in Christ Jesus" (6:11)—assumes the work of the Spirit.

It is the Spirit who brings Christ's life to life.

For Further Reading

Ellis, E. Earle. *Pauline Theology: Ministry and Society.* Grand Rapids: Eerdmans, 1989. Ellis suggests that for Paul Christian ministry is an activity of the Holy Spirit. In the context of this assertion, the second chapter of his book, Ellis explores the functions of the Spirit: baptism in the Spirit, the fruit of the Spirit, the gifts of the Spirit, and the final regeneration of the believer and of creation. A good introduction.

Fee, Gordon D. *God's Empowering Presence: The Holy Spirit in the Letters of Paul.* Peabody, Mass.: Hendrickson, 1994. The most comprehensive examination to date of references to the Spirit in Paul's letters. Every reference is identified and analyzed, including those in Ephesians and the Pastorals. The second part of this tome is synthetic, organizing the references under various categories such as the Spirit as eschatological fulfillment and the Spirit as God's personal presence.

———. *Paul, the Spirit, and the People of God.* Peabody, Mass.: Hendrickson, 1996. This is not a summary of *God's Empowering Presence* but rather an attempt to understand the heart of Paul's approach to the Spirit. Fee notices, for instance, that in what is most basic to Paul's theology the Spirit plays a leading role, and Fee ponders the significance for Paul of the Spirit signifying the return of God's personal presence among God's people. Very accessible.

Munzinger, André. *Discerning the Spirits: Theological and Ethical Hermeneutics in Paul.* Cambridge: Cambridge University Press, 2007. Munzinger provides an examination of the relationship between the human mind and the Spirit in Paul. He concludes that Paul understands the Spirit (with the cooperation of the human mind) to be capable of revolutionizing believers' understanding of self, others, God, and the world, and so of transforming their behavior.

Yates, John W. *The Spirit and Creation in Paul.* WUNT 2/251. Tübingen: Mohr Siebeck, 2008. Yates investigates the background of Paul's description of the life-giving work of the Spirit and conducts an inquiry into what Paul means by that description. In particular, is Paul referring to something that happens at conversion, or that will happen at resurrection? This is an in-depth analysis of 1 Cor 15, 2 Cor 3, and Rom 8.

GOD'S COVENANT FAITHFULNESS TO ISRAEL

E. Elizabeth Johnson

Christianity was born as a sect of Judaism and remarkably quickly—within the first few years—began to welcome non-Jews into its fellowships without expecting them to embrace the Judaism that was the church's heritage. This was both a source of its attractiveness to the outsiders who joined and a cause of internal debate as Christians who never stopped being Jews reflected on the implications of the church's including both Jews and Gentiles. How should Christian Jews who honor God's law relate to their Gentile Christian brothers and sisters? Should Gentile Christians, like their Jewish brothers and sisters, refrain from eating food "polluted by idols, ... whatever has been strangled, and from blood," as Luke thinks (Acts 15:20; cf. also Rev 2:14, 20)? Or should they consider that they may eat any food offered them, as Mark and Paul teach (Mark 7:19; Rom 14:1–12; 1 Cor 8:1–11:1)? More significantly, if God welcomes Gentiles into the church without requiring them first to become Jews, then what are we to say of God's covenantal relationship with Israel? Has God perhaps withdrawn covenant loyalty from Israel and given it to the church, as John's and Matthew's gospels suggest? Or, as Paul says, is God's faithfulness to Israel so centrally part of God's character as to require a more nuanced understanding?

Paul writes Romans to a group of house churches he does not know and has never visited (Rom 1:10; 15:22), although he greets twenty-eight friends who are among them, people he knows from somewhere else (16:3–16). He writes to introduce himself and his message to these people who largely know nothing about him, although apparently some have heard troubling rumors about his work (3:7–8). Why he writes this particular letter to these particular house churches in the capital city is not self-evident. He says, on the one hand, that he is eager to "reap some harvest" among the Romans as he has among other Gentile Christian groups (1:13), and, on the other hand, that it is his practice not to preach in churches founded by other apostles (15:18–21; cf. also 1 Cor 3:5–15). The harvest he seeks in Rome has at least partly to do with the westward movement of his mission work. Phoebe, the minister of the church at Cenchreae—a suburb of Corinth, where Paul is as he writes—carries his letter to Rome as his emissary, commissioned to set up a base of operations for him as he plans to travel to Spain (15:22–29; 16:1–2). The letter thus functions, at least in part, as the apostle's *curriculum vitae*, the credentials he lays before the Roman Christians as he asks for their support in his apostolic mission. It does not detail the full extent of his message, of course; it lays out his theology of mission in order that the Romans might join him in the spread of the gospel.

Paul consistently describes himself as apostle to the Gentiles (Rom 1:5, 13; 11:13; 15:16) and says elsewhere that he and Peter divided the mission field on ethnic terms at the direction of God (Gal 2:8). He nevertheless writes as a Jew who never relinquishes that identity. At Rom 9:4 and 11:1 he claims the designation "Israelite" rather than "Jew." "Israelite" is a theological rather than simply ethnic or cultural designation for the covenant people of God. Although he addresses his listeners explicitly as Gentiles (1:13; 11:13), his letter speaks de facto to a mixed audience of Gentile and Jewish Christians.

From the statement of his theme in 1:16–17, Paul repeatedly makes two parallel affirmations: God is utterly impartial, dealing with Jew and Gentile on precisely the same terms, and God is also abidingly faithful to Israel. The gospel is the power of salvation "to everyone who believes," without regard to ethnic identity or religious behavior, and it is also "to the Jew first" (1:16). He asserts God's impartiality five times (1:16; 2:11; 3:9, 22; 10:12) and names Jew and Gentile side-by-side nine times (1:16; 2:9–10; 3:9, 29; 9:24, 30–21; 10:12; 11:25; 15:10). Throughout the first four chapters, God judges Jews and Gentiles alike to be under the power of sin and similarly justified by faith. Specifically at 3:29–30, he asks, "Or is God the God of the Jews alone? Is he not the God of the Gentiles also? Yes, of Gentiles also, since God is one."[1] So also, throughout Romans, Paul affirms God's enduring faithfulness to Israel and reiterates the primacy of the covenant people ("to the Jew first," 1:16; 2:9–10; cf. 3:1–2; 9:4–5). This balanced tension between divine impartiality toward all and faithfulness

---

1. All translations, unless otherwise indicated, are from the NRSV.

to Israel drives not only chapters 9–11 but the entire argument of the letter to the Romans. Just as Paul begins the letter by describing the dynamic equilibrium between God's impartiality and faithfulness in the thematic statement of 1:16–17, so he returns to it in the conclusion to chapters 1–11:

> A[1] On the one hand, as regards the gospel, they [non-Christian Jews] are enemies for your [Christian Gentiles'] sake,
> B[1] but on the other hand, as regards election, they are beloved for the sake of the patriarchs and matriarchs,
> C[1] because the gifts and election of God are irrevocable.
> A[2] Just as you were once disobedient to God, but now you have received mercy because of their disobedience,
> B[2] so they are now disobedient because of your having received mercy, in order that they also might receive mercy,
> C[2] because God has shut up all to disobedience in order to have mercy on all (11:28–32, my translation).

The two C lines that interpret the A and B lines set God's faithfulness to Israel and God's impartial treatment of all side-by-side without resolving the tension. This means that God's impartiality cannot nullify God's covenant promises to Israel, and neither can God's faithfulness be construed as loyalty that can somehow be manipulated by human behavior or identity. God's mercy is just and God's justice is merciful.

Such a theological balancing act, however, is a delicate one:

> If God deals with all impartially yet remains faithful to Israel, why is the church full of Gentiles and Jews are staying away in droves? The danger is twofold: either God has ceased to keep promises to Israel and thus cannot be trusted to keep promises to the church, or God has become partial to Gentiles, since it is they who believe Paul's gospel, in which case God is neither impartial nor faithful.[2]

Paul has just brought the argument of chapter 8 to an impassioned close in 8:31–38 with a confident vow that absolutely nothing in all creation "will be able to separate us from the love of God in Christ Jesus our Lord" (8:38).

---

2. E. Elizabeth Johnson, "Divine Initiative and Human Response," in *A Critical Reader in the Theological Interpretation of Scripture* (ed. Stephen Fowl; Cambridge: Blackwell, 1997), 359.

Could it be that Jews who do not trust the faithfulness of Christ[3] have in fact separated themselves from God's love? Were that so, then Paul's parallel claims about God's impartiality and faithfulness could not be sustained. If God rejects Jews who do not trust the faithfulness of Christ, then God does not keep covenant faith with Israel; if Gentile Christians only—or primarily—are the people of God, then God is no longer impartial and has transferred loyalty from Israel to the Gentiles. Neither of these options is possible theologically for Paul.

Romans 9–11 begins and ends with the praise of God who is "above all" (9:5) and from whom, through whom, and to whom are "all things" (11:36). The whole of chapters 9–11 is structured internally by a series of three rhetorical questions, each of which is followed by further questions that develop the theme or meet potential objections:

(1) 9:6—God's word has not failed [has it?][4]
    9:14—There is no injustice with God, is there?
    9:19—Why then does God still find fault?
(2) 9:30-32—Why did Gentiles who did not pursue righteousness receive it, while Jews who pursued the law did not attain it?
    10:14-15—How are they to call upon one whom they have not believed?
    10:18—They have heard, have they not?
(3) 11:1—God has not rejected his people, has he?
    11:11—Israel has not stumbled so as to fall, has it?

Paul's first question poses his theological problem sharply. Has God's covenant promise collapsed (9:6)? Does the fact that so many Jews are not in the church mean that God cannot be trusted to stay in relationship with Israel? The answer is no. God's inclusion of Gentiles in the people of God

---

3. The phrase translated by the NRSV as "faith in Jesus Christ" at 3:26 (cf. also Gal 2:16; Phil 3:9) is more properly rendered "the faithfulness of Jesus Christ." For a helpful summary of the debate, see the essays by Richard B. Hays, "*Pistis* and Pauline Christology: What is at Stake," James D. G. Dunn, "Once More, *Pistis Christou*," and Paul J. Achtemeier, "Apropos the Faith of/in Christ: A Response to Hays and Dunn," all three in *Looking Back, Pressing On* (vol. 4 of *Pauline Theology*; ed. E. Elizabeth Johnson and David M. Hay; SBLSymS 4; Atlanta: Scholars Press, 1997), 35–92.

4.Although 9:6 is not put in the grammatical form of a question, "it is not as though" denies one possible answer to a question much like that posed in 3:3: "does their [that is, the Jews'] faithlessness nullify God's faithfulness?"

does not mean the exclusion of Jews. The historic people of God have never been defined solely by biological descent, he says, but always by God's sovereign and gracious election. Although Abraham fathered two sons, Ishmael and Isaac (see Gen 16–17), only Isaac and his descendents are called heirs of the patriarch (Rom 9:7–9). Similarly, Isaac's elder son Esau, by all conventional rights his heir, was supplanted by his younger brother Jacob (9:10–13). This is God's consistently surprising way of composing the covenant people. It is not human beings, because of what they do or who they are, who merit God's election, but God who freely elects. This is not unjust, Paul says (9:14), because God alone is in control of the world. The responsibility is "not of the one who wills nor of the one who runs but of the God who has mercy" (9:16, my translation). Even Pharaoh, Israel's worst enemy (see Exod 1–15), was but an instrument of God. The purpose of Pharaoh's hardened heart was to demonstrate God's saving power (Rom 9:17). God's call of Gentiles into the church is made on the same basis as God's earlier election of Israel. God is not unfair but is rather shockingly consistent.

Such a portrait of the deity might reduce human beings to mere pawns in a cosmic chess game—and thus relieve them of responsibility in their relationship to God—were it not for the fact that God's power is always power to save. Paul's metaphor of the potter and clay in 9:20–24, borrowed from the Prophets (Isa 29:1; 45:9; Jer 18:1–11) and reshaped by the Wisdom literature (Wis 12:12–13; 15:7; Sir 33:13), says that God's sovereign molding of human beings serves the purpose of showing God's mercy. Verses from Scripture originally applied to Israel now apply, on Paul's reading, also to Gentile Christians whom God has called in precisely the same way that God elected Israel. Those who belonged in the category of "not my people," that is, Gentiles, have become God's people, solely on the basis of God's loving mercy (9:25; cf. Hos 2:23, the passage from which Paul gets the designation "not my people").

Paul reprises the image of the runner from Rom 9:16 and expands it in 9:30–33, where he describes God's dealings with Israel and the Gentiles as a footrace. The stronger runner, Israel, faces a vastly weaker competitor, Gentiles who do not even train for the event. Astonishingly, God places an obstacle in the racetrack that trips up the favorite so that the underdog reaches the finish line first. The "stumbling block" God places in Israel's path is the gospel message of God's impartial treatment of all by means of the death and resurrection of Jesus. (The phrase the NRSV translates "whoever believes in him" in 9:30 should instead read "whoever believes in it," that is, the gospel.) In 10:1–4, Paul explains the failure of Israel to arrive at the "law of righteousness" it pursued, as well as the unexpected arrival of the Gentiles at the righteousness they did not pursue. Although genuinely zealous for God, Israel mistook the righteousness of God's law for something they did rather than something God does (10:3). When he says at 10:4 that "Christ is the end of the law so that there may be righteousness for everyone who believes," he means that the Christian message is the goal, the destination, the end toward which God's law, God's covenant with Israel, has always been directed.

As he does so often in Romans, Paul turns again to the Bible to support his argument.

> Moses writes concerning the righteousness that comes from the law, that "the person who does these things will live by them." But the righteousness that comes from faith says, "Do not say in your heart, 'Who will ascend into heaven?'" (that is, to bring Christ down) "or 'Who will descend into the abyss?'" (that is, to bring Christ up from the dead). But what does it say? "The word is near you, on your lips and in your heart" (that is, the word of faith that we proclaim); because if you confess with your lips that Jesus is Lord and believe in your heart that God raised him from the dead, you will be saved. (9:5–10)

One might get the impression from Israel's Scriptures that the one who should "do these things" is the person reading the Scriptures, that is, a human being. On the contrary, however, it is God who "ascend[s] into heaven" and "descend[s] into the abyss" by sending Christ and raising him from the dead. It is God alone who is righteous and who makes righteous all who trust God's righteousness. That is the reason the preaching of the gospel is so urgently needed and the reason Paul needs the Romans' help to go to Spain. He says, "I no longer have any room for work in these regions" (15:23 RSV), not because he has preached to every single person in the eastern provinces of the empire, but because he has successfully established churches that accomplish that work. What he tells the Thessalonian Christians, for example, is not hyperbolic: "For the word of the Lord has sounded forth from you not only in Macedonia and Achaia, but in every place your faith in God has become known, so that we have no need to speak about it" (1 Thess 1:8). So in Rom 10:14–21, he explains that the Christian mission is indeed going into the world and God has determined that the Gentiles' response will make Israel "jealous" of that response (10:19), even while God reaches out continually to the covenant people (10:21, quoting Isa 65:2).

Chapter 11 opens with the most pointed question so far. If God has deliberately held Israel back from responding to the gospel so as to allow the Gentiles to believe and thus to provoke Jews to jealousy, does that mean that God has rejected Israel? The answer is an emphatic "By no means!" His first response is to point to himself, "an Israelite, a descendant of Abraham, a member of the tribe of Benjamin" (11:2; cf. Phil 3:5), and he proceeds to describe his ministry in terms reminiscent of the prophet Elijah's. Just as Elijah pleaded with God on the people's behalf, so does Paul, and he too receives the assurance that God unfailingly preserves a "remnant according to the election of grace" (11:5, my translation). In Rom 11:4 Paul adds and changes words from the verse he quotes from 1 Kgs 19:18 to underscore God's preservation of the people rather than either the prophet's—or the apostle's—work or the people's faithfulness: "I *have kept for myself* seven thousand who have not bowed the knee to Baal." First Kings 19:18 reads, "Yet *I will leave* seven thousand in Israel, all the knees that have not bowed to Baal." Paul has added "for myself" and changed the time of God's action from the future to the present in his interpretation to say again that God is the lead actor in this drama and may be trusted to bring it to a just conclusion.

The remnant of Israel are those Jewish Christians who in Paul's day stand as proof that God's covenant faithfulness to Israel is intact. They are not sufficient to prove his point, however. He goes further to say that the current hardening of part of Israel (which recalls God's hardening of Pharaoh in Rom 9:17–18) serves a redemptive purpose. The fact that some Jews do not yet accept the Christian message means salvation for the Gentiles and "riches for the world" (11:12). Their "full inclusion" (11:12), which foreshadows what Paul will say in 11:25–27, will mean nothing less than "life from the dead" (11:15). This is why Paul is an apostle: "he is devoting his energies to Gentiles because, like God, he has not given up on Israel."[5]

A widely shared tradition among Jews of Paul's day contends that, at the moment Israel becomes truly faithful to God, the new age will be inaugurated, bringing with it God's judgment and salvation of the whole world. Were the "word of faith" that Paul and the other apostles preach (10:8) to reach Israel alone, the non-Jewish world would be left out of God's redemption. Because God is the God of the whole world, though, and not of Israel alone (3:29–30), this cannot be. So God engages in this mysteri-

---

5. Leander E. Keck, *Romans* (ANTC; Nashville: Abingdon, 2005), 271.

ous process of alternating between giving attention to Jews and then giving attention to Gentiles that Paul has been discussing. The gospel is indeed "to the Jew first," because, after all, the Scriptures that bear witness to that gospel are granted first to Israel (3:2), and the Messiah himself comes from Israel (9:5; 11:26). It is nevertheless to be preached in the entire world, to Gentiles as well as Jews. Gentile Christians are the current beneficiaries, but Israel too will finally share in God's redemption.

To warn against his Gentile listeners' being or becoming contemptuous of Jews who are outside the church, Paul employs yet another metaphor, this one agricultural, to describe the same back-and-forth dynamic of God's dealings with Israel that the footrace image portrayed in 9:30–33. Israel is a cultivated tree, another image familiar from the Bible (Ps 1:3; Jer 11:16–17; cf. Isa 5:1–7, where the picture is of a vineyard). Branches from a wild olive tree—the Gentiles—have been grafted onto this cultivated olive tree that is Israel, which means that, against all odds and contrary to nature (11:24), they share in the riches of Israel's heritage, God's promised redemption. Although some of the original branches have been broken off (Jews who do not accept the gospel), God has the power to graft them back in, just as the wild branches have been included.

Finally, Paul makes explicit the conviction that has guided his argument since Rom 9:6. It was revealed to him by God as a "mystery" (11:25), he says, not a puzzle to be solved with clues, but a heavenly disclosure of divine wisdom.

> So that you may not claim to be wiser than you are, brothers and sisters,
> I want you to understand this mystery: a hardening has come upon part
> of Israel, until the full number of the Gentiles has come in. And so all
> Israel will be saved; as it is written, "Out of Zion will come the Deliverer;
> he will banish ungodliness from Jacob." "And this is my covenant with
> them, when I take away their sins." (11:25–27)

The clause "and so all Israel will be saved" is better translated "and in this way all Israel will be saved," because Paul is describing the historical movement he has been describing for three chapters. God's hardening of some Jews, or causing them to stumble over the gospel, allows the Gentiles to hear the message and to respond. It is not clear what the "full number of the Gentiles" means, nor what Paul thinks will happen when they arrive. Does he envision that Jews will see that Gentile Christians experience the Spirit of God in worship, or perhaps does he anticipate their reaction to the Gentiles' being welcomed symbolically by the Jerusalem church when he delivers the collection he is taking there? He does not say. He is certain, though, that when the Gentile mission is complete, according to God's plan, "all Israel" will be caught up into the redemption God has initiated in the death and resurrection of Jesus Christ. Christian response to Jewish unbelief is therefore not more ardent proselytizing of Jews but rather concentration on the Gentile mission.

Paul draws this section of his letter to a close by quoting a hymn that he draws from the worship life of the synagogue.

> O the depth of the riches and wisdom and knowledge of God!
>   How unsearchable are his judgments and how inscrutable his ways!
>   "For who has known the mind of the Lord? Or who has been his counselor?"
>   "Or who has given a gift to him, to receive a gift in return?"
>   For from him and through him and to him are all things.
> To him be the glory forever. Amen. (Rom 11:33–36)

The hymn praises God's wise—if inscrutable—plan to save the world with words quoted from Isa 40:13 and Job 41:11 and expresses his confidence that all things are in God's hands. The theological problem of Jewish resistance to the Christian message is finally God's to solve and Paul is confident that God can be trusted.

Since the first century, the church has often been less confident than Paul that God's faithfulness to Israel is "irrevocable" (Rom 11:29). Other New Testament voices—notably those of Matthew, John, and Hebrews—have frequently spoken more loudly than Paul's.[6] Particularly when Christians began to outnumber Jews around the Mediterranean, perhaps in the third or fourth century, they began to interpret the refusal of their Jewish neighbors to become Christians as evidence that God had instead transferred faithfulness to themselves and to approve and eventually participate in increasingly vile persecution of Jews. Some contemporary theologians have suggested, in the sobering decades since the Holocaust, that Christians ought to consider God's covenant with Israel to be untouched by the death and resurrection of Jesus, that is, that God's promises to Abraham and Moses abide for Jews and that Christians may trust God's independent

---

6. E. Elizabeth Johnson, "Jews and Christians in the New Testament: John, Matthew, and Paul," *RefR* 42 (1988–1989): 113–28.

promises to the church. Paul would find such a solution highly unacceptable because it excludes Christians from their God-given identity as Israel and it deprives Israel of its own Messiah. This is precisely the arrogance he condemns in Rom 11:17–20, if perhaps softened by a separate-but-equal attitude, condescending though that is. Paul's argument in Rom 9–11 can be helpful in addressing the sibling rivalry that has historically characterized relationships between Christians and Jews precisely because he focuses his attention on the character of God's righteousness that is constituted by both God's impartiality and God's faithfulness to Israel.

For Further Reading

Bartlett, David L. *Romans*. Louisville: Westminster John Knox, 1995. A wise and perceptive reading of the letter that is very accessible to nonspecialists.

Bassler, Jouette M. *Navigating Paul: An Introduction to Key Theological Concepts*. Louisville: Westminster John Knox, 2007. Designed to orient the beginning reader to Paul's ways of thinking about the God of Israel, the gospel of Jesus Christ, and Christian life.

Grieb, A. Katherine. *The Story of Romans: A Narrative Defense of God's Righteousness*. Louisville: Westminster John Knox, 2002. A reading of the letter that makes significant scholarship on Romans available to nonscholars.

Johnson, E. Elizabeth. "Jews and Christians in the New Testament: John, Matthew, and Paul." *RefR* 42 (1988–1989): 113–28. A comparison of three New Testament writers' understandings of God's relationships with the church and non-Christian Jews.

Keck, Leander E. *Romans*. ANTC. Nashville: Abingdon, 2005. Perhaps the best commentary on Romans in English, based on the Greek text, but with sufficient explanation that non-Greek readers can easily profit from it.

Meeks, Wayne A. "On Trusting an Unpredictable God." Pages 103–24 in *Faith and History: Essays in Honor of Paul W. Meyer*. Edited by John T. Carroll, Charles H. Cosgrove, and E. Elizabeth Johnson. Eugene, Oreg.:

Wipf & Stock, 2004. A reflection on Rom 9–11 from a major scholar that considers both exegetical and theological aspects of Paul's argument.

Meyer, Paul W. "Romans." Pages 1038–73 in *The HarperCollins Bible Commentary*. Edited by James L. Mays et al. Rev. ed. San Francisco: HarperSanFrancisco, 2000. A brief commentary on the letter that makes significant observations about its theological content.

"A Light to the Nations":
The Role of Israel in Romans 9–11

Caroline Johnson Hodge

It used to be fairly standard to consider Rom 9–11 as ancillary to Paul's main arguments, which were laid out in Rom 1–8. These first eight chapters were thought to articulate the central points of Paul's theology: in the search for salvation, justification by faith trumps the keeping of the law. The contents of Rom 9–11—including Paul's emotional declarations, his scolding of Jews for their lack of belief, and his seemingly contradictory claims about Israel's continued privileges—were often neglected because they were considered difficult to understand and incongruent with traditional readings of Paul. This began to change with the publication of Krister Stendahl's now classic essay, "The Apostle Paul and the Introspective Conscience of the West."[1] Stendahl and those who followed him called attention to the importance of Rom 9–11 and argued that these chapters constitute not just key arguments, but the very climax of the letter.

One of the reasons that Stendahl held this view of Rom 9–11 is that he interpreted Paul differently from many others. He argued two important points that became the foundations of the "new perspective" on Paul, and more specifically the "radical" new perspective: (1) Paul writes exclusively to Gentiles, or non-Jews, in his letters, and (2) Paul does not intend to replace or even reform Israel in a fundamental way. These points encourage us to reorient Paul in our thinking, and to imagine him not as a Christian loyal to the church (which does not yet exist), but as a Jew faithful to Israel.

---

1. Krister Stendahl, "The Apostle Paul and the Introspective Conscience of the West," *HTR* 56 (1963): 199–215.

My interpretation of Paul has been shaped by this perspective. Therefore, I see Romans not as a letter written to all people about how to be saved but as a letter to Gentile believers on how they have been made right with God and, specifically in chapters 9–11, how they fit in with God's larger plan for the salvation of Israel. Beginning with his call, which he describes in Gal 1, Paul understands himself as apostle to the Gentiles. The major theological problem to which he responds is that Gentiles have a broken relationship with the God of Israel. Baptism into Christ is the solution to this problem, the means of linking Gentiles to Israel. As Paul describes in Rom 4 and 8, as well as in Gal 3 and 4, , Gentiles are adopted into the larger family of Israel, made into "sons" (Gal 4:7) or "children" (Rom 8:16) of Abraham through baptism into Christ. This new birth creates a kinship where there was none before, a new relationship sanctioned by God, a merciful solution to the Gentile problem.

In Rom 9–11, Paul maps out the salvation histories of Jews and baptized Gentiles, distinct ethnic peoples who are now linked by their loyalty to the God of Israel. Paul understands that Christ's death and resurrection signal the coming of God's judgment of the world and the time for the ingathering of nations, as foretold in the prophets. The time has come for Israel to fulfill its role as "a light to the nations."[2] Through scripture, footrace imagery, and agricultural metaphors, Paul reiterates several points in these chapters: Gentiles have been included through Christ; many in Israel have not recognized this as God's plan; and this lack of understanding was planned by God in the first place. The tension created between these two peoples propels them both toward this salvation. The larger goal is not the creation of the church or Christianity, but the salvation of Israel.

AUDIENCE: TO WHOM DOES PAUL WRITE?

Reading Paul's letters as constructed for Gentiles alone goes against most scholarship on Paul, which assumes that Paul writes to Jews and non-Jews alike, to all people, and his advice can therefore be applied to humanity in general. Is Paul calling for *all people* to be baptized into Christ and not keep the law? Or is he offering ethnically-specific advice, aimed at *Gentiles* who think they can be made right with God through the law?

---

2. See Isa 2:2–4 and Zech 8:21–23. Pamela Eisenbaum discusses this theme in *Paul Was Not a Christian: The Original Message of a Misunderstood Apostle* (New York: HarperOne, 2009), 96–98, 250–55.

Everyone agrees that Paul is writing to Gentiles; he addresses them explicitly in several places, including once in chapters 9–11 (Rom 1:5–6, 13; 11:13; 15:6). Furthermore he sees himself as called to the Gentiles (Rom 11:13; 15:1–6). So there is a consensus on this point: Paul tells us he is writing to Gentiles and scholars generally accept this to be the case. Many scholars think, however, that Paul is also addressing Jews, even though he does not indicate this. They argue that Jews were in the communities to which he wrote and he knew that. Or they argue that Paul talks about Jewish law, uses Jewish Scripture or terminology, so he must have been writing to those who would understand these cultural references.[3]

I think it is possible for Jews to have been in the historical audience, and for Paul to have used references to Scripture, and still to understand Paul's arguments aimed solely at Gentiles. Indeed there are Jews among the believers in Rome, as is clear from Rom 16 where Paul greets some of them, but this does not mean he is necessarily addressing them. And he often uses Scripture and discusses the law, but this makes perfect sense in a missive to people who have pledged loyalty to the God of Israel. Paul even talks *about* Jews, especially in Rom 9–11, but not *to* Jews.

Why does it matter to whom Paul writes? It matters because how we understand the audience radically changes how we read Paul. If his audience is both Gentiles and Jews, then Paul's advice is aimed at all people, Jews and non-Jews (which then can be extrapolated to include humanity in general). This means that his critique of the law applies to all, including Jews, which implies that he can be read as replacing, or at least reforming, Judaism with Christianity. According to Paul, all humanity is broken and all need Christ. An audience of both Gentiles and Jews makes this traditional reading possible.

If his audience includes Gentiles only, then the reading changes. If Paul's advice is aimed at this specific group, then his critique of the law pertains to *Gentile* use of Jewish law, and Paul argues that keeping the law the way Jews do is not right for Gentiles. Gentiles, who by definition have no covenants, no relationship with the God of Israel, are in desperate need of help, and Paul argues that it is baptism into Christ, and not law-keeping, that will make them right with God. Paul has in mind the other Jewish

---

3. For more detailed discussion of audience, see Stanley K. Stowers, *Rereading of Romans: Justice, Jews, and Gentiles* (New Haven: Yale University Press, 1994), 21–33; Caroline Johnson Hodge, *If Sons, Then Heirs* (New York: Oxford University Press, 2007), 6–9.

teachers of Gentiles who teach a different gospel, teachers who insist on circumcision and other Jewish practices for Gentiles-in-Christ, and he argues vehemently against this approach (Rom 2:17–2:29). Paul's task is not to fix Jews, but to fix Gentiles. The good news that he proclaims is not that humanity is sinful and needs redemption, but that the God of Israel has mercifully made room for Gentiles through Christ. Christ makes it possible for Israel to be a "light to the nations," a crucial step in the restoration of Israel.

I agree with those who insist on taking Paul at his word that he writes to Gentile believers, according to his call. Regardless of the makeup of the community of believers in Rome in the first century, which may well have been a mix of Jews and Gentiles, the audience Paul constructs in the letter itself is a Gentile one.

Importance of Ethnicity

As the above discussion of audience hints, ethnic identity is crucial to Paul's thinking. Indeed, ethnicity and theology are inseparable in Romans because Paul understands the relationship between humans and the divine explicitly in terms of kinship and ethnicity. As we will see, one's ethnic identity, according to Paul, is determined by one's relationship to the God of Israel.

Many agree that Paul preaches a universalizing gospel, yet there are different ways to understand this universalism and the role of ethnic identity within it. Some resist the idea that ethnicity matters to Paul. They see Paul's universalizing message as erasing ethnic differences: all are welcome in Christ. Another way to see his universalism is precisely in terms of ethnic particularity: he argues that God includes multiple ethnic groups, not just Jews. This kind of universalizing does not erase specific identities but includes them within the larger network of God's people.

Let us look at Paul's language. Like other Jews in his time, Paul thinks of the world's peoples in terms of "us" (Jews) and "them" (non-Jews or Gentiles). Jews are those loyal to the God of Israel: they descend from the same founding ancestors, they keep God's sacred laws, and they are the recipients of the covenants and promises (Paul lists these blessings in Rom 9:4–5). Gentiles (or "nations," "peoples"), by contrast, are all those who are not loyal to the God of Israel: they worship other gods and are unable to control their passions (Rom 1:18–26; 1 Thess 4:4–5; 1 Cor 6:9–11).

The urgent theological problem for Paul is that Gentiles are not in good standing with the God of Israel. Paul describes this situation in Rom 1:18–26, where he details the fate of those who rejected or did not recognize God: God turned them over to their passions and idols. Without God, these people are stuck in their idolatry and immoral behavior. These characteristics define them as Gentiles, and they will not survive God's judgment when the time comes (which is soon, according to Paul, as signaled by Christ's life, death, and resurrection). For Paul, as for his contemporaries, ethnic identity and status before God are inextricable.

If the theological problem is defined in terms of ethnicity, so also is the solution: baptism into Christ. In Rom 4 (and Gal 3), Paul presents baptism as a ritual of adoption that creates new kinship ties. Through Christ, the baptized become descendants of Abraham (which Jews already are) and therefore recipients of the promises foretold in Scripture. With this new heritage, they take on many of the characteristics of Jews: loyalty to the God of Israel, descent from the founding ancestors of Israel, the ability to live moral lives. A shift has taken place in their identity; they have not become Jews, but they are no longer the same Gentiles they once were. They are now "in Christ," which is not ethnically neutral, but a category that connects them to Israel. They are now eligible for salvation when Christ returns. Thus, instead of being sidelined or downplayed, ethnic categories define the parameters of Paul's mission.

A Note on Salvation

Often the Bible is read by Christians today as a way to understand the answer to the question: "How can I be saved?" Many Christians imagine a kind of personal salvation, God's response to the inevitable moral flaw in all humans. It is extremely difficult not to import these modern notions into these first-century letters. But Paul had something else in mind. As an apocalyptic Jew, he believed that the God of Israel had plans to set the world right, to vanquish Israel's enemies and to bring the nations, or non-Jews, into God's fold. Thus for Paul, salvation refers—at least in part—to surviving the destruction of the evil age, which requires being made right with God beforehand.[4] Paul's urgency in his mission work stems from his

---

4. This notion is reflected in the basic meanings of the Greek term Paul uses for salvation, *sōtēria*, which comes from the verb *sōzō*, meaning "to save from death," "to rescue," "to preserve."

belief that this plan was already set in motion, signaled by Christ's life, death, and resurrection, the firstfruits of a larger renewal. Thus when Paul speaks of salvation, or being saved, he has these events in mind.

For apocalyptic Jews like Paul, who expected the Messiah to defeat Israel's enemies and usher in a new age, Jesus' life and death is unexpected. Jesus' story certainly does not sound like that of Israel's Messiah. As we will see in Rom 9–11, Paul acknowledges this discrepancy between expectations and what God has done and understands himself as one of a few who understand God's larger plan. It is helpful to think of Paul's version of God's plan for salvation in two stages: phase 1, which is Christ's life, death, and resurrection (for Gentiles); and phase 1, which is Christ's return as the Messiah (for all of Israel and for baptized Gentiles). As Christianity developed over the decades after Paul, and Christians faced the reality of living in this world in the long term, more emphasis was placed on the salvific power of phase 1, Christ's death and resurrection. Paul, however, seems to associate salvation more with phase 2, when Christ returns (see Rom 5:9–10). Phase 1 is indeed an unexpected and merciful act on the part of God, a pause in the flow of salvation history, so that the Gentiles have a chance to come in. According to Paul, baptism into Christ makes them eligible for salvation, which they were not before. Paul's own mission exists in the interim between the two, and he awaits phase 2 eagerly.

ROMANS 9–11: STEPS IN THE ARGUMENT

As we shall see as we look more closely at Rom 9–11, Paul's understanding of God's plan for salvation is not so easy to explain. In these chapters, Paul tries to work out for his Gentile audience how they fit in to God's larger plan for Israel. This task is made particularly tricky by the fact that many members of Israel do not share Paul's view, which saddens him. The contrast with chapter 8 is striking: one moment Paul's language uplifts and inspires as he describes the Gentiles' new life in the Spirit; the next moment he is despondent, saying, "I have great sorrow and unceasing anguish in my heart" (Rom 9:2).[5] Paul's goal in the next three chapters is to account for most of Israel's failure to understand who Christ is and how he fits into God's plan for salvation of both Jews and Gentiles. In a rather laborious manner, Paul presents the following argument: Israel's inability to recog-

---

5. Translations here and throughout are my own in consultation with the NRSV.

nize God's righteousness (that is, God's plan to put the world right) is actually planned by God, foretold in Scripture, and is crucial not only to the salvation of the Gentiles but also to the salvation of Israel itself. Because this is the larger goal, and because Gentiles-in-Christ are dependent upon Israel, they should recognize their subordinate position.

Salvation of both peoples, Paul argues, depends upon the distinct ethnic identities of Jews and faithful Gentiles. The tension between these two groups, which perhaps Paul witnessed in his work as a missionary, propels both toward salvation. In what follows we will look at the steps of Paul's argument, highlighting his main points and always keeping in mind that he is speaking to Gentiles.

Blessings of Israel (9:4–5)

Immediately following Paul's confession of sorrow in 9:2 and his own heartfelt wish to sacrifice even his tie to Christ for his people in 9:3, he lists the many blessings of the Jews: "For they are Israelites, to whom belong the adoption as sons and the glory and the covenants and the lawgiving and the cult worship and the promises, to whom belong the fathers and out of whom Christ was born" (Rom 9:4–5). This list highlights the asymmetry between Jews and Gentiles: not only do Jews already have kinship and covenants with God, but they are the source of the Messiah. This asymmetry makes more difficult the situation he is about to explain, that the Gentiles have been made right with God out of faithfulness and Israel has not (9:30–31). This simultaneous expression of his affection for Israel and his sadness at this turn of events launches Paul's explanation of how God is orchestrating the larger drama of salvation.

Chosen Lineages (9:6–16)

In order to begin explaining how it is that the word of God has not failed (9:6), Paul turns to scripture, to stories of the chosen ancestors Isaac and Jacob. In the story of Isaac told in Genesis, which Paul cites in 9:7, God makes clear to Abraham that his descendants will come from Isaac, not from Ishmael. One son is chosen over the other. Likewise, God chooses Jacob over his twin brother, Esau (9:11–13). Descent from Abraham, it turns out, is not determined solely by human biological relationship ("flesh" is the word Paul uses) but by the promise of God (9:7–13). This promise can include manipulating biological relationships, creating descendants when there are none, or privileging certain descendants over others. In turn, this promise is not based on the particular characteristics of one son, but simply on God's choice. Paul clarifies that this is the work of a just and merciful God (9:14–15) and declares that election "depends not on human will or exertion, but on God who shows mercy" (9:16). This mercy may even include "hardening the hearts" of some (9:18), a hint as to why Paul is so sorrowful.

These examples from Israel's history help Paul explain two things: (1) why alien peoples, the Gentiles, are now adopted by the God of Israel, and (2) why some members of Israel do not accept Paul's gospel and do not understand Christ's role for the Gentiles. These stories of the patriarchs and matriarchs set up his argument in 9:16–29, which is that God has a larger, merciful plan, and different groups play different roles in it, according to God's will. So it is not human actions that earn status, nor is it typical biological relationship. Instead, God maintains these relationships through gifts of the promise and the Spirit according to his will.[6] Paul cites Hosea to illustrate this pattern:

> As it says in Hosea: "I will call those who are not my people 'my people' and the one not loved, 'loved.' And it will be in the place where it was said to them, 'You are not my people.' There the sons of the living God will be called." (Rom 9:25–26; citing LXX Hos 1:10)

Furthermore, antagonists—like Pharaoh, like those Israelites who turn against God—are all a part of God's ultimate plan to call new people to him.

RACE TO THE FINISH LINE (9:30–10:4; 11:11–15)

In 9:30, Paul finally describes the tragedy to which he first alluded in 9:2. The reason for his sorrow, the reason for his discussion of chosen lineages and God's mercy and judgment, the reason for his recollection of biblical accounts of God's judgment against Israel, is that it appears that the Gentiles have beaten Israel to the goal:

---

6. Although I would not otherwise use gendered pronouns for God, I do so in this discussion of Paul's views both to stay close to his language (and conception of God) and for grammatical ease.

What then are we to say? Gentiles, who did not pursue righteousness have attained it, that is, righteousness that comes from faithfulness; but Israel, who did pursue the law of righteousness, did not arrive first at the law? Why not? Because they did not strive for it out of faithfulness, but instead out of works. They have stumbled over the stumbling stone. (Rom 9:30–32)

The basic idea of this passage, which is notoriously tricky to translate (see commentaries for a detailed discussion of the issues involved), is that Paul proposes the impossible: Gentiles have the upper hand over Israel. He makes this proposition using agonistic imagery, alluding to a footrace between two competitors. Both Jews and Gentiles pursue a goal, and one takes the lead while the other stumbles. As Paul will explain, the tension created by the competition is necessary to the larger process.

Two important terms in this passage are "righteousness" and "faithfulness." The goal of both peoples is "righteousness," a term which Paul uses for at least two related concepts: being reconciled (or being "made right") with God (from the perspective of those who need reconciliation), and God's overall plan to reconcile the world (to make things right). Paul argues that Gentiles, who by definition are alienated from God, have been offered reconciliation out of faithfulness, even though they did not seek it.

The concept of "faithfulness" (or "faith," as some translate the Greek word *pistis*) is pivotal in Paul's overall understanding of how Gentiles are included in God's people.[7] In 9:30–32, faithfulness is instrumental to the process of being made right with God. Those who seek righteousness "based on faithfulness" succeed; those who fail to do this do not succeed. What does Paul mean by "faithfulness" here? The traditional answer is that Paul is talking about a believer's faith in Christ (as opposed to works of the law), which is the key to being made right with God both for Gentiles and Israel. In my view, this underestimates what Paul means here. In these verses, where righteousness depends upon faithfulness (indeed, Paul speaks of faithfulness as source or foundation for righteousness), *pistis* refers to the initiatives and actions of God, Christ, and Abraham more than those of believers in Christ.

---

7. I think "faithfulness," "loyalty," or "steadfastness" are better translations of *pistis* than "faith" or "belief" because these nouns imply a commitment that is manifest in actions, not just an interior state. For more discussion, see my *If Sons*, 82–84.

Paul spends the most time discussing *pistis* in Rom 4, where he develops a multi-layered concept of the term "faithfulness." He begins with Abraham, who "was faithful to God and it was reckoned to him as righteousness" (Rom 4:3; Gen 15:6). At this moment of calling, it is not just Abraham who is claimed by God but a whole people who are born of this relationship, as God promises Abraham an heir and many descendants. *Pistis* is thus Paul's shorthand for his understanding of how God works in the world, by calling whole peoples to him through faithful ancestors. Paul uses Abraham to illustrate how this works and to offer a model for understanding Christ: his faithful obedience to God resulted in his death and resurrection and extended God's blessings to the Gentiles. Abraham's and Christ's generative faithfulness is a product of the "faithfulness of God" (Rom 3:3) who calls peoples to be his own. Finally, Paul adds that Gentile believers, too, are called to respond with faithfulness to God for all he has done through Christ (Rom 4:23–25).

While the faithfulness of believers is certainly important, it is the faithfulness of Abraham and Christ—and of course of God in the first place—that establishes relationships between humans and God. This is the principle on which righteousness depends in Rom 9:30–32, as opposed to works or biological relationship or anything else that humans can control.

The problem seems to be, as Paul explains in 9:31–32, that Israel has not understood this principle. The issue is not the goal, "the law of righteousness," but in how it was pursued, "out of works" instead of "based on faithfulness." He further comments on this mistake in 10:3: "For being ignorant of God's righteousness and seeking to establish their own, they have not submitted to the righteousness of God." Paul blames them not for their lack of commitment to God ("they have a zeal for God") but for their inability to perceive the situation correctly (they are "unenlightened" and "ignorant").

What exactly do they misunderstand? We can imagine how Paul may have been trying to make sense of the fact that most Jews around him do not interpret Christ's death the way he does; they do not see Christ as God's Messiah who, although put to death by the Romans, would soon return to vanquish Israel's enemies. They do not understand how God plans to set the world right; they do not recognize the power of Christ's faithfulness, for Gentiles (in phase 1) and then for all of Israel (in phase 2).

Another more specific explanation emerges when we notice the many connections between these passages and the discussion with the fictive Jewish teacher in 2:17–3:9. Using speech-in-character, a common rhetorical device in diatribe, Paul stages an argument with a character of a rival Jewish teacher of Gentiles. This interlocutor teaches that in order to be made right with God, Gentiles need to keep the law. Paul proves him wrong, of course, and the argument serves to show his Gentile audience that righteousness comes from faithfulness, from God's mercy, and not from law-keeping. The Jewish teacher misunderstands how God works.[8] In chapters 9–10, Paul levels these same critiques at Israel. Perhaps he has those in mind who insist that Gentiles, upon their baptism into Christ, need to keep the law as Jews do. This fundamental disagreement over Gentiles and the law is a central theme for Paul and could explain what Paul means when he says Israel pursued righteousness "out of works."

Whether the stumbling is a misunderstanding of who Christ is on the part of many in Israel, or a mistaken insistence that Gentiles keep the law on the part of believing Jewish teachers, or some combination, is difficult to tell. While the mistake upsets Paul, he places it within the larger context of the history of Israel, in which the people have turned away from or misunderstood God's call before. Furthermore, he knows that this current "stumbling" is all part of God's larger plan. Indeed, it was God who put the "stumbling stone" in Israel's path (9:32b–33). This stumbling, this failure to understand and submit to God's plan to make the world right, turns out to be a necessary part of the unfolding of salvation for all peoples.

What Israel does not understand, Paul explains in 10:4: "For Christ is the goal (*telos*) of the law with respect to righteousness for all who are faithful." *Telos* is a term that can mean a variety of related things: end, goal, finish line, termination. Traditionally, *telos* in 10:4 has been translated as "termination"; Christ brings an end to the law. This interpretation makes little sense in light of Paul's own commitment to the law (Rom 3:31; 7:12). Christ and the law are not in opposition to each other—you choose one or the other—but Christ fulfills what was promised in Scripture or Torah. Therefore, "goal" or even "finish line" is a better translation of *telos*, especially in light of the footrace imagery at work in this passage.

Paul returns to the footrace metaphor in chapter 11 to explain in further detail that Israel has only stumbled, not fallen, and only temporarily so:

Therefore I say, "surely they did not stumble so as to fall?" No indeed. But by their misstep salvation came to the Gentiles with the purpose of

---

8. See Stowers, *Rereading*, 143–58, 286.

> making [Israel] jealous. If their stumbling offers riches for the world and
> their failure offers riches for the Gentiles, how much more will their own
> fulfillment offer? (Rom 11:11–12)

Here we begin to see the outline of a larger, complex plan that depends on competition between Israel and the Gentiles. The Gentiles, who entered the race late (with their baptism into Christ), are spurred on by Israel's stumbling. This Gentile gain in turn makes Israel jealous and thus inspires them to push on harder toward the goal. And of course the whole thing was arranged by God in the first place, whose aim was to reconcile the world, including not only Israel but also faithful Gentiles. As Paul explicitly reminds the Gentiles in 11:13–14, the whole point of his ministry to them was to contribute to this larger plan. They would do well to remember that they are not at the center of the plan but only a part of it.

Remnant (9:27–29; 11:1–6)

Interspersed between footrace passages, Paul turns to Scripture to explain the situation. Within the context of Jewish history, the idea of protagonists and antagonists acting for and against God's will is a familiar one. And, as Paul argues, God always supplies a "remnant" who will remain faithful to God and who will ensure the salvation of all of Israel. Two times Paul evokes a remnant theology in these chapters, Rom 9:27–29 and 11:1–6, and these examples are crucial for how Paul wants the Gentiles in Rome to understand what is currently happening.

Thus before Paul explains the competition between Gentiles and Israel, he recalls Isaiah in Rom 9:27: "And Isaiah cries out on behalf of Israel: 'Though the number of the sons of Israel were like the sand of the sea, a remnant of them will be saved.'" And again in Rom 11:2–3, in order to reiterate that Israel's stumbling is temporary and intended for the good of the larger whole, Paul cites the story of Elijah, who stands alone in his faithfulness to God. Paul reminds his audience that God secured a remnant then as well, "seven thousand who have not bowed the knee to Baal" (Rom 11:4, citing LXX 3 Kgdms 19:18 = 1 Kgs 19:18 in NRSV). God always has a plan to deliver Israel, even when Israelites have turned away. These remnant passages thus contextualize this particular moment of tension described in 9:30–10:4; it is a part of a long history in which, from time to time, numbers of Israelites turn away from God, leaving only a few who remain loyal. These remaining few, these remnants, speak God's truth, call those who stray back to God, and thus maintain Israel's status before God. And of course these passages also bolster Paul's own status as they imply that he is the remnant, the one who truly understands God's purposes for Israel and for Gentiles.

BRANCHES OF A TREE (11:17–24)

In 11:13, Paul mentions his audience explicitly, as though reminding them (and it should remind us as well!) that although he writes to them, they play only a supporting role in the divine drama taking place.[9] To show them where they stand, Paul uses an agricultural image to illustrate the relationship he envisions among Jews, Gentiles, and God. He has just explained how God's plan for reconciliation of the world has placed Gentiles, at least temporarily, ahead of Jews. He immediately warns, however, that they are not to think too highly of themselves. He compares them to a "wild olive shoot" that has been grafted onto a larger olive tree:

> If you boast remember that you do not support the root but the root supports you. Therefore you will say, "The branches have been broken off so that I might be grafted on." True. They have been broken off by unfaithfulness, but you have stood by means of faithfulness. Do not consider high things, but be afraid. For if God did not spare the natural branches, he will in no way spare you. See the kindness and severity of God: severity upon those who have fallen, but the kindness of God upon you. Unless you remain in his kindness, you will be cut off. Also those people, if they do not remain in unfaithfulness, they will be grafted on. For God is able to graft them on again. For if you are cut off from an olive tree which is wild by nature, and, beyond the bounds of nature,

---

9. Some have interpreted Rom 11:13 as Paul turning from one epistolary audience (either the whole audience or the Jewish members of the audience) to Gentiles at this point. The NRSV translation seems to be influenced by this reading, initiating a new paragraph with v. 13 and translating it: "Now I am speaking to you Gentiles." As Stanley Stowers has shown (*Rereading*, 287–89), this interpretation does not adequately translate the Greek, which indicates that the contents of vv. 11–14 belong together as three connected ideas and that the sense of vv. 13–14 is, "'Yes, I am addressing you Gentiles in this letter but you should understand that my very ministry to the Gentiles has direct relevance to the salvation of my fellow Jews and their salvation to your own'" (Stowers, *Rereading*, 228). This makes sense given that Paul is turning at this point in the letter to correct any haughtiness on the part of the Gentiles.

you are grafted onto a cultivated tree, how much more will these natural branches be grafted onto their own olive tree. (Rom 11:18b–24)

In this agricultural image, Paul compares baptized Gentiles to grafted plants. Their baptism is an adoption, in which they join the lineage of Abraham. Thus they are like shoots of a wild olive becoming a part of a cultivated one. The main point of this passage is to remind Gentiles of their subordinate place. They are a part of a larger structure, and although they have been granted this new status, it is by no means guaranteed to be permanent. Paul uses the powerful image of God as a gardener pruning his garden to deliver the same message as the stories of Isaac and Jacob: God decides who is in and who is out.

Paul has drawn for his readers an ethnic family tree, which arranges Jews and Gentiles as related but distinct peoples of the God of Israel. In this family tree, some groups are "natural" and some are "grafted." As recent adoptees, baptized Gentiles are the grafted branches, and Paul reminds them of their dependence on the root that sustains them. Both the natural and unnatural members, however, are subject to the power of God, who is like a horticulturalist grafting on new branches or chopping off existing ones. God's mercy and judgment fall on both.

It is true that some branches have been cut off, which continues Paul's theme in these chapters about the failure of at least part of Israel to understand who Christ is. But Paul is clear that this is not a signal that Israel—the tree itself—has fallen or that God has abandoned or rejected Israel. Likewise, although the Gentiles in Christ currently "stand by means of faithfulness," they should nevertheless be wary, for God can easily cut them off and graft others on again.

By associating Gentiles with the wild olive tree and Jews with the cultivated one, Paul establishes a hierarchy between these two peoples. Paul frames this difference in terms of proximity to the source: your own grafting was "beyond the bounds of nature"; imagine how much easier to graft the natural branches back onto the tree (11:24). The Jews constitute the "natural" branches from God's original tree, whose roots provide nourishment for all the branches. The grafting of the Gentiles, by contrast, is unnatural and somewhat precarious.

Thus Jews and Gentiles are distinct peoples and remain so; the Jews claim their link to Abraham by birth (and God's promise) and the Gentiles by adoption (and God's promise). Yes, Gentiles have now been included and yes, some Jews have stumbled, but this is no reason to boast, Paul reminds his Gentile audience. The olive tree metaphor reminds them of where they stand in the larger order. They are connected to Israel, grafted in through baptism into Christ, but they are subordinate to the other branches.

SUMMARY OF THE PLAN (11:25–31)

If Paul's message of the last few chapters, as he recounts mistakes and issues warnings, has been unsettling and at times hard to understand, clarity comes in Rom 11:25–26a: "So that you may not claim to be wiser than you are, brothers and sisters, I want you to understand this mystery: a hardening has come upon part of Israel, until the full number of the Gentiles has come in. And so all Israel will be saved." This succinct statement summarizes everything Paul has argued since 9:1. It describes how Paul understands this interim period between phase 1 and phase 2: it is a time for the ingathering of nations which is to take place before the Messiah returns. Note that Paul's point here is to further accentuate his warning to Gentiles. Your own gains, he says to them, as well as Israel's mistakes, are simply a part of a larger plan to restore Israel.[10]

Paul articulates again the dual responsibilities of Israel: they are "enemies of the gospel" but they play this role for the sake of the Gentiles (11:28). Indeed, their gifts and their calling are irrevocable, and they are still God's beloved, elect people (11:28–29). Jews and Gentiles have participated in a mutually beneficial disobedience, arranged by God, and the disobedience of each people has resulted in mercy for the other (11:30–32). These two ethnic peoples, traditionally opposed to one another, have interdependent salvation histories. The God of Israel has orchestrated a roundabout scheme to execute his justice and his mercy not only on Jews (which is expected), but also on Gentiles (which is Paul's good news). At the end of Rom 11, Paul himself acknowledges that this plan is not straightforward, as he exclaims about God, "How unsearchable are his judgments and how inscrutable his ways!" (11:33b). Yet also, Paul declares, how deserving is God of praise for this merciful plan, as he closes the argument with a prayer: "For from him and through him and to him are all things. To him be the glory forever. Amen" (Rom 11:36).

---

10. Mark Nanos argues this point in *The Mystery of Romans: The Jewish Context of Paul's Letter* (Minneapolis: Fortress, 1996), 239–88.

FINAL THOUGHTS

One question that arises in this interpretation of Paul is what exactly is the relationship, if any, between Jews and Christ. Is there any point at which Jews must align with Christ, in Paul's view? What exactly is the good news that Peter is to proclaim among the "circumcised" in Gal 2:7? In my reckoning, Paul is simply not explicit about this. And this makes sense because Paul is not fundamentally concerned about Jews: their status before God is already taken care of by covenants and promises that will not be rescinded, despite the unfaithfulness of some. Instead, Paul is concerned about Gentiles, those whose status before God is uncertain, those who will not survive Christ's return unless they are made right with God. So he does not tell us exactly what he thinks about how Jews should relate to Christ.

There are some in the radical new perspective who think that there are two paths for these two people: Christ for Gentiles and continued covenantal faithfulness through keeping the law for Jews.[11] In this understanding, the law and the gospel are mutually exclusive. I do not think this is the case. Instead, I think Christ plays two interdependent roles in Paul's understanding, related to what I have called phase 1 and phase 2 of salvation. The ultimate goal is phase 2, where Christ will do the work of the long-awaited Messiah in defeating Israel's enemies and establishing a new age. In phase 2, Christ is the Messiah for all of Israel and for those Gentiles who are attached to Israel through him. Phase 1, Christ's life, death, and resurrection, however, serves as a merciful surprise, an early appearance of the Messiah to offer a chance for the "full number of Gentiles" to come to the God of Israel. Phase 1 is a necessary step in the larger restoration of Israel, a chance for Israel to be a "light to the nations." Thus the gospel is not on a separate track from the law, but it helps to fulfill the promises to Israel in the law.

Romans 9–11 serves as Paul's explanation of where things stand in the interim period as they await the return of Christ. Gentiles have been offered inclusion into the ethnic genealogy of Israel, into God's people, and they have been aided by the temporary mistakes of some in Israel. Paul, as apostle to the Gentiles, has remained true to God's purposes and reminds Gentiles that their experience is only part of the larger story of Israel.

---

11. John Gager, *The Origins of Anti-Semitism: Attitudes toward Judaism in Pagan and Christian Antiquity* (New York: Oxford University Press, 1983), 247.

This interpretation requires a shift in how we think about Paul, from a founder of Christianity to a faithful Jew helping to implement God's plan. For us reading Paul today, it is almost inconceivable to imagine that Christianity did not develop as it did. But this is exactly what we must do to understand how Paul was thinking. Paul himself was not imagining a new religion, centered on Christ, that would understand itself as a replacement for or fulfillment of Judaism and that would last for thousands of years. Quite the opposite. As he explains in Rom 9–11, Paul understood that he lived at a crucial moment in Israel's history, in which God was about to inaugurate a promised new age. Christ's life, death, and resurrection were signs that this was happening. As foretold by the prophets, when the time was near, the *ethnē* (the nations or Gentiles), would come to the God of Israel. In Paul's view, this is happening through Christ and through Paul's ministry in his name.

FOR FURTHER READING

Buell, Denise Kimber. *Why This New Race: Ethnic Reasoning in Early Christianity*. New York: Columbia University Press, 2005. Buell examines how Christian authors in the second and third centuries employ "ethnic reasoning" to construct Christian theologies and identities.

Eisenbaum, Pamela. *Paul Was Not a Christian: The Original Message of a Misunderstood Apostle*. New York: HarperOne, 2009. Eisenbaum argues that Paul did not convert to a new religion but remained a faithful Jew who promoted God's plan to bring together Jews and Gentiles.

Gager, John G. *The Origins of Anti-Semitism: Attitudes Toward Judaism in Pagan and Christian Antiquity*. New York: Oxford University Press, 1983. Gager explores the roots of anti-Jewish thinking in early Christian literature and argues that Paul himself did not hold anti-Jewish views.

———. *Reinventing Paul*. Oxford: Oxford University Press, 2000. Gager presents a clear explanation of the traditional view and the new perspective view of Paul and argues that the latter is the better interpretation.

Gaston, Lloyd. *Paul and the Torah*. Vancouver: University of British Columbia Press, 1987. Gaston argues for the importance of audience in interpreting Paul and that Paul writes specifically to Gentiles. Paul's view of the law must be seen in this context—it does not work for those outside the covenant. He makes the case that Paul does not reject Judaism for Christianity.

Johnson Hodge, Caroline. *If Sons, Then Heirs: A Study of Kinship and Ethnicity in the Letters of Paul*. New York: Oxford University Press, 2007. Johnson Hodge focuses on Paul's kinship and ethnic language in Galatians and Romans. She argues that this terminology supports the idea that Paul was writing to Gentiles to help implement God's plan to include them, along with Jews, as peoples of God.

Nanos, Mark D. *The Mystery of Romans: The Jewish Context of Paul's Letter*. Minneapolis: Fortress, 1996. Nanos argues that Paul is a devout Jew who continues to be Torah-observant even after his call to be an apostle to the Gentiles. He shows that Paul is concerned with the behavior of Gentiles who are in Christ.

Stendahl, Krister. "The Apostle Paul and the Introspective Conscience of the West." *HTR* 56 (1963): 199–215. Stendahl critiques the Augustinian/Lutheran reading of Paul and challenges the tendency to interpret Paul using anachronistic theological concepts. This is a foundational article for the new perspective.

Stowers, Stanley K. *A Rereading of Romans: Justice, Jews, and Gentiles*. New Haven: Yale University Press, 1994. Stowers poses a challenge to traditional readings of Paul through a serious effort to interpret Paul in his historical context. He shows how one's reading of Paul changes when the interpreter recognizes that Paul uses ancient literary devices, modes of argumentation, philosophical concepts and categories of identity.

Zetterholm, Magnus. *Approaches to Paul: A Student's Guide to Recent Scholarship*. Minneapolis: Fortress, 2009. Zetterholm examines the new perspective and its various branches but also lays out earlier, traditional views and recent reactions to the new perspective.

Living to God, Walking in Love:
Theology and Ethics in Romans

Victor Paul Furnish

Almost all of the ethical appeals in Romans come toward the close of the letter, in 12:1–15:13.[1] For years, even centuries, many interpreters tended to view this section as general moral advice based on what Paul had given his own churches and which, he assumed, could benefit the Roman Christians as well. On this reading, Romans is important primarily because of the "theological doctrines" spelled out in chapters 1–11, and the "practical" topics in chapters 12–15 are by and large incidental.

This view, however, is no longer widely held. The apostle himself indicates a connection between these two sections of the letter when he opens the second by saying, "I *therefore* implore you, brothers and sisters" (12:1 NRSV mod.).[2] And this connection is not merely formal. What Paul says about the gospel (literally, "good news") in Rom 1–11 provides the theological foundation and shapes the actual content of the ethical appeals that follow. The present discussion seeks to demonstrate this by highlighting some of the principal points in Romans where "theology" and "ethics" intersect.

Living to God (Romans 1:1–11:36)

Paul makes two important statements about the gospel in the opening paragraphs. In the first, perhaps quoting from a creed with which

---

1. The admonitions in Rom 16:17–20 are probably a non-Pauline addition to the letter; see Robert Jewett, *Romans* (Herm; Minneapolis: Fortress, 2007), 986–88; Leander E. Keck, *Romans* (ANTC; Nashville: Abingdon, 2005), 27–28, 377–78.

2. Unless noted otherwise, all biblical quotations are from the NRSV, although occasionally with some modification (= "NRSV mod.").

the addressees were familiar, he says that the good news concerns "Jesus Christ our Lord," who "was declared to be Son of God with power according to the spirit of holiness by resurrection from the dead" (1:3–4). In the second, which opens the body of the letter and states its theme, he declares that this good news is "the power of God for salvation to everyone who believes" and the means by which God's righteousness is revealed (1:16–17 NRSV mod.).

Beginning in 3:21 Paul elaborates on these claims about the gospel, argues in support of them, and responds to possible misunderstandings and objections. In advance of that, however, he explains why the whole of humankind stands in need of the good news that he proclaims.

Humanity's Plight (1:18–3:20)

According to Paul, the whole of humankind is in bondage to the death-dealing power of sin, which he views as humanity's rebellion against the one God by whom all things exist and to whom every human being is ultimately accountable (3:19). Convinced that rebellious self-assertiveness is the universal human condition (3:20, 22b–23), he maintains that sin's power is evident both in the idolatry and licentiousness of those (Gentiles) who are ignorant of God's law (1:18–32) and in the hypocrisy and self-righteousness of those (Jews) who exult in their possession of it (2:17–29). Paul therefore holds that the whole of humankind needs to be delivered from sin, rescued from the divine wrath that sin elicits, and restored to its proper relationship with God.

The Revealing of God's Righteousness (3:21–5:11)

Having established that humanity has fallen into the clutches of sin and rebelled against God, Paul turns to his proper subject, which is the good news of God's righteousness (rectitude) and power to save (1:16–17). In Pauline usage, the noun usually translated "righteousness" ordinarily refers to the state or practice of *rightness, justice,* and *fairness*; the related verb, which is usually translated as "justify," means to *put, make,* or *show* to be right; another related term, which is usually translated as "justification," refers to the *action* of putting, making, or showing to be right. The apostle has said that God's power to put things right does not work through the law (3:19–20), and later he will explain why it cannot: precisely in exposing sin the law brings sin to life, allowing it to exercise its own deadly power (7:7–25). He therefore declares that God's righteousness has been disclosed "apart from law," even though "the law and the prophets" bear witness to it (3:21).

For Paul, the righteousness that the law cannot impart is bestowed as a gift of God's grace, through Jesus Christ, on "all who believe" (3:22–26). This much is clear whether the ambiguous phrases in verses 22 and 26 are interpreted, respectively, as "*faith in* Jesus Christ" and "the one who has *faith in* Jesus," or "*the faith of* Jesus Christ" and "the one who has *the faith of* Jesus." Either way, Paul is saying that through God's Son, raised from the dead (1:3–4), sinful humanity has been released from sin's power and put right with God (3:22–24a). Speaking metaphorically, he calls this deliverance "redemption" and portrays Christ's death as a "sacrifice [*or* place] of atonement" that reveals God's "righteousness" and "forbearance" in dealing with sins (vv. 24b–25). Rather than explaining these images, however, he repeats his basic claim: Christ's death is compelling evidence "that [God] himself is righteous and that he rectifies the one who has faith in [*or* the faith of] Jesus" (v. 26 NRSV mod.).

That righteousness depends on faith is also Paul's theme in chapter 4, where he presents Abraham's believing as exemplary for both Jews and Gentiles. The faith that was "reckoned" to Abraham as righteousness was his absolute *trust*—itself elicited and strengthened by God's promise— that he and Sarah, although "as good as dead" because of their age (v. 19), would be blessed with countless descendants. In believing, therefore, Abraham was *entrusting himself and his future entirely and unconditionally to God.* By specifying that Abraham trusted in the God "who gives life to the dead and calls into existence the things that do not exist" (v. 17), Paul connects even the content of his faith with the faith of those "who believe in him who raised Jesus our Lord from the dead, who was handed over to death for our trespasses and was raised for our justification" (vv. 24–25).

Moving on (5:1–11), Paul says that the righteousness bestowed through Christ's death and resurrection brings both "peace with God" and "hope" (vv. 1, 2b). By "peace" he means more than the cessation of hostilities. In response to the enmity expressed in humanity's rebellion, God has extended himself in love to bring about reconciliation (vv. 8, 10a, 11). And by "hope" he means more than wishful thinking. He speaks of the confidence, grounded in the presently experienced reality of God's love (v. 5), that one's destiny is not to incur God's wrath (vv. 9b, 10b) but to share in God's glory (v. 2b).

Although Paul addresses this letter "to all God's beloved in Rome" (1:7) and has characterized Christ's death as an act of "divine forbearance" (3:25–26; cf. 2:4), his first specific declarations about God's love (*agapē*) occur here (5:5, 8), and they are of exceptional importance. The statement that "God confirms his love for us in that while we still were sinners Christ died for us" (v. 8 NRSV mod.) identifies Christ's death as the definitive expression of God's unconditional, reconciling love—the kind that embraces precisely the "ungodly" who position themselves as God's "enemies" (vv. 6, 10). The statement that "God's love has been poured into our hearts through the Holy Spirit" (v. 5) both affirms the abiding presence of God's love and suggests why Paul can describe believers as continuing to "stand" in grace (v. 2).

THE REIGN OF GRACE (5:12–7:6)

Paul argues that Adam's primal disobedience brought condemnation and the reign of sin and death, while Christ's obedience, which led to his death and resurrection, brought righteousness and the reign of grace that leads to eternal life (5:12–21). But if, as the apostle also claims, more sin brings more grace (5:20), why not simply "continue in sin" (6:1)? He responds that such a conclusion is invalidated by what believers themselves have experienced (6:2–7:6).

Portraying baptism as the burial of the sin-dominated self that has been "crucified with" Christ (6:4, 6), Paul reasons that because Christ died "to sin, once for all" (6:10), those who belong to him have also "died to sin" (6:2b) and are released from its power (6:7). Moreover, "just as Christ was raised from the dead by the glory of the Father," they, too, have been granted "newness of life" (6:4). Although Paul stops short of claiming that the baptized have been resurrected with Christ,[3] he views their new life as genuinely eschatological (end-time) existence, for it has been granted by the same power of God that raised Christ from the dead.

Paul's argument reaches a conclusion of sorts in his first explicit appeal: believers are to *actualize* the new reality that they are "dead to sin and alive to God in Christ Jesus" (v. 11). Two further appeals draw attention to the inherently moral character of this new life (6:12–13):

---

3. For Paul, resurrection is an end-time event and an object of hope; note 1 Thess 4:14, 16; 1 Cor 6:14. Interpreters differ on whether the future tenses in Rom 6:5, 8 are "logical" or "eschatological."

Do not let sin exercise dominion in your mortal bodies, to make you obey their passions. No longer present your members to sin as instruments of wickedness, but present yourselves to God as those who have been brought from death to life, and present your members to God as instruments of righteousness.

Paul supports these appeals with the assurance that believers have been placed under the jurisdiction of grace (6:14). He warns again, however, that grace does not license sin. Rather, life under grace means both freedom *from* slavery to sin (and, thereby, from the passions of one's mortal body, 6:12) and freedom *for* obedience to God (and, thereby, for God's "free gift" of righteousness, 6:16, 18; cf. 5:15–17). Believers have been emancipated from their old master so they can bind themselves to another, the God by whom they have been delivered from sin and graced with righteousness (6:16–18, 20–22). So to his three earlier appeals Paul adds a fourth: "Just as you once presented your members as slaves to impurity and to greater and greater iniquity, so now present your members as slaves to righteousness for sanctification" (6:19b).

Concluding, Paul refers to the situation of a widow who, upon the death of her husband, is "discharged from the law" that would have made her an adulteress had she been unfaithful to him while he lived (7:1–3). Similarly, he suggests, those who have died with Christ are no longer bound to the law through which sin exercises its power (7:4–6). They have been freed to "belong to another," the resurrected Christ (cf. 2 Cor 11:2). In order to emphasize the moral dimension of this new relationship, Paul contrasts the offspring of those who are bound to the law with the offspring of those who belong to Christ. Those who live "in the flesh" where "sinful passions" are stirred up by the law "bear fruit for death." Those who belong to Christ, now described as "slaves … in the new life of the Spirit" (7:6), "bear fruit for God" (7:4).

Life in the Spirit and the Invincibility of God's Love (8:1–39)

Paul's further comments about "the new life of the Spirit" (8:3–17) are consistent with what he had written in Gal 5:16–25 about the opposing desires of the flesh and of the Spirit (Gal 5:16–25). Although there are no direct appeals to live according to the Spirit like those in Galatians, there is nonetheless imperative force in the assertion that submitting to the Spirit's control brings life, while submitting to the control of the flesh brings death (vv. 5–11). The same is true of the statement that "we are debtors, not to the flesh, to live according to the flesh" (v. 12), even though Paul does not continue with the expected, "but we are debtors to the Spirit, to live according to the Spirit." Still, what crowds out this expected but missing statement has its own significance. Concerned to emphasize the moral claim that is inherent in God's bestowal of the Spirit, Paul declares that "if by the Spirit you put to death the deeds of the body, you will live" (v. 13; cf. 6:12–13, 19).

The apostle's description of those who live according to the Spirit as "joint heirs with Christ" (8:17a) accords with earlier statements about sharing in Christ's death and life (6:5, 8). While he now acknowledges that believers also suffer with Christ (8:17b), he attests that such sufferings are slight in comparison with the coming glory (8:18–30) and that the ground and guarantee of this hope is God's invincible love (vv. 31–39; cf. 5:5). And now, as earlier (5:8), he cites as the evidence of this love God's giving up "his own Son ... for all of us" (vv. 31–32)—"Christ Jesus, who died, yes, who was raised, who is at the right hand of God, who indeed intercedes for us" (v. 34). There is nothing "in all creation," he says, that "will be able to separate us from the love of God in Christ Jesus our Lord" (vv. 35–39).

THE WONDER OF GOD'S FAITHFULNESS AND MERCY (9:1–11:36)

Continuing and concluding his exposition of the gospel, Paul admits to "great sorrow and unceasing anguish" because most of his fellow Jews have not accepted it (9:1–5). While he had touched on this subject earlier (3:1–4), he now addresses it at some length, determined to show that God has in no way "rejected his people" (11:1). He argues, to the contrary, that the refusal of the gospel by Jews is integral to God's plan for salvation, because it opens the way for the good news to be accepted by Gentiles (11:7–12). And he is equally insistent that the mercy God shows toward the disobedient Gentiles will be extended also to the disobedient Jews: "For God has imprisoned all in disobedience so that he may be merciful to all" (11:25–32).

Two premises underlie Paul's reasoning here. The first is that humanity's well-being "depends not on human will or exertion, but on God who shows mercy" (9:16), by which he means, on God's love (note his pairing of scriptural texts in vv. 13, 15) as it is revealed in Christ (cf. 15:8–9). The second is that mercy (love) is what God *does* and that God is "merciful to all" (11:32). In thus affirming God's faithfulness to Israel, Paul is also affirming the inclusiveness of God's "mercy" (9:15–16, 18, 23; 11:30–32; cf. 11:5–6, 22) and, in effect, reaffirming the invincibility of God's love.

The apostle concludes this discussion—and the whole expository section of his letter—not with some creed-like summary (e.g., "Therefore, we believe that…"), but with expressions of wonder (11:33–36). Consistent with the good news of God's love that has been his subject, he extols the awesome generosity of God's mercy (v. 33; cf. 2:4; 10:12; 11:12); and in concluding with a doxology (v. 36), he seems to suggest that what is left for the beneficiaries of God's mercy to offer in return is nothing else, and nothing less, than their unending praise.

Walking in Love (Romans 12:1–15:13)

With the opening words of Rom 12, exposition gives way to exhortation, yet Paul's subject remains the good news of the saving power of God's love revealed in Christ. Especially in his comments about the new life that is bestowed in Christ and conducted according to the Spirit (e.g., 6:1–7:6; 8:1–17), Paul has called attention to the moral imperative that is inherent in God's grace. Now he proceeds to indicate various ways in which God's grace should be manifested in the daily lives of those who belong to Christ.

This second main part of Romans extends from 12:1 through 15:13. Two introductory appeals (12:1–2) link the preceding exposition to the following exhortations. The initial exhortations (12:3–13:14) cover a number of topics and, with one exception, are offered with little or no discussion. The ones that follow (14:1–15:13) occur within an argument that Paul develops in response to a specific issue that was unsettling the Christian community in Rome.

"Therefore …" (12:1–2)

The introductory appeals deserve close attention for what they show about the relationship between the expository and exhortatory sections of Romans and, therefore, about Paul's understanding of the moral imperative that lies at the heart of the gospel.

> I therefore implore you, brothers and sisters, by the mercies of God, to present your bodies as a sacrifice that is living, holy, and acceptable to God, which is your reasonable worship. Do not be conformed to this present age, but rather, let yourselves be transformed in the renewing of

the mind, so that you may discern what is the will of God—the good and
acceptable and perfect. (NRSV mod.)

In this context the apostle's "therefore" (v. 1) has theological weight, for it
indicates that what follows is required by the gospel that has been his subject since the beginning of the letter. His mention of the "mercies of God"
connects this appeal in the first instance with claims in chapters 9–11
about the constancy and scope of God's mercy. Yet because he makes no
distinction between God's mercy and God's love (e.g., 9:13, 15; cf. 15:8–9),
this phrase connects his appeal just as certainly with everything that he
has said about Christ as the one in whom God's love is definitively revealed
(5:8; 8:31–39; cf. 3:21–26).

Paul's summons to "present your bodies … to God" is a variation
of the earlier appeals to "present yourselves to God … and present your
members to God as instruments of righteousness" (6:13; also v. 19b, "present your members as slaves to righteousness…"; cf. v. 16). Now, using the
verb "present" in its cultic sense, he calls on believers to offer up to God
their own "bodies" as a "living sacrifice." Here, "body" refers not just to
the physical body but, more comprehensively, to one's whole *self*, one's
"being in relation to the world."[4] The remarkable image of a sacrifice that
is "living" specifies that the selves to be put at God's disposal in the world
are precisely those which, having "been brought from death to life" (6:13),
are indwelt by the life-giving Spirit (8:1–13) and are "alive to God in Christ
Jesus" (6:11). Paul's description of this self-offering as "reasonable [*or* spir-
itual] worship" both commends it as suited to one's nature as a rational
being[5] and distinguishes it from worship that is based on "a lie" rather than
the "truth about God" (1:25).

In the second appeal, Paul indicates that putting oneself at God's disposal requires the reorientation of one's life from "this present age" to
the "will of God" (v. 2). In accord with Jewish apocalyptic-eschatology,
he presumes that the "present evil age" (Gal 1:4) is destined to come to
an end and be replaced by the "kingdom of God" (see, esp., 1 Cor 15:24,
50). Yet Paul's outlook differs from the traditional view in that he regards
the eschatological (end-time) power of God as already revealed in Christ's

---

4. Ernst Käsemann, *Commentary on Romans* (ed. and trans. Geoffrey W. Bromiley; Grand Rapids: Eerdmans, 1980), 327.

5. See the translation and comments of Joseph A. Fitzmyer, *Romans* (AB 33; New
York: Doubleday, 1993), 637, 640.

death and resurrection; the coming age has already broken into the present (see "But now," introducing Rom 3:21–26, and in 6:22; 7:6). Simultaneously, the "present form of this world is passing away" (1 Cor 7:31) and the day of salvation is coming nearer (Rom 13:11); and in this overlapping of present and future there is already, in Christ, access to grace (5:2) and "newness of life" (6:4)—"a new creation" (2 Cor 5:17; Gal 6:16).

This "already and not yet" dynamic of the new life in Christ gives to Paul's exposition of the gospel an "ethical" as well as a "theological" aspect. It requires him to consider how believers can put themselves wholly at God's disposal when they must constantly face the temptations, responsibilities, and risks of living in "this present age." Significantly, Paul does not follow his warning about conforming to this age with an appeal to separate from society (in 1 Cor 5:9–10 he dismisses this as unrealistic). Rather, he calls on believers to let the transformation that is already taking place in their lives (cf. 2 Cor 3:18) renew their minds as well, so that they may "discern what is the will of God" in their present situation.

Like his contemporaries, Paul uses the word "mind" to refer to the human capacity for thinking, reasoning, and making critical judgments. The "renewing of the mind" would therefore be the restoring of an "undiscerning mind" (Rom 1:28 NAB) so that it can function as it should. Paul has in view the task of moral discernment and the specific goal of distinguishing what conduct accords with the will of God. Here, to "discern" does not mean to acquire information from an established body of knowledge, like the law (note Rom 2:18) or the Jesus traditions. It means, rather, to engage in a process of inquiry, critical appraisal, and reasoning.

Accordingly, Paul does not convey the moral advisories that follow in 12:3–15:13 as though they are rules drawn from an established code of conduct. He does not mean to preempt the process of moral discernment but to guide it. Even though he claims apostolic authority ("by the grace given to me," 12:3; cf. 1:1), he presents the commended actions to his audience as responsibilities that *are inherent in their belonging to Christ*, and he provides reasons why they should themselves be able to recognize them as such.

RESPONSIBILITIES WITHIN AND BEYOND THE BODY OF CHRIST (12:3–13:14)

The counsels in 12:3–13:14 deal with such broad topics and in such a general way that they could have been directed to almost any first-century church. Indeed, some also appear in other Pauline letters, and a number echo moral traditions that were at home in both Hellenistic Judaism (and its Scripture) and Hellenistic moral philosophy. But even though this section is rather loosely organized, it is not utterly haphazard, and all of the counsels are given a decidedly Christian stamp by christological references in the opening and closing paragraphs.

In the opening paragraph (12:3–8), Paul declares that believers, though "many," are "one body in Christ" and therefore "members one of another," graced with various gifts that should be used to benefit all (vv. 4–8). The background of this "one body" imagery is a baptismal formula, likely known to the Roman Christians, that Paul had employed in earlier letters. As cited in Galatians, it portrays baptism as being "clothed" with Christ and transferred into a community where "there is no longer Jew or Greek, … slave or free, … male and female; for all of you are one in Christ Jesus" (3:27–28). As cited in 1 Corinthians, it portrays believers as "many" and yet "one," because they are "all baptized into one body"—the "body of Christ" (1 Cor 12:12–13, 27). Baptismal imagery is also reflected in the closing paragraph (Rom 13:11–14), where Paul underscores his call for good conduct by exhorting his audience to "put on the Lord Jesus Christ" (v. 14).

The apostle's declaration that believers constitute "one body in Christ" supports his advice "not to think of yourself more highly than you ought to think, but to think with sober judgment, each according to the measure of faith that God has assigned" (v. 3). By "measure of faith" he probably means the strength and character of one's particular relationship with God, which is necessarily unique even though it is also necessarily experienced and lived out within a believing community (see 14:4, 22–23).[6] This call for sober self-assessment and humility is reinforced with two subsequent injunctions: "do not be haughty, but associate with the lowly; do not claim to be wiser than you are" (12:16bc). And it is complemented with exhortations concerning love, living in concord, and striving for peace (12:9–21; 13:8–10).

The appeal in 12:9, "Let love be genuine; hate what is evil, hold fast to what is good," is comprehensive enough to stand as a heading for all of the counsels that follow through 12:21. Some pertain to conduct within the "one body in Christ" (vv. 10–13a), others to relationships with nonbelievers (vv. 14, 17–21), and a few could apply to both (vv. 13b, 15–16).

---

6. Following Jewett, *Romans*, 742.

Throughout this paragraph, the accent falls on love: it is the subject of the initial appeals (*agapē*, v. 9a; *philadelphia*, v. 10a) and, implicitly, of subsequent appeals to show "honor" (12:10b), bless one's persecutors (12:14), live together in harmony (12:16a), and live peaceably with everyone (12:18). Moreover, here, as elsewhere in Paul's letters, love is the principal referent of the "good" (vv. 9, 21).

Paul himself highlights love as the believers' fundamental obligation when he identifies the commandment to "love your neighbor as yourself" (Lev 19:18) as summing up all other commandments (13:8–10). Significantly, he does not cite Jesus as the source of this teaching (or of the instruction to bless one's persecutors, 12:14), even if he is familiar with such a tradition (cf. Mark 12:28–34). In Galatians, where he also singles out this commandment (5:13–14), he links it, rather, to the crucified and risen Christ through whom God grants deliverance from sin (5:1; cf. 1:4), bestows righteousness (5:4–5; cf. 2:15–21), and sets love in motion (5:6; cf. 2:20). The same is true here in Romans. Paul's emphasis on loving the neighbor in all of the ways he specifies in 12:9–21 is rooted in his belief that Christ's death-resurrection is the event through which God's love "for us" has been confirmed (5:8; 8:31–39). Given this understanding of the "good news" of Christ, the new life of those who are "united with him in a death like his" (6:4, 5) can be nothing else than a life that is conformed to the love by which it has been generated and is sustained.

But what does love have to do with the advice that everyone should "be subject to the governing authorities" (13:1a)?[7] This is the only Pauline letter in which there is such an instruction, and this is the only instruction in chapters 12–13 that Paul backs up with an argument (vv. 1b–7). While this passage continues to be vigorously debated, a few matters are relatively clear.

First, Paul's topic is not political authority or, in particular, Roman imperial authority. It is, more concretely, whether believers are obliged to accept the authority of civic officials and adhere to the laws and regulations they administer. While he argues that they do have this obligation (vv. 1, 3c, 5, 7), the ensuing discussion shows that he does not regard it as absolute.

---

7. Although most interpreters accept this paragraph as Paul's, a few regard it is a non-Pauline addition; e.g., William O. Walker, *Interpolations in the Pauline Letters* (JSNTSup 213; Sheffield: Sheffield Academic Press, 2001), 221–31.

Second, he assumes that the primary responsibility of civic officials is to maintain the public welfare by supporting "good" conduct and punishing "bad" conduct and, further, that officials are, as a rule, just and wise in fulfilling this responsibility (vv. 3–4). He does not raise the question of what to do about officials who are corrupt or who govern unjustly or unwisely.

Third, he declares that all political authority has been instituted by God, for "there is no authority except from God" (v. 1). He, therefore, repeatedly identifies civic officials as God's "servants" (*diakonos* in vv. 4a and 4b; *leitourgoi* in v. 6), thereby implying that they are *accountable* to God.

Fourth, like all of his moral advisories in 12:3–13:14, Paul's instruction to be subject to the governing authorities is radically qualified by the appeal in 12:2. Rather than conforming to the claims of "this present age," believers should seek to discern the will of God through careful inquiry, reflection, and the judicious weighing of options. Clearly, then, whatever subjection to civil authorities may require in any given instance must not be at odds with the believers' understanding of their responsibility before God. Indeed, Paul's comment that one should "be subject" not just from fear of punishment but "because of conscience" (v. 5) suggests that he views subjection to political authority as always conditional on its being in accord with God's will.

The advice in 13:1–7 can be read either as following from the instructions about dealing with enemies (12:14, 17, 19–21) or from the instruction to live in peace with everyone, whenever it is "possible" and "depends on you" (12:18). It is unclear, however, why Paul gives special attention—and only in this letter—to the civic responsibilities of believers. Conceivably, the Roman Christians had lingering fears about the governing authorities because, several years earlier (in 49 c.e.), some of them, along with members of the Jewish community, had been expelled from the city by an edict of the emperor, Claudius.[8] But however that may be, some of the other counsels in chapters 12–13 do seem to anticipate the specific situation that Paul subsequently addresses in 14:1–15:13.

---

8. Thus Sylvia C. Keesmaat, "If Your Enemy Is Hungry: Love and Subversive Politics in Romans 12–13," in *Character Ethics and the New Testament: Moral Dimensions of Scripture* (ed. Robert L. Brawley; Louisville: Westminster John Knox, 2007), 141–58.

Dealing with Differences (14:1–15:13)

Paul is concerned that the Roman Christians are "quarreling over opinions" (14:1). Some abstain from meat (thinking it pollutes) and regard one day as holy (14:2b, 5a), others do not (14:2a, 5b), and neither group respects the views of the other (14:3, 10). It is possible, but not certain, that most of the observant were Jewish Christians and most of the nonobservant were Gentile Christians. The apostle's own views are clear, for he describes the observant as "weak in faith" (14:1–2; cf. 15:1) and says that he himself does not regard anything as inherently unclean (14:14a; cf. v. 20b). Yet he also declares that something *is* unclean for those who believe it to be (v. 14b). And he never calls on the weak to change their views. Rather, three key appeals, which call for unity but not for uniformity, shift the focus of moral concern from ideologies to relationships.

First, "Welcome one another." This comprehensive appeal, addressed to both the observant and nonobservant, frames the whole discussion (14:1; 15:7a). Paul's reminder that God has welcomed them all in Christ (14:3b; 15:7b–8) both validates the appeal and suggests that the welcoming he commends means extending oneself to "the other" in unconditional love and a spirit of reconciliation. Accordingly, he also urges that those on each side of the issue refrain from dismissing or condemning the views of those on the other side, because judgment belongs to God, to whom all of them are accountable (14:3a, 4, 10–13). Looking back, one sees these counsels anticipated by earlier ones, like the advice to "live in harmony with one another" and "not claim to be wiser than you are" (12:16).

Second, "Let all be fully convinced in their own minds" (14:5b). This, too, is addressed to both the observant and the nonobservant. What Paul means is suggested by his later remark that every believer must remain true to her or his own considered judgment about what is right: "The faith that you have, have as your own conviction before God. Blessed are those who have no reason to condemn themselves because of what they approve" (14:22). In the phrase, "what they approve," Paul employs the same Greek verb that in 12:2 refers to the task of discerning the will of God. He is, therefore, not talking about one's personal moral preferences or offhand opinions. He is referring to convictions that are formed and tested as believers, together, think through the implications of the new life they share in Christ.

The process of moral discernment does not, of course, guarantee unanimity, and Paul does not press for it. What he does urge is that actions accord with actual convictions and that convictions accord with one's relationship to God—one's "measure of faith" (12:3b); for "whatever does not proceed from faith is sin" (14:23b). The critical matter is not belonging to one group or the other, but belonging to Christ, who "died and lived again, so that he might be Lord of both the dead and the living" (14:9). And further, that one's conduct can be offered to God in thanksgiving, as genuinely expressive of one's belonging to the Lord (14:6–8).

Third, "Let us then pursue what makes for peace and for mutual upbuilding" (14:19). Like the discussion as a whole, this exhortation directs attention to what Paul regards as one's primary moral responsibility, which is to serve Christ (14:18) by serving one another, for mutual upbuilding. In context, this instruction applies to the nonobservant, who are being cautioned that they are "no longer walking in love" if their eating causes the "ruin" of anyone "for whom Christ died" (14:15). Behind this warning lies Paul's view that it is not religious knowledge (beliefs) but the working of love that "builds up" (1 Cor 8:1), and that love calls for being patient (1 Cor 13:4!) with the "weak" (see also 15:1; cf. 1 Cor 8:9–13).

In 15:2 Paul generalizes this instruction so that it applies to the "weak" as well: "Each of us must please our neighbor for the good purpose of building up the neighbor." His wording here echoes the commandment to "love your neighbor," which he has identified earlier as the sum and substance of what God requires (13:8–10). And here again (cf. 14:15) he invokes the selfless love revealed in Christ, "who did not please himself" (this is love's way, 1 Cor 13:5), as the decisive ground of his appeal and the definitive model for Christian conduct (15:3; cf. vv. 5, 7–8).

•••

The intersecting of theology and ethics in Romans is most evident in the four exhortations that stand within the expository section of the letter (6:11–13, 19b), in the theological warrants that are invoked in the exhortatory section (e.g., 12:5; 13:14; 14:9, 15, 17, 18; 15:3, 7–8), and in the appeals that mark the transition from exposition to exhortation (12:1–2). Yet the word "intersection" cannot do justice to the organic relationship of theology and ethics that one sees in Romans. To highlight this, it may be best to set aside even the terms "theology" and "ethics" (neither occurs in Romans) in favor of the apostle's own word, "gospel." As he presents it in Romans, the "good news" is that the saving power of God's unconditional love, revealed in Christ, brings deliverance from sin and death and new life under the reign of grace. Accordingly, God's love is viewed as both intrinsic to the gospel and constitutive of the new life in Christ; and "walk[ing] in newness of life" (6:4) means, necessarily, "walking in love" (14:15).

FOR FURTHER READING

Betz, Hans Dieter. "The Foundations of Christian Ethics according to Romans 12:1–2." Pages 55–72 in *Witness and Existence: Essays in Honor of Schubert M. Ogden*. Edited by Philip E. Devenish and George L. Goodwin. Chicago: University of Chicago Press, 1989. Betz argues that Romans presents the "final version" of Paul's thinking about the theological foundations of Christian ethics.

Du Toit, Andrie B. "Shaping a Christian Lifestyle in the Roman Capital." Pages 167–97 in *Identity, Ethics, and Ethos in the New Testament*. Edited by Jan G. van der Watt. BZNW 141. Berlin: de Gruyter, 2006. Du Toit emphasizes "Christian identity" as the basis for ethics in Romans.

Elliott, Neil. *The Arrogance of Nations: Reading Romans in the Shadow of Empire*. PCC. Minneapolis: Fortress, 2008. Elliott provides a political reading that accents the letter's "counter-imperial aspects" and focuses on Paul's "sustained interaction" with the topics of *empire, justice, mercy, piety*, and *virtue*.

Furnish, Victor Paul. *The Moral Teaching of Paul: Selected Issues*. 3rd ed. Nashville: Abingdon, 2009. Passages in Romans that address ethical issues are discussed, especially in chapters 3 ("Homosexuality?") and 5 ("The Church in the World").

Horrell, David G. *Solidarity and Difference: A Contemporary Reading of Paul's Ethics*. London: T&T Clark, 2005. This is an important and scholarly study of Paul's ethics, which includes insightful discussions of Rom 14–15 (in ch. 6) and Rom 1–2; 13:1–7 (in ch. 8).

Jewett, Robert. *Romans*. Herm. Minneapolis: Fortress, 2007. This sociohistorical and rhetorical commentary combines detailed exegetical analysis with wide-ranging proposals about Paul's missionary goals.

Käsemann, Ernst. "Worship in Everyday Life: A Note on Romans 12" and "Principles of the Interpretation of Romans 13." Pages 188–95 and 196–216 in *New Testament Questions of Today*. Philadelphia: Fortress, 1969. These are classic studies that probe theological and ethical issues of continuing importance.

Keck, Leander E. *Romans*. ANTC. Nashville: Abingdon, 2005. This accessible commentary is particularly attentive to the letter's theological aims and outlook.

Matera, Frank J. *Romans*. PCNT. Grand Rapids: Baker, 2010. Matera's exposition is impressively comprehensive, balanced, and lucid.

AUTHOR INDEX

Subject Index

Abraham, 54, 55, 58, 83, 104, 105, 116, 117, 118, 161, 163, 165, 170, 173, 175, 177, 178, 182, 189

Adam, 7, 54, 73, 102, 111, 125–38, 126 n. 3, 125 n. 1, 125 n. 2, 126 n. 5, 127 n. 6, 129 n. 10, 129 n. 12, 130 n. 14, 133 n. 20, 134 n. 23, 134 n. 24, 136 n. 29, 147 n. 16, 190

adoption, 146, 147, 151, 153, 173, 175, 182

agriculture, 164, 170, 181, 182

ashamed, 5, 52, 66, 69, 70, 92, 102, 112

atonement, 73, 74, 78, 79–82, 84–91, 152, 189

audience, 12, 14, 21, 22, 23, 24, 27–41, 43–46, 52, 54, 55, 88, 110, 111, 139 n. 1, 140, 152, 158, 170, 171, 171 n. 3, 172, 174, 179, 180, 181, 183, 185, 195, 196

Augustus, 16, 53, 56, 64

baptism, 66, 69, 76, 132, 155, 170, 171, 173, 174, 179, 180, 182, 183, 190, 196

body, 117, 136, 137, 145, 150, 191, 192, 194

Caesar, 16, 20, 21, 50, 52, 53, 55, 56, 62

Caligula, 54

children
of Abraham, 118
of God, 56, 145, 147, 149, 150, 151, 153, 154, 170

Chrestus, 18, 20, 40, 41, 42, 43, 44

Christ
body of, 39, 195, 196–98
death of, 6, 62, 65, 66, 67, 69, 70, 71, 73, 74, 75, 76, 77, 79, 80, 81, 82, 84, 85, 86, 88, 89, 90, 91, 92, 101, 117, 120, 136, 140, 141, 155, 161, 165, 170, 173, 174,178, 184, 185, 189, 190, 192, 194–95, 97

faith in, 5, 6, 68, 71, 82, 105 n. .21, 120, 132, 160 n. 3, 177, 189

faithfulness of, 6, 7, 14, 65, 66, 71, 73, 76, 85, 86, 88, 91, 160, 177, 178, 182

life in, 66, 94, 132, 142, 155, 195, 201

resurrection of, 6, 26, 52, 62, 65, 66, 67, 69, 70, 71, 73, 75, 76, 80, 95, 96, 117, 119, 120, 124, 135, 136, 140, 140 n. 5, 145, 146, 155, 161, 165, 170, 173, 174, 178, 184, 185, 188, 189, 190, 190 n. 3, 195, 197

church, 1, 2, 3, 4, 6, 7, 8, 11, 12 n. 4, 15, 16, 30, 31, 31 n. 2, 39 n. 21, 48, 50, 56, 62, 63, 65, 71, 75, 76, 82, 85, 90, 99, 140, 157, 158, 159, 160, 161, 162, 164, 165, 166, 169, 170, 187, 195, 201

Claudius, 16, 19, 20, 22, 26, 28, 30, 40, 41, 42, 43, 44, 46, 48, 198

Claudius edict, 19, 22, 26, 30, 40, 42, 43, 44, 46, 48–49, 198

clean and unclean, 35, 36, 84, 199

cleanse from sin, 74, 75, 84, 88, 122

condemn, condemnation. *See* judgment

covenant, 5, 7, 11, 23, 26, 49, 50, 65, 69, 70, 71, 74, 75, 76, 77, 81, 83, 86, 87, 88, 114, 118, 119, 121, 128, 157, 158–65, 186

creation, 55, 56, 68, 69, 71, 127, 129, 130, 132, 135, 136, 137, 138, 153, 154, 155, 159, 170, 192

creation, new, 76, 100, 138, 156, 192

CPSIA information can be obtained
at www.ICGtesting.com
Printed in the USA
BVHW031935011221
623024BV00005B/122